THE ROLE OF
RELIGION
IN 21ST-CENTURY PUBLIC SCHOOLS

COUNTERPOINTS

Studies in the Postmodern Theory of Education

Joe L. Kincheloe and Shirley R. Steinberg
General Editors

Vol. 374

PETER LANG
New York • Washington, D.C./Baltimore • Bern
Frankfurt am Main • Berlin • Brussels • Vienna • Oxford

THE ROLE OF
RELIGION
IN 21ST-CENTURY PUBLIC SCHOOLS

EDITED BY
STEVEN P. JONES
& ERIC C. SHEFFIELD

PETER LANG
New York • Washington, D.C./Baltimore • Bern
Frankfurt am Main • Berlin • Brussels • Vienna • Oxford

Library of Congress Cataloging-in-Publication Data

The role of religion in 21st-century public schools /
edited by Steven P. Jones, Eric C. Sheffield.
p. cm. — (Counterpoints: studies in the postmodern
theory of education; vol. 374)
Includes bibliographical references.
1. Religion in the public schools. 2. Prayer in the public schools.
3. Church and education. 4. Church and state.
I. Jones, Steven (Steven P.) II. Sheffield, Eric C.
LC107.R65 379.2'8—dc22 2009033488
ISBN 978-1-4331-0765-8 (hardcover)
ISBN 978-1-4331-0764-1 (paperback)
ISSN 1058-1634

Bibliographic information published by **Die Deutsche Nationalbibliothek**.
Die Deutsche Nationalbibliothek lists this publication in the "Deutsche
Nationalbibliografie"; detailed bibliographic data is available
on the Internet at http://dnb.d-nb.de/.

The paper in this book meets the guidelines for permanence and durability
of the Committee on Production Guidelines for Book Longevity
of the Council of Library Resources.

© 2009 Peter Lang Publishing, Inc., New York
29 Broadway, 18th floor, New York, NY 10006
www.peterlang.com

All rights reserved.
Reprint or reproduction, even partially, in all forms such as microfilm,
xerography, microfiche, microcard, and offset strictly prohibited.

Printed in the United States of America

Table of Contents

Acknowledgments vii

1. The Role of Religion in 21st–Century Public Schools 1
   Steven P. Jones

2. Understanding Unbelief as Part of Religious Education 19
   Nel Noddings

3. Seven Things the Establishment Clause Does Not Require 33
   Jordan Lorence

4. Religion, Identity, and Morality in Public Schools 51
   T. Jeremy Gunn

5. Metaphysics, Metaphor, and Meaningfulness: How to "Teach the Controversy" in Science Class 57
   Steve Broidy

6. College Fraternities and Expressive Association: Discrimination, Diversity, and Education 71
   Daniel Cohen

7. Prayer in Public Schools: Forming a More Perfect Union?.. 103
    Susan E. Waters

8. Thwarting the Court: A Historical Perspective on Efforts to Undermine the Supreme Court's School Prayer Decisions and the Effects on Religious Minorities.. 127
    Craig A. Smith

9. To Hell and Back: Teaching Faith-Based Literature to the Devout... 149
    Ryan Kennedy

10. The Necessary Role of Religion in Civic Education... 163
    Craig S. Engelhardt

11. Seeking Spaces for Emotionally Connected Rationality Amongst Dogmatic Belief Systems................ 187
    Andrew N. McKnight

12. Holding Tight with Open Hands—Education at Humlehaveskolen: A Majority Christian Culture and a Minority Muslim Culture Together in a Danish Public School.. 203
    Karla J. Smart-Morstad & David P. Morstad, Jr.

Contributors.. 225

Acknowledgments

In October 2007, the Academy for Educational Studies hosted the third annual Critical Questions in Education conference on the campus of Missouri State University. Sixty-five presentations over the two-and-a-half-day conference addressed different aspects of the critical theme question that year—What should the role of religion be in 21st-century public schools? The essays in this book are drawn from essays presented at the conference and represent the diversity of arguments and positions articulated at the conference.

We wish to thank those who support the Critical Questions in Education conference, especially Dennis Kear (Dean of the College of Education at Missouri State University), Fred Groves (Chair, Reading, Foundations & Technology at Missouri State University), and departmental office staff who help us put the conference together. Our keynote speakers at the conference—Nel Noddings, Jordan Lorence, and Jeremy Gunn—provided thought-provoking addresses and sparked comments and discussion among conference attendees, and we thank them for an excellent job. We also wish to thank Chris Myers, Sophie Appel, and all the staff at Peter Lang for their patience and professionalism as we worked through this publishing process. We thank our authors who were patient with us as we put the book together and arranged its publication. Last, but most importantly, we wish to thank all those who attended our conference who engaged in dialogue, asked questions, uncovered truths, and offered suggestions on the role of religion in the public schools.

Please see the website of the Academy for Educational Studies (http://education.missouristate.edu/acaded/) for information about the Academy and the next Critical Questions in Education conference.

Steven P. Jones
Eric C. Sheffield
Springfield, MO
September, 2009

CHAPTER ONE

The Role of Religion in 21st–Century Public Schools

Steven P. Jones, Missouri State University

No other educational issue hits a more sensitive nerve with the American public than the role of religion in the public schools. This is the issue that causes parents to storm school board meetings and science teachers to duck and cover. It's the issue that keeps newspaper editors busy all day and school administrators awake all night—the one stoking the public fire, the other trying to figure out what to say to a group of parents who demand that the upcoming graduation ceremonies be opened in prayer.

We shouldn't be surprised that such issues evoke strong responses from people involved directly and indirectly with the public schools. The public schools have always been a public arena where people with vastly different political, moral, and religious ideas and understandings send their children for assistance with a task that could not be more precious or dear to them—the education of their children. Parents and other community members contend with one another and with those responsible for educating their children so insistently about the presence of religious ideas and activities in the public schools because something vital is at stake—the moral (and, perhaps, spiritual) development of their children, at least part of which happens in the public schools.

Parents think and wonder almost continuously during the years they are raising their children about the kind of persons their children will become and the kind of life each will lead. "Will my child be happy in the living of his or her life?" is always a first question they ask themselves, and so, too, "Will my child be healthy?" These are not usually questions that generate much controversy. We have a generally clear idea of what we mean by "health," and we only disagree about what it means to be "happy" if we start to think about it too much. As long as we mean by "happy" the feeling that exists when one is relatively free from pain or anxiety or when a reasonable state of well-being is maintained—and as long as we agree that each of us has an unencumbered right to pursue what it is we believe will make us happy—then there is not much about which to argue.

It's when we ask the third important question natural to all parents in thinking about their children that the trouble starts. The third question is "Will my child be a good person?" Like the other two, this third question has a correlate question: "How do I help my child become a good person?" It may be, in a certain sense, that this question is like the one about happiness—as long as we don't think about what we mean by a "good person" very hard we can all agree. If by being "good" we have in mind only a sort of low-level civic responsibility—basic law abidingness or a minimal tolerance of those we don't especially care about—then we're probably on safe ground.

But most parents have a more particular idea of the kind of "goodness" they want for their children. For most religious people, in most religious communities in the United States, the goodness they want for their children is bound up in a life of religious faith. For them, being "good" involves (at least to some extent) living a life that is in accord with the law or with the teachings of a god that has revealed to members of the religious community what it is they are to believe and how they are supposed to live their lives. The sacred texts of received religions set out an ideal, or an "ought," for how one should live. Christians, for example, are taught they should strive to live a "Christ-like existence," and the Bible is filled with lessons on what that means and how it should be done. But traditional, organized religions ask much more from believers than obedience to scriptural law. The gods that speak to believers in sacred texts demand faith and worship—they ask for the giving over of heart and soul with the promise of what that will bring, now and in the future.

While, for the sincerely religious, faith is at the center of living a "good life" or being a "good person," it is no doubt true that a good life for such a person may and almost always does involve other things beyond religious faith—patriotism or love of country, for example. But religion gives the religious person a "second language" with which he or she can articulate the commitments, intentions, and actions that he or she believes constitute a good person and the living of a good life (Bellah, 1985). Our natural, instinctive "first language" is individualistic—an "I" language of personal wants, desires, and choices. But the second languages we also speak tie us to particular communities, traditions, and understandings. These suggest other duties and obligations that sometimes ameliorate and sometimes conflict with the self-oriented first language that is natural to us. Traditional, received religions and the teachings and support of local congregations may be more or less clear or compelling for those who profess faith, but it is the usual hope of parents who desire a religious upbringing for their children that those communities will provide a conception, even if rudimentary, of how one should live (Bellah, 1985, p. 239).

The question, "How do I help my child become a good person?," then, has an obvious answer for the religious parent: Do what is necessary to see that one's child learns the tenets of the faith and encourage and support his or her faith development. This may, as we know, be accomplished in any number of ways—first of all, when parents take their children to churches (or synagogues or mosques) where the children in some systematic and time-honored way are initiated into the faith and learn the beliefs and tenets of the religion. Parents try to inculcate certain faith practices in the daily routines of their children's lives, such as regular prayer and time for reading scripture. They craft activities—such as singing groups, youth groups, or softball teams—for their children to enjoy with other members of the faith community. Sometimes these activities become evangelistic, sometimes not—but effort is always made to conduct such activities in ways that are consistent with the religious understandings of the community.

Religious teaching and the understandings of faith communities also give parents a standard by which they can, and do, measure and judge the value and appropriateness of things outside the immediate control and influence of the family or faith community—with special interest on the part of parents in those things they believe might influence the moral and spiritual development of their children. Parents examine popular movies, television shows, video games, fairy tales, books, magazines, and the music played on the radio—scouring them for language, themes, or images they believe might be detrimental to their children. But they also scour political issues and political candidates in the light of religious understanding. They scour career and educational paths for their children, too, and how the "dating scene" looks to them when their children become teenagers. What they think about these things, and what this thinking decides for them about how to raise their children, they communicate to children by means of such things as dinner-table talk, solicited and unsolicited advice, behavior expectations, family rules, and the privileges or opportunities that will (or will not) be made available to their children.

And, so, these religious parents often (usually) send their children off to the public schools, and just as they scour books and movies and political candidates for public teaching that may be at odds with the religious teaching that is at the heart of family life, these parents scour all the goings-on of the public school. They look at children's literature books and science textbooks. They look at curricular materials used in elementary reading programs and high school "Marriage and Family" classes. They look at moral routines chosen by the school, like the saying of the Pledge of Allegiance at the start of the elementary school day and the presence (or absence) of a prayer at high school graduation ceremonies. They look at high school club activities, like Bi-Gala and the Fellowship of Christian Athletes. They want to know what their tax dollars actually buy in the school setting, and they tend to support those things they believe contribute to the vision they want for their children, and they tend not to support those they see as detrimental. They want teachers and school administrators to support and contribute to the vision they have for their children, or at least not work counter to it.

And so they come to school board meetings to talk about graduation prayers and the Pledge of Allegiance and the high school biology textbook. They complain about the Bi-Gala club that shares space and institutional support with the Fellowship of Christian Athletes. They seek to ban certain books from the library, they mount heated campaigns for school board elections, they get teachers fired, and they hire lawyers to advocate their cause and pursue justice as they see it. They do these things because they want their children to live good, godly lives—and they believe the school should contribute to this.

Of course, not all parents who would describe themselves as being religious or who share a god-centered conception of "goodness" for their children see all this in the same way. In the public discussion of the role of religion in the public schools a second group of religiously oriented parents and community members is generally recognized—one that does *not* want the public school involved in matters of religious faith and practices. These parents fear those controlling the schools may invoke or insist upon tenets of faith, religious practices, and religious understandings that are contrary to those shared by their particular religious communities. For such parents, the graduation prayer or the religious song programmed at the choir concert is not problematic because it is religious, but because it might undermine the particular religious understanding the parents wish their children to acquire.

But it is impossible to capture, in such a short summary, all the reasons why religiously inclined parents seek to affect school policy, in one way or another, in regard to matters of religious faith. General descriptions, such as the one offered here, do not do justice to the complexity of what is a highly individual and personal matter. It is just as difficult to describe the understandings of those parents who are not religious—those parents who would answer the questions "Will my child be a good person?" and "How do I help my child become a good person?" in ways that have nothing to do with religious conceptions

Parents not oriented by religious understandings do the same kinds of things as religious parents as they try to make their children into good people. They institute certain regular family practices and organize youth activities, and they scour movies, television shows, music, and video games for the same kind of language, ideas, or images the religious parent might deem inappropriate for his or her children. They, too, make decisions about political issues and political candidates in the light of deeply held commitments, commitments that guide their thinking about career and educational paths for their children and the rules and guidelines they institute when their children start dating. And they do all this for many, even most, of the same reasons as religious parents. They do so as guardians of the moral development of their children. They do it with hopes their children will grow up to be good people living good lives.

Nonreligious parents, too, send their children off to public schools, and there they watch over the content and practices of their children's education. They are interested in the stories their children read in elementary school, and they want to know about what the biology textbook says about evolution or creationism. They care about how sexual relations are discussed in health and "Marriage and Family" classes, and they monitor the kinds of clubs or fellowship offered to their children. And they are as interested as the religiously oriented parent in whether or not their tax dollars and the practices of the school support or fail to support the vision they have for their children.

And they, too, go to school board meetings and advocate for their positions. They enter into debate about whether or not books should be banned or if Bi-Gala should be allowed to share space and resources with the Fellowship of Christian Athletes. They are as apt to rally the community for school board elections as any other group, and they, too, hire lawyers and challenge school policies in court.

But while the intentions and actions of the religious and non-religious parents and community members overlap a great deal as they conceive of the good people they want their children to become, there is no apparent overcoming of their differences regarding the place of religious faith and religious life in that vision. Non-religious parents do not use religious language to describe the basis of their moral commitments and their hopes for the moral life their children will lead. Other second languages are available to them, each suggesting a community to serve, and each with the power to circumscribe our first instincts for radical autonomy. There is, for instance, the language of the civic republican tradition that articulates commitments and practices that can powerfully shape character. These commitments and practices establish interconnections between people, joining people to families, friends, communities, and churches—making each individual aware of his reliance on the larger society (Bellah, 1985, p. 251). The second languages of social responsibility and social justice suggest other commitments, duties, and obligations that can shape "the habits of the heart" of young people. Religious people have recourse to these same second languages, and most of us speak a mix of second languages as we try to articulate the commitments that bind us to one another and suggest duties and obligations central to the living of a good life.

People of faith committed to religious second language sometimes intend to disparage the ideals articulated by those who use other second languages by calling those ideals "secular humanism." In the pejorative sense of the term, these other languages speak a "mere" secular humanism, the pejorative sense pointing to how these languages are unmoored to divine revelation that can be taken as the absolute ground for human action and understanding. This, of course, points to the sticking point between the religious and the secular humanists—the "God question." The question is this: Is God at the center of a vision of goodness and the living of a good life, or is he (or she) not? And because they cannot agree on the answer to this question, they cannot agree on an answer for its correlate: Should God, and/or religious faith, be at the center, or any part of, the moral and spiritual upbringing of children? They cannot agree, then, that religious faith should be at the center of curriculum or practices in the public school.

So, the group of parents and community members that wants faith-based understandings for their children press the school administrator to open graduation ceremonies with what they deem to be an appropriate prayer. The group of parents and community members that insists the school not endorse or inculcate faith-based understandings—the secular humanists and those with religious understandings who worry school people may be forced to endorse only limited and particular understandings—press those same administrators to deny the request for the opening prayer. And so the newspaper editor churns out his paper. And so the school administrator tosses in her sleep, unable to please everyone.

Does Man Need God in Order to be Good?

The question of God—about whether or not one should be raised to believe in God or some form of higher power—is a central educational question. We cannot will it away. That is because we cannot escape thinking about the kinds of questions with which this essay opens—about the happiness and health and goodness we want for our children. The moment we start thinking about the kind of good life we want our children to lead—the kind of good people we want them to become—is the moment we start down the road that leads to the god question. Why should man be good? Why should he be compassionate? Why should he care as much or more about others as he does himself? We ask these things in the frame of thinking about our children. We also ask them when we think about ourselves. Why should I be kind to others, even when I feel myself being abused? Why should I care about my children when the care goes unrewarded? Why should I come home every night to my wife instead of going somewhere else? Do I do these things because I have faith in a god who teaches me to do them and gives me reason for doing so, or do I do these things because I have some other conception of or reason for goodness?

Every important educational philosopher, from Plato on, has dealt with these questions. And, in America, every important thinker worried about the function and purpose of the public school has dealt with them, from the founding fathers on. And, as it turns out, these thinkers couldn't disagree more about the place of religious faith in the education of the young.

It will perhaps be useful, as we think about how and why this "God question" is so central to the education of our children, if we remind ourselves of the contours of the arguments put forth by some central educational thinkers. How is it possible our best educational thinkers could disagree so radically on such an important issue? A brief look at the ideas of Plato, Rousseau, and the founders of the common schools in America may help expand our ways of viewing this question.

In Plato's *Republic*, the rich and powerful young men of Athens—the young men who aspire one day to come to power and rule the city—gather around Socrates, first of all, to talk about the nature of justice and political power. To these ambitious and potentially dangerous young men, Socrates offers to describe the "perfect city" and the "perfect men" who will inhabit it. In the perfect city that will satisfy the longings of these young men, Socrates describes the perfect guardians and how they must be educated. The perfect guardians are, of course, the ones perfectly suited by nature to be fierce defenders of the city. They are characterized by *thymos*, or a warlike spiritedness that makes them fearless and invincible in the defense of the city (375b)—the same kind of fearlessness we see in a guard dog that will die in defense of his (or her) owner or the property it takes to be its own. In humans this *thymos* can appear as anger, or rage, or zeal. We recognize *thymos* in the spiritedness of the war hero, fearless in attacking the enemy even when he knows he may die in the attempt.

But just as the dog, willing to attack (and kill) the "enemies" come to do harm to its owner, is a gentle and affectionate dog with the people it knows and loves, so, too, must the perfect guardian—the ferocious defender of the city—be gentle and affectionate toward his fellow citizens. This becomes the first educational task in Socrates' perfect city: to make the guardians into *kaloagathos*, or gentlemen, who are gentle when among their countrymen, but fierce and full of *thymos* when defending the city from its enemies. While not an easy education to effect, it is, perhaps the most critical, as we see in our own time. We know the dramatic, even tragic, consequences of failing to conduct this education properly whenever we learn of some general in a third world country—tired of his own political impotence or urged on by the soldiers beneath his command—who conducts a military coup and comes to power. Absent the right education, the noble dog can and will turn on its owner.

To guarantee the fidelity of the guardians to the people, Socrates insists their first education be about the gods of the city—and the stories about the gods must be carefully chosen. The young guardians are not to hear all the awful stories about what the gods did to one another and to the humans who worshipped them—only the stories that depict the gods of the city in the most admirable and perfect ways. These stories, Socrates says, will make the young men into warriors who honor the gods and ancestors, and they will become men who are serious about their friendship with one another. The guardians will have proper opinions about the gods and will become pious and just (Bloom, 1968, p. 353).

But while this teaching about the gods is sufficient for the guardians of the city, it is not sufficient for those young men who might one day lead the city—the philosopher-kings. For the philosopher-kings, the gods are useful and necessary to the peaceful and orderly operation of the city, and they deserve respect and receive public homage. But the goal for the philosopher-king is not to come to have "proper opinions," or "true opinions," about the pious and the just, as it is for the guardians. The education of the philosopher-king is to lead him to knowledge (*episteme*), specifically, to knowledge about the truth of things. The way to the truth of things, for Socrates, was not divine revelation—it was through reasoning (*logos*). The education of the philosopher-kings was always aimed at perfecting this reasoning ability. The philosopher-king, liberated from the cave of opinion, was one day to come to know the *idea of the good*—that perfect, ultimate knowledge of the whole, of the one and the many.

The young men gathered to talk to Socrates (especially Glaucon, the particular favorite in the dialogue) are not interested in becoming guardians—they want to be philosopher-kings, and they picture themselves as such even as they may fail to possess the capacities outlined by Socrates as he discusses the nature of the philosopher-king. Throughout the course of the dialogue, Socrates shows these young men something much better for them than what they thought they wanted at the beginning of the dialogue, which was political power—specifically, the power of the tyrant who is able to command whatever it is he believes he wants. Superior to political power, Socrates convinces them, is knowledge, or wisdom—the life of the philosopher—and by the end of the dialogue they turn away from their tyrannical ambitions in favor of the pursuit of wisdom. Here, religious faith or adherence to the teachings of the gods does not make the young men good—the perfection of their reason does. Even the erotic Glaucon now has reason to subdue his passions and be "stronger than himself" (431a) because now he knows something better and more worthy of his strongest desires. The guardians and the artisans (the *hoi polloi*) need faith in and fear of the gods in order to subdue their passions and become good, but the elite few need only the power of their reason. With the arguments of Socrates and Plato and a commitment to untrammeled reason, the Western tradition begins. Faith in reason and the rational discovery of the truth of things led to philosophy and natural science as we know them.

An inheritor and great critic of that tradition, especially a critic of the Enlightenment and its understanding of man based on tenets of natural science, stands Jean-Jacques Rousseau, the great Romantic who protested that those who understood man simply as some great reasoning animal were simply setting aside what most animates and distinguishes man—his passions. In *Emile*, Rousseau proposes to make not the elite philosopher-king—the man with perfected reason who knows the truth of things—but the man most necessary to his own time, the modern democratic man. Rousseau proposed to make the man who was good for himself and good for others, the man who had sure judgments about things, the man who would be able to stand independent of others yet be compassionate to those in need. Rousseau proposed to make the natural man—not the man completed by a vision of perfected reason—but the man completed by following the dictates of nature. According to Rousseau, nature establishes both the goals and the limits of the education we should contrive for our children.

And what does nature tell us about ourselves? "Natural man is entirely for himself," Rousseau writes early in *Emile*. From the infant's first cry, to the self-interested demands the child makes of his parents, to our desire to be the most preferred when we seek to capture the interest of a mate, we operate on the basis of our own self-interest. Rousseau calls this "self-love," and according to him there are two kinds—*amour de soi* and *amour-propre*. *Amour de soi* is the natural self-love given us at birth, a self-interested love that reveals itself primarily in our instincts to preserve ourselves. It is not a self-love we should be ashamed of, and we could not overcome it even if we sought to. *Amour-propre*, on the other hand, is a comparative kind of self-love—a love of self with a view to how others see and esteem us. It is self-love with a preferential demand that others love us more than they love themselves. The baby who cries because he is hungry or wet and seeks remedy for his condition cries out of *amour de soi*; the baby who cries as a demand for his mother to pick him up and pay attention to him—a demand for his mother to prefer him over herself—cries out of *amour-propre*. The child, in a famous passage in *Emile*, who runs a foot race against fellow competitors so as to gain the prize for the victor—sweet cakes that are a favorite of his—competes out of *amour de soi*; the child who runs the race to receive the accolades accorded to the victor, and so as to see himself as superior to the other competitors, competes out of *amour-propre*. The one is a healthy, inescapable, entirely natural self-love. The other is a function of pride and vanity. The one, Rousseau claims, is given by "the Author of things"; the other is a relative sentiment, artificial, and born in society. The educational object, then, is to preserve the healthy self-love given us by nature and to do all we can to prevent the development of the unhealthy self-love—to prevent the development of pride and vanity (See Bloom, 1979, p. 483–84). Now, all this is neither possible, nor, in the end, desirable. *Amour-propre*, after all, must come to be in a man's sexual life when he wants a woman to prefer him to all other men (and vice versa), and it can powerfully motivate his actions. Still, delay of, and then delicate control of, emergent passions is the primary task of the tutor, and this the tutor, Jean-Jacques, provides for his pupil Emile.

But how is a "natural man, entirely for himself" to be made good for others? Even *amour de soi*, a healthy self-love, is "entirely" self-interested. How is such a self-interested man to be made compassionate? Why would a self-interested man be willing to accept duties and obligations that come with being a citizen, a member of a community, someone's son, or someone's husband or father? Is there a place here for religion and faith in God in the moderation or elimination of man's instinctive self-interest?

Not according to Rousseau—at least not as we typically conceive of the ways religion counteracts the native impulses of men. In the long "Profession of Faith of the Savoyard Vicar" Rousseau addresses religious faith, though the text makes it clear that the profession of the good Vicar would be more valuable and appropriate for a corrupt adolescent (such as Rousseau was, himself) than for Emile who has received protection from the corruptions of society. In his profession the Vicar speaks of "inner sentiment" and "conscience" as being natural to us. These are innate senses of justice and virtue, deep in our souls, and they are not contrary to our self-love, but come to be natural expressions of it (Dent, 1988, p. 234–242). Cruelty and injustice are the result of an enflamed *amour-propre*, and in the person with such inflamed self-love the development of conscience and compassion for others is problematic, if not altogether doubtful. But in the man Emile becomes, these passions are not inflamed, and his natural compassion for others is an expression of the divine gift given him at birth. His passions need careful education—there is danger of corruption all around. But these passions can be sublimated, or lifted up, to lead Emile to see his duties and obligations to be as sweet as they are necessary (Bloom, 1979, p. 15–16). Emile has no need of a pastor, or a Catholic priest, sermonizing on the evils of pride and submission to a forgiving god. He will recognize, thank, and even praise god as the giver of the gifts he enjoys, but it is doubtful one would ever find him, on any given Sunday, sitting in church.

The founders of the common schools in America—careful readers, all, of both the Greeks and Rousseau—were less sanguine about the natural goodness of man and the possibility of his perfected reason. Carl Kaestle writes about the ideology these founders shared—their common ideas about human nature and society that allowed them to interpret complex human problems and devise solutions to them (Kaestle, 1983, p. 76). This ideology, he argues, gravitated around three poles—republicanism, Protestantism, and capitalism—but the name he gives this thinking is "Native Protestant ideology." In this conception, human beings were "born malleable and potentially good but need much careful guidance"—exactly opposite the thinking of Rousseau. These founders believed all men are equal in some formal ways, but they also believed some groups are more able, wise, and refined than others. This meant, in education and other arenas such as economics and politics, that institutions be shaped to maintain the values and leadership of cultivated, native, Protestant Americans (Kaestle, 1983, p. 95).

"The survival of the American republic depended upon the morality of its people," Kaestle writes, "not in armies or constitutions or inspired leadership—but in the virtue of the propertied, industrious, and intelligent American yeoman" (Kaestle, 1983, p.79). Schooling was to stress unity, obedience, restraint, self-sacrifice, and the careful exercise of intelligence (p. 81). Here, moral education overlapped citizenship education (p. 97), and moral education was bound up with Protestant religious understandings, these understandings being its source and ground. The founders had a common understanding about the moral purposes for common schooling, among them that moral education was to produce obedient children, reduce crime, and discourage vice (p. 101).

The historical record is pretty clear: God used to be in the common public schools. Protestant understandings were evident, directly or indirectly, in the readers given to children in the one-room schoolhouse, in the citing and rehearsal of Bible verses, in the moral asides of teachers and schoolmasters, in the explanations of expected behavior given to students, and in school prayers. Protestant ideology and its place in the common school was extolled from the pulpit, demanded in the town hall, explained in domestic manuals, and proposed in educational texts.

The historical record is no less clear about how, from the very beginning, this native Protestant ideology was deeply problematic and the source of contention. The efforts to establish a common culture and a national unity, underpinned by a distinctly Protestant theology, caused anger and resentment from ethnic and religious groups with very different understandings, especially the Catholics. Even Protestants who might affirm much of the prevailing ideology could disagree with one another in quite vociferous terms about the conduct of their local common schools. Localists who disputed with those who favored centralized schooling objected on several counts. Many objected because they wanted to limit the costs of education that came with centralization, but many objected, as well, because they detected the sacrifice of their own traditions and the elimination of their own prerogatives as parents or members of minority groups (Kaestle, 1983, p. 148).

Explorations Undertaken in This Volume

People engaged in the current public discussion of the role of religion in the public schools don't worry too much about the ideas of Socrates and Rousseau—at least not directly. The thinking of the founders of the public schools—like the thinking of Washington, Jefferson, Adams and the rest of our political founders—seems more salient to the current discussion than the thinking of an ancient Greek and a crazy, idealistic Romantic. It is certainly the case, as the article by Susan Waters (Chapter 7) makes clear, that founding thought is taken very seriously in the contemporary debate. How central was God to the political and educational understandings of the founders, and what was the place, constitutionally, they intended to allow for God and religious faith in public life? The very fact that God and religious faith used to be so present and central to the conduct of public schools is reason enough, for some, to argue for a return to God-centered public schools. Craig Engelhardt traces some of this thinking in his argument for the necessary role of religion in civic education (Chapter 10).

Much of what the founders intended as they drafted our founding documents—especially, of course, the Constitution—gets argued in the continuing line of court cases involving the different roles of religion in the public school. What the school administrator decides to do when assailed by parents about graduation prayers is determined in no small way by Supreme Court decisions. The essay by Craig Smith (Chapter 8) details many of the Supreme Court decisions about the issue of school prayer. But the Supreme Court never seems quite done with cases about religion

The Role of Religion in 21st–Century Public Schools 15

and the schools. This is because new issues keep coming up, like whether or not state-supported university fraternities and sororities can enforce "Christian only" admissions. This new issue is explored in depth in Daniel Cohen's essay (Chapter 6). The Supreme Court is also never quite done with this issue because "Christ-centered" legal alliances, like the Alliance Defense Fund, keep bringing new cases through the court system in their attempts to develop a more central place for religious understandings in the public schools. In this volume, Jordan Lawrence, a constitutional attorney who works for the Alliance Defense Fund, outlines seven things the Establishment Clause of the Constitution does *not* require of government and school officials, enabling school officials to allow more religious activities in the school (Chapter 3). Jeremy Gunn, Director of the Program on Freedom of Religion and Belief for the American Civil Liberties Union (ACLU) offers an opposing view. Gunn seeks to remind religious conservatives that the youth of this country were not quite so moral in the years *before* the Supreme Court ensured that public schools would largely be "godless" (Chapter 4).

The issue of religion and the public schools can put into question the faith Socrates and the rest of the Greeks had in the power of man's reason, but educators are not usually without hope about the abilities of human beings to use and develop their reasoning abilities and come to reasoned understandings. In this volume's second essay, Nel Noddings, America's pre-eminent philosopher of education, argues students need, deserve, and can thoughtfully consider not only aspects of traditional religious instruction, but also arguments for agnosticism, atheism, and secular humanism (Chapter 2). Similarly, Steve Broidy argues that teachers should *not* avoid that most controversial of topics—the evolution/creationism debate, especially in science classes. Broidy argues, instead, that teachers ought to "teach the controversy" and give students the tools for understanding the reasons for religious and scientific understandings of our beginnings (Chapter 5).

Rousseau's concerns about man's passions—his pride and his vanity, especially when a cherished and central belief seems as if it is being challenged or undermined—this human drama appears, too, as the issue of the role of religion in the public school is pushed and prodded. Andrew McKnight's essay examines the difficulties he faces in his teacher education classes when students who, in thinking about themselves as teachers, profess intolerance for students who do not share their Christian understandings (Chapter 11). Ryan Kennedy's essay documents his experiences teaching Dante's *Inferno* in a rural church-going town and tells about another teacher, a Catholic, who lacked the courage to teach Milton's *Paradise Lost* to anti-Catholic students (Chapter 9). Only the essay by Karla J. Smart-Morstad and David P. Morstad, Jr. seems to offer evidence of Rousseau's faith that man can set aside his pride and vanity and act compassionately to others who are very different. Smart-Morstad and Morstad, Jr. document their research on a Danish public school that has successfully adapted to a growing number of Muslim students (Chapter 12).

Concluding Thoughts

"Will my child be a good person?" and "How do I help my child become a good person?" These *are* inevitable questions that both parents and school people must answer. And, as I have suggested above, the God question is just as inevitable: Is faith in God necessary and central to being a good person and living a good life? The religious person and the nonreligious person are never going to see eye-to-eye on this central question, and so they are likely not to see eye-to-eye on the place of religious teaching and activities in the public school.

The religious person is likely not to share Plato's confidence in the power of human reason to lead people to see, understand, and embrace the good and to want to live a good life. Neither is the religious person likely to share Rousseau's faith in the natural goodness of man and his capacity to live a good and compassionate life when that goodness is nurtured and preserved. Plato's understanding conflicts with the religious man's commitment to faith over reason in providing answers to man's important questions. Rousseau's understanding conflicts with the doctrine of original sin and the idea that man needs faith and religious commitment in order to overcome his sinfulness and live a worthy life. Neither is the nonreligious person likely to share the beliefs and practices of the founders of the public schools who believed their own Protestant religion necessary to redeem man's flawed nature and make him fit both to be an American citizen and a servant of God, and who saw the public school as a legitimate and important place for such teaching.

None of these different ways of conceiving the possibility for human goodness and the way to the living of a good life is silly, stupid, or unreasonable. Each argument has a place in our tradition, and each shapes our current understanding and our current conflict. If the truth be told, many parents no doubt borrow something from each of these understandings in thinking about how to help their children live good lives. They may believe they see a natural goodness in their children they want to preserve and protect, and they may believe the development of the child's reason can lead to informed choice and compassionate adult behavior. They may also believe that religious teaching and religious faith may help their child along the way, perhaps as an anchor for the child's understanding and choice of action. This might be mere confusion on the part of parents. It may also be, however, an amalgam of understandings that shape the policies, theories and practices of schools and the well-intentioned people in them who want the best for the children they serve.

Those who work in public schools, or who send their children to them, or who try to think carefully about them, have some reason to try to be clear about their own understandings about the role of religion and the public schools, and they have reason to be clear about the understandings of others. Each of us has an opportunity to enter the discussion and debate about this issue in a knowing, reasonable, and sensitive way. We hope this book contributes to the careful discussion of this most important topic.

BIBLIOGRAPHY

Bellah, R. N., et al. (1985). *Habits of the heart: Individualism and commitment in American life*. Berkeley: University of California Press.

Bloom, A. (1968). *The Republic of Plato*. New York: Basic Books.

Dent, N. J. H. (1988). *Rousseau: An introduction to his psychological, social and political theory*. Oxford: Basil Blackwell.

Kaestle, C. (1983). *Pillars of the Republic: Common schools and American society, 1780–1860*. New York: Hill and Wang.

Rousseau, Jean-Jacques (1762/1979). *Emile, or on education*. A. Bloom, trans. New York: Basic Books.

CHAPTER TWO

Understanding Unbelief as Part of Religious Education

Nel Noddings, Emeritus, Stanford University

It is often recommended that courses in world religions and Bible literacy be taught in our public schools. Even Richard Dawkins (2006) approves of the latter for its contribution to the understanding of literature. However, it is rarely suggested that students should gain some understanding of deism, agnosticism, atheism, and secular humanism.

Too many adults—even supposedly well-educated adults—express scorn and contempt for unbelievers. It is widely held, and probably true, that a confessed unbeliever could not be elected president of the United States today. No matter what candidates really believe, if they hope to be elected in the United States, they had better say that they believe in God. Students are expected to learn respect, or at least tolerance, for all religions, but little is said about tolerance for unbelief.

I'll begin this paper with a discussion of terms that should be understood and their frequent misapplication. Then I'll consider briefly the intellectual and moral reasons people have offered for rejecting religion. Finally, I'll consider some possible ways to improve communication between believers and unbelievers. In all that follows, I'll speak of unbelief in the context of Christianity, although many of my comments might easily be transposed to other religions.

The Language of Unbelief

In his fascinating study of teenagers and religious belief, Christian Smith found that students sometimes declared themselves to be deists but contradicted themselves in responding to his questions: "22 percent of teen 'deists' in our survey reported feeling close or very close to God (the very God they believe is not involved in the world today). Go figure" (Smith, 2005, p. 42). Apparently, these kids had little understanding of the belief they professed.

Some confusion over the term *deism* is understandable. Over the five centuries or so that it has been used, its meaning has varied, but today it refers to belief in a God indistinguishable from nature or to a God who created the world but does not intervene in its affairs. The first interpretation is found in Spinoza and, much more recently, in Einstein. The second, differing only slightly, is reflected in the writings of the American Founding Fathers—Washington, Jefferson, Franklin, Paine, and Adams. These men spoke of a "creator" but did not believe in a God who watches over humans, hears prayers, or responds with rewards and punishments. We may quibble over whether Jefferson should be labeled an atheist and Adams a Unitarian Christian, but evidence abounds that all of them rejected the central beliefs specific to Christianity.

The deistic beliefs of the founders (and, likely, of Abraham Lincoln) are widely denied, and many Americans insist on calling them "Christians" and the United States a "Christian" nation, even though Washington explicitly denied that the nation was founded on Christian principles (Allen, 2006; Jacoby, 2004). Such false beliefs should be challenged in history courses, and at least a few brief original writings should be used to dispel them.

The term *agnostic* is, of course, derived from the Greek, but our use of the label is usually traced to Thomas H. Huxley, and Huxley's view greatly influenced Darwin. Agnostics hold that we do not know, and probably can never know, whether God exists. Their position seems both admirably humble and scientifically reasonable. Yet they are attacked from both ends of the belief spectrum. Many Christians simply lump them with atheists; atheists accuse them of fence-sitting.

Atheists think there is so little evidence (some argue there is none) for the existence of God that the only logical conclusion to draw is that there is no God. Martin Gardner, a philosophical theist, acknowledged that his faith was "unsupported by logic or science" (1983, p. 209). Indeed, he admired Bertrand Russell's definition of faith as "a firm belief in something for which there is no evidence" (quoted in Gardner, 1983, p. 209). In the writings of the theist Gardner and the atheist Russell, we see possibilities for meaningful dialogue between believers and unbelievers.

Some contemporary atheists—Dawkins, 2006; Dennett, 2006; Harris, 2004, 2006; Hitchens, 2007—make such dialogue difficult. Many of their points are well made, and one wonders why they fall on deaf ears. One wonders, that is, until one reflects on how any of us feels when her deepest convictions are not only challenged but mocked. In contrast to the heavy-handedness just mentioned, E. O. Wilson (2006) invites serious dialogue between Christians and secular humanists. I'll return to Wilson's approach in the last section of this paper.

Secular humanists (as contrasted with religious humanists) reject religion and a God-centered notion of human perfectibility. They put their efforts into improving earthly life for humans and, increasingly, into preservation of the earth and all living things. There are opponents who refer to the "religion of secular humanism," but this is wrong and adds to the confusion surrounding the language of unbelief. Most sociologists studying religion recognize that the best line of demarcation between religion and other belief systems is the inclusion or exclusion of a supreme being, God (Stark & Bainbridge, 1985). Still, this is in itself a discussion to which students should be introduced. In addition to the faulty labeling of secular humanism as a religion, some people have even called Marxism a religion because it has an eschatology—a predicted end-stage. It is indeed odd to classify a Godless ideology as a religion.

Intellectual Objections to Religion

Many thoughtful people give up (or never adopt) belief in God because they find no evidence for its acceptance. All the great attempts at logically establishing the existence of God have been demolished. Some of these proofs can be legitimately explored in math classes. In geometry, teachers might mention that a great philosopher, Immanuel Kant, used Euclidean geometry as an example of logico-mathematical certainty. Actually, at about the time of his writing, non-Euclidean geometries were being invented, and their invention proved Kant wrong in his claim of certainty. However, Kant—like many great philosophers—was also interested in religion, and he successfully destroyed all three of the traditional proofs of God's existence.

Students, unaware of these "proofs," may point at one of them intuitively. There is the world, they may say, a whole universe. Must there not have been a creator? But, then, who or what created the creator and, if the creator created himself, why could we not suppose the same of the universe? Kant answered these questions poignantly:

> We cannot put aside, and yet also cannot endure, the thought that a being, which we represent to ourselves as supreme amongst all beings, should as it were, say to itself: I am from eternity to eternity, and outside me there is nothing save what is through my will, but whence then am I? All support here fails us. (1781/1966, p. 409)

Without expecting high school students to master the details of various attempts at proof, we can induce awareness of them. An outline of Descartes' version of the ontological proof can also be engaged in math class, for example. It should, of course, be pointed out that attempts to prove that God does *not* exist have also failed, but attempts are still made (Martin & Monnier, 2003). Awareness of these logical exercises, like Bible study, can be thought of as part of religious literacy.

The argument from design has to be discussed somewhere in high school. My own preference would be to discuss creationism and intelligent design in science classes—not *as* science but as part of an on-going challenge that scientists still face. Too often the decision to teach evolution and omit intelligent design is made by school boards, and students are left ignorant about the exciting history of the debate. Or the issue might arise briefly in social studies class—a "current events" treatment bereft of both passion and science.

In an honest discussion, students would learn that, although many scientists are secular humanists, many others retain belief in a personal God, and some provide evolutionary evidence for the existence of God. Simon Conway Morris, for example, offers powerful evidence of a pattern in evolution that leads inexorably to intelligent life. In concluding, he writes:

> None of it presupposes, let alone proves, the existence of God, but all is congruent. For some it will remain as the pointless activity of the Blind Watchmaker, but others may prefer to remove their dark glasses. The choice, of course, is yours. (2003, p. 330)

The Morris book is far too difficult for high school students, but excerpts from it could be read—so, too, the lovely lines from Kant—and readings of this sort could serve as models for generous discussion. We need not attack one another with nasty, disparaging remarks but, unfortunately, both sides have been guilty of this. Christian fundamentalists have equated atheism with evil and immorality, and some of today's atheist writers heap ridicule on believers. Educating for intelligent belief or unbelief requires a more thoughtful, considerate approach (Noddings, 1993, 2003, 2006).

Students should also learn that they may, if they wish, retain their religious affiliation even if they reject some of its beliefs. (This is not true of all religious institutions, of course, but it is of many Christian subgroups.) They should hear of cases in which priests and ministers have doubted the virgin birth, the miracles reported in the New Testament, the trinity, the existence of hell, the correctness of infant baptism, the bodily ascent of Mary into heaven, transubstantiation, and many other ideas held by some to be essential beliefs. Scholars have labeled some of these beliefs "maximally counterintuitive" (Slone, 2004), and they are studying how religious groups maintain such beliefs.

As a matter of fact, we cannot conclude what people actually believe from their church attendance or even from their public statements. We know, for example, that some of the Founding Fathers, despite their church membership, did not believe in a personal God and, although the large majority of people in the United States today claim belief in such a God, we do not know what they might say in the company of highly respected unbelievers. In such circumstances, they might well feel comfortable expressing some doubt. As Daniel Dennett (2006) has argued, many believers seem to believe in belief, not in particular beliefs.

Science fiction might be used to expand the range of students' thinking. Is it utterly impossible to imagine another dimension in which a whole world of godlike entities exist? Might some of them now and then take notice of human affairs? Why is monotheism favored over polytheism, and whose interests have been served by the elevation of monotheism?

The enduring concern about matters of spirit should be addressed. Atheists and agnostics are not devoid of a sense of wonder and spiritual awe. Bertrand Russell regarded the universe with awe, and his daughter described his life as a spiritual quest (Ryan, 1988). Believers, if they think, are assailed by doubt and unbelievers, if they accept their emotions, are deeply affected by "spirit." Miguel De Unamuno captured the conflict:

> "Is there?" "Is there not?"—these are the bases of our inner life. There may be a rationalist who has never wavered in his conviction of the mortality of the soul, and there may be a vitalist who has never wavered in his faith in immortality; but at the most this would only prove that just as there are natural monstrosities, so there are those who are stupid as regards heart and feeling, however great their intelligence, and those who are stupid intellectually, however great their virtue...(1954, p. 119)

Moral Objections to Belief

In the late nineteenth century, many erstwhile Christian believers turned against religion. "Declarations of unbelief often sounded more like acts of moral will than intellectual judgments," writes James Turner (1985). Oddly, Christian churches at the time had made a discernible shift from stern practices toward more humane messages emphasizing the relief of suffering. The anticruelty sentiment was then turned against religion itself. Newly confessed unbelievers cited both the cruelty of nature and the cruelty of religion as reasons for their unbelief.

Darwin, for example, was certainly shaken by the cruelty and indifference of the natural world, but he was pushed even harder into agnosticism by the cruelty of Christian beliefs. He wrote:

> I can indeed hardly see how anyone ought to wish Christianity to be true; for if so, the plain language of the text seems to show that the men who do not believe, and this would include my father, brother and almost all my best friends, will be everlastingly punished. And this is a damnable doctrine. (quoted in Browne, 2002, p. 432)

Today there are Christian groups that do not require belief in hell, but most still do, and thoughtful believers are likely to become unbelievers when they consider the question: What sort of God would say to his creatures, "Believe in me, or go to hell"? Karen Armstrong (1995), for example, revolted at the task she was given by the Catholic Church—to fill children with guilt and teach them doctrines through fear.

The public schools cannot speak out directly against the practices of any religious institutions (except when they violate state laws), and they should not indoctrinate either for or against religion, but they should protect children from religious cruelty by exposing them to a variety of views that may help them eventually to reject harmful beliefs such as the one on hell. I agree with Dawkins (2006) that teaching children to believe in eternal punishment in hell is a form of child abuse. In explaining why he was not a Christian, Russell, too, spoke on this: "There is one very serious defect to my mind in Christ's moral character, and that is that He believed in hell" (1957, p. 17).

An important intellectual problem arises in discussion of belief in hell. Many theologians recognize that we cannot logically hold to all three great characteristics so often attributed to God: omniscience, omnipotence, and all-goodness. Indeed, while the existence or nonexistence of God cannot be logically proved, the coexistence of these three attributes has been effectively demolished. Something has to be given up. What bewilders so many unbelievers is that few believers consider questioning God's "all-goodness"—the one attribute that is contradicted by a clear look at the natural world. When people are wiped out by tsunamis, babies are born with horrible defects, and people of all ages suffer dreadful illnesses, how can we speak of a good and merciful God? What sort of God would create a world in which its creatures must eat one another to stay alive? Even C. S. Lewis (1962) had a hard time with questions of animal pain, and he answered them badly. Indeed, although I believe that students should be exposed to Lewis as well as Russell, it might happen that, paradoxically, reading *The Problem of Pain* (1962) would convert some believers to unbelief.

Another moral objection to Christianity is its habit of placing itself above history—claiming that moral offenses by Christian groups are aberrations or misunderstandings and that Christianity is a "religion of peace." (Christianity is not alone in this, of course. Every day now we hear Moslems threatening violence when they are accused "falsely" of embracing a violent religion.) From this perspective, wrongs done in the name of Christianity are distortions, but Christians seldom ask themselves what it is in Christian doctrine that grounds such distortions, and why it is that Christian history is loaded with violence, intolerance, and cruelty. There is too little discussion of contradictions in the Bible—for example, the Prince of Peace claiming, "Think not that I come to send peace on earth: I came not to send peace, but a sword" (Matthew 10:34). The verses that follow this are not comforting, and terrible threats appear again in Matthew 11:22, 23; 12:30, 31; 13:40–42, 50. The disavowal of peace is repeated in Luke 12: 51–53.

The frustration of unbelievers is directed at the Christian God when we read Matthew 25: 35–46 where Jesus promises salvation to believers who act compassionately to "the least of these my brethren." Compassionate unbelievers want to know why God does not follow his own commands. What is he doing for the least of these my brethren?

Thoughtful readers can see what so angers Dawkins and Harris and before them Robert Ingersoll and Russell. Yet, if we mean to educate, we must find a way to communicate honestly and compassionately across the gulf of belief and unbelief.

Communicating to Educate

E. O. Wilson's *The Creation* (2006) is a model of attempted communication. Written as a letter from a secular humanist (Wilson) to a nameless southern Baptist pastor, it is "a call for help and an invitation to visit the embattled natural world in the company of a biologist." Wilson wants the pastor to join him in saving life on earth. The technique is one recommended by savvy diplomats; it was also recommended by John Dewey. The idea is to talk about something on which we might agree—to admit our differences but to join together in some significant task.

Wilson starts right out stating the differences:

> You are a literalist interpreter of Christian Holy Scripture. You reject the conclusion of science that mankind evolved from lower forms. You believe that each person's soul is immortal, making this planet a way station to a second, eternal life. Salvation is assured those who are redeemed in Christ. (2006, p. 3)

Wilson then identifies himself:

> I am a secular humanist. I think existence is what we make of it as individuals. There is no guarantee of life after death, and heaven and hell are what we create for ourselves, on this planet. There is no other home. Humanity originated here by evolution from lower forms over millions of years...

And

> For you, the glory of an unseen divinity; for me, the glory of the universe revealed at last...You have found your final truth; I am still searching. I may be wrong, you may be wrong. We may both be partly right. (p. 4)

It could hardly be said better, but we have to care enough for one another to start the conversation. In contrast to Wilson's approach, consider what Sam Harris says in his *Letter to a Christian Nation*:

> Nonbelievers like myself stand beside you, dumbstruck by the Moslem hordes who chant death to whole nations of the living. But we stand dumbstruck by you as well—by your denial of tangible reality, by the suffering you create in service to your religious myths, and by your attachment to an imaginary God. (2006, p. 91)

His letter is not an invitation to join in a mutually recognized project—saving Darfur, rescuing Katrina survivors, ending war. Rather, it is an attempt to re-educate, to show people how backward they have been and still are. I happen to agree with his main points. I, too, think beliefs should be anchored in evidence. I, too, believe religion has outlived its usefulness and does more harm than good. But if you believe in it, then—like Wilson—I would prefer to say, "You may be right; I may be right, but let's put that aside (we'll come back to it) and tackle this problem on which we can both work." And we should come back to the differences over belief; we should question and answer each other honestly but only when we have reached the point at which it is unthinkable to harm each other.

Harris claims that our schools have failed "to announce the death of God in a way that each generation can understand" (2006, p. 91). Imagine our schools trying to do this! The *New York Times* recently (Dec. 18, 2006) ran a story on a U. S. history teacher in New Jersey who told his students that evolution and the Big Bang are not scientific, that dinosaurs were aboard Noah's ark, and that only Christians have a place in heaven. "If you reject his gift of salvation, then you know where you belong...If you reject that, you belong in hell." (quoted, p. B 6). School administrators told the teacher to desist, but students and parents in the community have "mostly lined up" with the teacher. Stories like this one tempt us to join Harris and Dawkins.

Similarly, many people seem to believe it is all right—perhaps even obligatory—to say dreadful things about unbelievers. The schools can do something about this by honestly and courageously sharing the actual words of unbelievers and the undeserved epithets hurled at them. Because Thomas Paine said, "My country is the world; to do good is my religion," did he deserve Theodore Roosevelt's condemnation as a "filthy little atheist"? Students should learn that many atheists are good people. What about Hitler and Stalin? they may ask. Well, Stalin was an atheist, but it isn't obvious that his atheism had much to do with his criminal leadership. On the other hand, it isn't clear that Hitler ever publicly rejected his Christian faith; some of his speeches appeal to Christianity to support his anti-Semitism, and many of his followers—even some in the Nazi high command—retained their Protestant affiliation (Steigmann-Gall, 2003). Much can be done in the study of history and literature to set the record straight and get students to think.

It is possible, also, to address these topics in math classes. As mentioned earlier, Descartes' version of the ontological proof and Kant's challenge to the cosmological proof could be studied. In discussion of logical puzzles and antinomies, interesting material on the life of Bertrand Russell could be introduced, including his objections to the concept of hell. Wilson is useful here, too. In a discussion of large numbers, we might share Wilson's comment on hell:

> The condemned will remain in hell...for a trillion trillion years, enough for the universe to expand to its own, entropic death, time enough for countless universes like it afterward to be born, expand, and likewise die away. And that is just the beginning of how long condemned souls will suffer in hell—all for a mistake they made in choice of religion during the infinitesimally small time they inhabited Earth. (p. 6)

Can students imagine a trillion years? A trillion trillion? Graphed against such an enormous number, what does the average human life span look like?

I am not suggesting that a special course or unit of study be organized around the topic of unbelief. That add-a-course strategy is our usual approach to new topics, but I think it is usually a mistake. Teaching explicit facts in history or special vocabulary in biology or technical details on metaphor and simile in English may actually explain the adult ignorance we so deplore in our citizens. Topics essential to human flourishing should pervade all of our subjects. It is entirely appropriate to diverge from prescribed math objectives to a discussion of the life of Descartes, Russell, Whitehead, or Erdos and to share information on their views of politics, religion, war, and nature. Similarly, science teachers should introduce students to the political issues involving evolution and creation. And in English classes, literature should be chosen for its contribution to an understanding of existential questions.

In the process of education, students should read the 23rd Psalm, but they should also read Darwin's concluding lines in *On the Origin of Species*:

> There is a grandeur in this view of life, with its several powers, having been originally breathed into a few forms or into one; and that, whilst this planet has gone cycling on according to the fixed law of gravity, from so simple a beginning endless forms most beautiful and most wonderful have been, and are being, evolved. (Darwin, 1859, p. 490)

We should, however, continue to ask questions of one another, to suggest the need for evidence and/or logical justification, to point out weaknesses in one another's positions. But we should try to limit the insults leveled at both atheists and fundamentalists. Alan Peshkin put it well in his study of a Christian fundamentalist school. Calling for civility, he wrote:

> Without compassion and civility, I may too readily dismiss you and your claims for survival as a nuisance, as a barrier to progress, and thereby deny that your stripe of humanity deserves the voice, the time, and the space to be heard and acknowledged as worthy. (1986, p. 291)

We must continue to seek an avenue of communication.

BIBLIOGRAPHY

Allen, Brooke. (2006). *Moral minority*. Chicago: Ivan R. Dee.

Armstrong, Karen. (1995). *Through the narrow gate.* New York: St. Martin's Press.

Browne, Janet. (2002). *Charles Darwin: The power of place*. New York: Alfred A. Knopf.

Darwin, Charles. (1859). *The origin of species*. London: John Murray.

Dawkins, Richard. (2006). *The God delusion*. Boston: Houghton Mifflin.

Dennett, Daniel C. (2006). *Breaking the spell*. New York: Viking.

Gardner, Martin. (1983). *The whys of a philosophical scrivener*. New York: Quill.

Harris, Sam. (2004). *Religion, terror, and the future of reason*. New York: W. W. Norton.

Harris, Sam. (2006). *Letter to a Christian nation*. New York: Alfred A. Knopf.

Hitchens, Christopher. (2007). *God is not great: How religion poisons everything*. New York: Twelve (Warner Books).

Jacoby, Susan. (2004). *Freethinkers*. New York: Metropolitan Books.

Kant, Immanuel. (1781/1966). *Critique of pure reason* (F. Max Muller, Trans.). Garden City, NY: Doubleday Anchor Books.

Lewis, C. S. (1962). *The problem of pain*. New York: Macmillan.

Martin, Michael & Monnier, Ricki (Eds.). (2003). *The impossibility of God*. Amherst, NY: Prometheus Books.

Morris, Simon Conway. (2003). *Life's solution: Inevitable humans in a lonely universe*. Cambridge: Cambridge University Press.

Noddings, Nel. (1993). *Educating for intelligent belief or unbelief*. New York: Teachers College Press.

Noddings, Nel. (2003). *Happiness and education*. Cambridge: Cambridge University Press.

Noddings, Nel. (2006). *Critical lessons: What our schools should teach*. Cambridge: Cambridge University Press.

Russell, Bertrand. (1957). *Why I am not a Christian, and other essays on religion and related subjects*. New York: Simon & Schuster.

Ryan, Alan. (1988). *Bertrand Russell: A political life*. New York: Hill & Wang.

Seigmann-Gall, Richard. (2003). *The holy Reich*. Cambridge: Cambridge University Press.

Slone, D. Jason. (2004). *Theological incorrectness: Why religious people believe what they shouldn't*. Oxford: Oxford University Press.

Smith, Christian. (2005). *Soul searching: The religious and spiritual lives of American teenagers*. Oxford: Oxford University Press.

Stark, Rodney & Bainbridge, William. (1985). *The future of religion*. Berkeley: University of California Press.

Turner, James. (1985). *Without God, without creed*. Baltimore: Johns Hopkins Press.

Unamuno, Miguel De. (1954). *Tragic sense of life* (J. E. Crawford, Trans.). New York: Dover.

Wilson, Edward O. (2006). *The creation: An appeal to save life on earth*. New York: W. W. Norton.

CHAPTER THREE

Seven Things the Establishment Clause Does Not Require

Jordan Lorence, Alliance Defense Fund

Faulty understanding of the Establishment Clause in the U.S. Constitution has created excesses where government officials needlessly censor religious expression in ways not required by the Constitution's text, relevant court decisions or common sense. Many government officials believe widely disseminated myths about the Establishment Clause and suppress religious expression in ways no court decision has required. Although debate over what the Establishment Clause requires will go on, there should be consensus on what it does **not** require.

1. The Establishment Clause Does Not Require the Government to Censor Private Religious Expression.

Religious speech expressed by regular citizens does not violate the Establishment Clause. The Constitution only regulates "state action"—government action by federal, state or local officials. In order for religious expression to pose a problem under "separation of church and state," the religious speech must come from the mouth of the government. Private speakers expressing or advocating religious ideas cannot violate the Establishment Clause because they are private citizens, not government officials. Government tolerance of private religious speakers does not violate the Establishment Clause if the speech is truly private speech. The Supreme Court correctly explained the difference this way:

> There is a crucial difference between *government* speech endorsing religion, which the Establishment Clause forbids, and *private* speech endorsing religion, which the Free Speech and Free Exercise Clauses protect. Board of Education of Westside Community Schools v. Mergens, 496 U.S. 226, 250 (1990).

In fact, government officials can violate the constitutional rights of private people by censoring their speech because of its religious content. The Constitution also requires government officials to respect the free speech rights of private speakers and to remain neutral about religion. Singling out for censorship speakers espousing religious speech does not show governmental "neutrality" towards religion.

2. The Establishment Clause Does Not Require the Government to Treat Religion as Inherently Dangerous and to Eliminate It from Public Life, No Matter What the Context.

Some people wrongly assume that the Establishment Clause requires the government to go on a search-and-destroy mission to eradicate all things religious from public life. They view religion as some sort of hazardous waste, like asbestos in the ceiling tiles. Religion, like these poisons, must be removed from public life, no matter what the context, they wrongly think. For example, a suburban New York public high school prohibited a student-led Bible study on campus. The high school students sued and lost. The Second Circuit ruled against the students and upheld the censorship, stating:

> Our nation's elementary and secondary schools play a unique role in transmitting basic and fundamental values to our youth. To an impressionable student, even the mere appearance of secular involvement in religious activities might indicate that the state has placed its imprimatur on a particular religious creed. This symbolic inference is too dangerous to permit. Brandon v. Bd. of Ed., 635 F.2d 971, 978 (2d Cir. 1980).

Now, Congress has overturned this ruling with passage of the Equal Access Act in 1985, which the Supreme Court upheld in Board of Education v. Mergens, 496 U.S. 226 (1990). However, other examples of the erroneous "religion-as-hazardous-waste" view abound.

Michael Newdow, the noted atheist, has resurrected his lawsuit to expunge the words "under God" from the Pledge of Allegiance. He argued that exposing his daughter to the words "under God" would be unconstitutional. (The school allowed her to opt out of saying it, so this was not a case of government coercion. However, the daughter is under the custody of her mother, who never married Michael Newdow, and she and her daughter ***do*** want her to say the full Pledge, with the phrase "under God."). It is reasonable to conclude that the use of "under God" in the Pledge of Allegiance is a statement of political philosophy, not religion. It states that our political liberties come from God and not the government, as the Declaration of Independence says. Michael Newdow reasons that the mere mention of God, no matter what the context, is inherently unconstitutional. This ignores context and superficially and mechanically views all religious references as per se violations of the Establishment Clause.

Zealots filing lawsuits to censor Christmas celebrations frequently exhibit this same wrongheaded mindset, that religion must be expunged from the public square no matter what the context or the identity (private or government) of the speaker. For example, the American Civil Liberties Union sued the Sioux Falls, South Dakota school district because it allowed the school choirs to sing religious Christmas carols. To the ACLU, it made no difference that the school officials had the students sing for educational and not devotional purposes. To the ACLU, it made no difference that school officials allowed objecting students to opt out of singing religious songs. The federal appeals court for South Dakota, the Eighth Circuit, ruled in favor of the school and against the ACLU's extreme position, stating that religious Christmas carols could be sung in the public schools when done for appropriate pedagogical (and not devotional) reasons. *Florey v. Sioux Falls School District,* 619 F.2d 1311 (8th Cir. 1980).

The organization that I work for, the Alliance Defense Fund, has dealt with many situations of Christmas censorship, usually government officials squelching private religious expression. These situations in the last few years included:

- In Mine Hill, N.J., Canfield Avenue School officials altered the words to the popular hymn "Silent Night" for their holiday concert, changing them from "Silent night, holy night" to "Silent night, winter night."

- In Northridge, Calif., school officials refused to allow the Good News Club at Andasol Elementary School to sing "Silent Night" or "Joy to the World" at the school's "Holiday Concert" because the songs "refer to God."

- In Monona, Wis., the manager of a retirement community that received some government grant money ordered the removal or covering of any religious Christmas decorations, such as those that depicted a nativity scene, angels, or the words "Merry Christmas." Residents restored their religious decorations after reportedly being told by the foundation that owns the building and by the office of U.S. Sen. Russ Feingold that they should ignore the order and display their decorations.

- In Memphis, Tenn., library officials told a woman that she could place a nativity scene on the community shelves as long as it did not include the "inappropriate figures." Library officials subsequently changed their minds and agreed to allow the figures as part of the displayed nativity scene.

- State officials in Wisconsin and Washington state prohibited local people to place religious ornaments on the big Christmas tree in their respective state capitols.

Equal access to government facilities is another example of extreme, erroneous misunderstandings of the Establishment Clause. Government officials wrongly believe that when they open their facilities for use by every type of community group, they must nonetheless single out religious groups for exclusion from the facility. But the Supreme Court has ruled at least five times since 1981 (with no countering decisions) that the government cannot exclude religious groups from meeting in a government building opened to all other community groups. Government accommodation of private religious speakers does not violate the Establishment Clause. See, for example, *Widmar v. Vincent*, 454 U.S. 263

(1981), which established that evangelical Christian college students must be allowed to meet on a Missouri state university campus on the same terms and conditions as other student groups; and *Good News Club v. Milford Central School*, 533 U.S. 98 (2001) where the court ruled that the evangelical Christian club must be allowed to meet after school in a Albany, New York-area school when the school allows other community youth groups to meet, like the Boy Scouts. The mindset of those who deny equal access to religious groups is that the Constitution requires censorship of religious expression because it is religious.

However, the inherent religiosity of speech does not determine whether it is constitutional or not. Context is important to determine whether something violates the Establishment Clause or not. Some expression can be deeply religious and totally appropriate for a public school. For example, an English class may be reading a novel where the author describes the main character as "Daniel in the lion's den" or "David against Goliath." It would be totally appropriate for the teacher to hand out copies of the actual biblical text of these stories in Daniel 6 and I Samuel 17. Although the teacher is having the students read words from the Bible, the pedagogical context of the classroom activity makes it totally appropriate. Even though this is uncut, hardcore "religious" stuff, its use in a public school would not violate the Establishment Clause.

The Supreme Court understands this as it has found that "the Bible may constitutionally be used in an appropriate study of history, civilization, ethics, comparative religion, or the like." *Stone v. Graham*, 449 U.S. 39, 42, (1980). Similarly, the Supreme Court wrote that:

> It certainly may be said that the Bible is worthy of study for its literary and historic qualities. Nothing we have said here indicates that such study of the Bible or of religion, when presented objectively as part of a secular program of education, may not be effected consistently with the First Amendment. *School Dist. of Abington Tp., Pa. v. Schempp*, 374 U.S. 203, 225 (1963).

Therefore, the main error with the "religion-as-hazardous-waste" view of the Establishment Clause is that it wrongly focuses on the inherent degree of religious content, assuming wrongly that more intensely religious content means the more it violates the

Establishment Clause. Rather, the critical constitutional issue is context. How and for what purpose is the government using the religious material? If the context is appropriate, then the use of highly religious materials would be constitutional. How can one learn music without studying the works of J.S. Bach? Handel's *Messiah* is one of the greatest works of music, yet all of its lyrics are Bible verses. Without looking to context, those viewing religion as a hazardous waste unnecessarily eliminate religion from appropriate places in our society.

3. The Establishment Clause Does Not Require Censorship of Religious Expression Because It Is Confusing to Others— Especially Impressionable Youth Who Might Not Understand That It Is Private Speech.

Many erroneously believe that the Establishment Clause requires the government to censor private religious speech in public places because some may be confused and attribute the religious speech to the government. When impressionable youth are present, some argue, the Constitution requires the government to silence private religious speakers in order to end the children's confusion. This is totally wrong.

The Supreme Court has rejected this "impressionable youth" veto justifying censorship of private religious speech in public places. It rejected a school district's argument that it must censor private religious speakers from a forum where impressionable youth are present in *Good News Club v. Milford Central School*, 533 U.S. 98, 119 (2001):

> We decline to employ Establishment Clause jurisprudence using a modified heckler's veto, in which a group's religious activity can be proscribed on the basis of what the youngest members of the audience might misperceive.

In an important, yet whimsical decision, the Sixth Circuit ruled that the government may not use a modified version of this concept—the "ignoramus' veto"—to exclude religious speakers from a forum:

> We believe that the plaintiffs' argument presents a new threat to religious speech in the concept of the "Ignoramus' Veto." The Ignoramus' Veto lies in the hands of those determined to see an endorsement of religion,

even though a reasonable person, and any minimally informed person, knows that no endorsement is intended, or conveyed, by adherence to the traditional public forum doctrine. The plaintiffs posit a "reasonable observer" who knows nothing about the nature of the exhibit—he simply sees the religious object in a prominent public place and ignorantly assumes that the government is endorsing it. We refuse to rest important constitutional doctrines on such unrealistic legal fictions. *Americans United For Separation of Church and State v. City of Grand Rapids*, 980 F.2d 538, 1553 (6th Cir. 1992).

The better way to deal with impressionable youth, or anyone else who is confused about whether the government endorses some private speaker's religious speech is to explain to them that the government does not endorse every viewpoint that it permits. Educate them about the First Amendment so that young people grow up seeing the government accommodating private religious advocacy, or any advocacy.

Also, the impressionable youth argument cuts both ways—government actions **excluding** religious groups communicates to impressionable youth that religion should be censored. The Supreme Court said in the *Good News Club* case:

> [W]e cannot say the danger that children would misperceive the endorsement of religion is any greater than the danger that they would perceive a hostility toward the religious viewpoint if the Club were excluded from the public forum. 533 U.S. at 118.

If impressionable youth witness repeated acts of government suppression of religious speech, they will learn that religious expression should be suppressed, not tolerated. After all, they are impressionable.

4. The Establishment Clause Does Not Require the Government to Suppress Religious Speech Because It Is Offensive to Others.

The Establishment Clause does not require the government to muzzle speakers who advocate ideas that others oppose. Claiming, for example, that we should follow the Law of Moses, or that Jesus is the only Savior that God has provided for us, can be offensive to some. To say that those offended have the right to have the government silence those espousing the offensive ideas is the "heckler's veto." The Supreme Court has forcefully condemned government actions to suppress public advocacy because others find their ideas offensive:

> But the fact that society may find speech offensive is not a sufficient reason for suppressing it. Indeed, if it is the speaker's opinion that gives offense, that consequence is a reason for according it constitutional protection. For it is a central tenet of the First Amendment that the government must remain neutral in the marketplace of ideas. *F.C.C. v. Pacifica Foundation*, 438 U.S. 726, 745–746 (1978).

Similarly, the Supreme Court has also stated:

> Accordingly a function of free speech under our system of government is to invite dispute. It may indeed best serve its high purpose when it induces a condition of unrest, creates dissatisfaction with conditions as they are, or even stirs people to anger. Speech is often provocative and challenging. It may strike at prejudices and preconceptions and have profound unsettling effects as it presses for acceptance of an idea. That is why freedom of speech, though not absolute (*Chaplinsky v. New Hampshire*, supra, 315 U.S. at pages 571–572) is nevertheless protected against censorship or punishment, unless shown likely to produce a clear and present danger of a serious substantive evil that rises far above public inconvenience, annoyance, or unrest. *Terminiello v. City of Chicago*, 337 U.S. 1, 4 (1949).

Additionally, those who seek to suppress government acknowledgement of our nation's religious heritage file lawsuits on behalf of "offended observers," seeking to eradicate these traditional governmental practices. Unless the government is doing more to harm these "offended observers" than merely allowing an opening prayer at a meeting or passively posting displays with religious content relevant to America's history, the courts should throw out these cases brought by "offended observers." They have suffered no real harm.

For example, the two Ten Commandments cases would not even have come to court except for the flimsy claims of offended observers. In the Texas case, a lawyer with an expired law license brought the lawsuit based on the fact that he must walk past a Ten Commandments monument on the state capitol grounds in Austin (located in an outdoor park with sixteen other nonreligious monuments) on his way to the law library. One of the sixteen monuments honors Confederate soldiers. If someone were offended by that monument, no court would entertain a lawsuit by an "offended observer" to remove it.

The Kentucky case, concerning a display on a courthouse wall, is even worse, in terms of no harm inflicted upon the offended observers. The American Civil Liberties Union (ACLU) filed this lawsuit on behalf of itself, representing its anonymous members in Kentucky who go to the courthouse in McCreary County to "transact civic business," such as "obtaining and renewing licenses, registering property, paying local taxes and registering to vote." (The quotations are from the complaint filed by the ACLU in federal court.) While at the county courthouse, these offended observers "*have occasion* to view the Ten Commandments display in their courthouse." What harm do these ACLU members suffer when they "view" the Ten Commandments? Persecution? Jail? Bad cell phone reception? Fire from heaven? Outbreaks of boils? The ACLU says "[e]ach plaintiff perceives this Ten Commandments display as a violation of the Constitution....Each plaintiff therefore is offended by the continued display." (I would be more offended by the sign at the courthouse saying, "Pay Taxes Here," but I digress).

Justice O'Connor wrote the following in Michael Newdow's case to eliminate "under God" from the Pledge of Allegiance when recited in a public school: "The Constitution does not guarantee citizens a right entirely to avoid ideas with which they disagree....no robust democracy insulates its citizens from views that they might find novel or even inflammatory." *Elk Grove Unified School District v. Newdow*, 542 U.S. 1, 44 (2004) (O'Connor, J., dissenting). The price we pay for a free society is that we must tolerate advocacy of ideas we find offensive.

The fact that the government and not a private individual presents the "offensive" message does not empower offended observers to silence the government. Someone will always object to any government message, even if they are benign messages that most Americans would support—such as, for example, "Support our troops," "Just say no to drugs," or "Liberty and justice for all." Being offended by walking by a message passively displayed does not demonstrate that someone has suffered actual concrete injury by the government's actions. A passive display does not constitute an "establishment of religion" because it does not compel anyone to do anything. If some find it offensive, then they should work to resolve the issue through the political process and through public debate in the media, etc. The government does not have to censor speech with religious content merely because someone is offended.

5. The Establishment Clause Does Not Require Exclusion of Religious Groups from Public Benefits Because of an Alleged Subsidy to Religion.

Contra Costa County California believes the following is a government "subsidy" of religion, rather than merely a religious group trying to utilize a benefit the government offers to all other community groups. Hattie Hopkins, a Christian evangelist from Sacramento, conducts religious meetings in nonchurch venues so that people unfamiliar with the Christian faith will feel more comfortable attending and hearing her Gospel message. In 2004, she requested to hold two of her meetings at a large meeting room at a branch of the Contra Costa County Library in Antioch, California, in the East Bay area near San Francisco and Oakland.

Many community groups used this room. For example, the local Democratic Party met there to chose candidates for public office. The local Sierra Club met to decide on their legislative priorities for the upcoming session of the California Legislature. A large number of neighborhood associations, hunting clubs and other community organizations met there.

When Hattie Hopkins conducted her first meeting, library officials realized that it was a "worship service" and told Hattie that she would not be able to hold her second meeting because of the religious content of the meeting. Hattie Hopkins contacted the Alliance Defense Fund, which won a preliminary injunction against the County. The Ninth Circuit reversed, ruling that the policy singling out worship services for exclusion was constitutional. The Supreme Court denied review of the case in October 2007.

Contra Costa County officials rejoiced. The attorney for the County said to a reporter that allowing worship services in the public libraries would amount to having taxpayers subsidize religious expression. Huh? Hattie's attempt to use a meeting room twice would be a government "subsidy" of religion?

This is strange reasoning because it stretches the concept of "government subsidy" to religion to a ridiculous extreme. No government money changed hands with a religious group. Even if one calls this a governmental "in-kind" contribution to religion, the argument fails because the government gives this in-kind "subsidy" to every community group.

For example, has Contra Costa County also "subsidized" the local Democratic Party when it met there? Maybe the County needs to comply with state campaign finance laws. Or, maybe the local Democratic Party is really just a community group availing itself of a government meeting room, widely available to all.

Did the County subsidize the local Sierra Club Chapter when it met there to plan legislative initiatives? Maybe the County needs to comply with state lobbying laws for this "in-kind contribution." Or, maybe the Sierra Club Chapter is really just a community group availing itself of a government meeting room, widely available to all.

There is no "subsidy" to religion if every community group gets the same "subsidy." The Supreme Court has rejected this subsidy argument because its forced application to a forum opened to everyone feels attenuated and exaggerated:

> We are not oblivious to the range of an open forum's likely effects. It is possible—perhaps even foreseeable—that religious groups will benefit from access to University facilities. But this Court has explained that a religious organization's enjoyment of merely "incidental" benefits does not violate the prohibition against the "primary advancement" of religion. *Widmar v. Vincent*, 454 U.S. 263, 273 (1981).

This subsidy argument makes no more sense than saying that the Social Security system violates the Establishment Clause because an old lady in Bismarck, N.D., gives part of her check to her church. But millions receive Social Security checks, so how one or a few recepients use their money does not implicate the Establishment Clause. It's their own private choices that result in the government funds of Social Security to flow to a religious group.

And this is a benefit widely available to all. Everyone gets the same "subsidy." The government does not "subsidize" religion when the synagogue hooks up to the local sewer system—and does not have to construct its own system—because *everyone* gets sewer hook-ups. The government does not "subsidize" religion when the fire department puts out a fire at the local Catholic Church, or the police investigate a break-in and burglary at the Buddhist monastery, because *everyone* gets fire and police protection. When religious groups partake of a benefit the government makes available generally to all, there is no governmental "subsidy" of religion.

6. The Establishment Clause Does Not Require the Government to Treat Christianity Worse Than Other Religions Because It Is the Majority Religion (or How Christianity Is Religious, While Other Religions Are Only Cultural).

Sometimes, in disputes about religion in public life, courts fall into a bad habit of viewing only Christianity as religion and viewing government support of non-Christian religions as acceptable because those religions are only "cultural." Only Christianity, they say, is "religious." For example, a school district in suburban Denver ordered a reading teacher to remove two Christian books from his bookshelves—an old illustrated book on the life of Jesus and an abridged Bible with comic book illustrations. Students who did not bring their own books to read during the silent reading time could pick one of the 350 or so books to read. The school board also ordered the teacher to stop his occasional silent reading of the Bible during the time when all students read silently.

But the teacher also had books of non-Christian religions (as well as plenty of books on nonreligious subjects) on the shelves—Buddhist, Native American, even Greek myths. The teacher also read plenty of other books during the silent reading time, some having nothing to do with religion, but also books on the life of Buddha and on Native American religious beliefs. The district court tried to explain why the Christian materials he read silently or that sat passively on a shelf had to leave the classroom, but how the other religious materials that he read silently or that sat passively on a shelf could stay:

> Roberts' teaching of American Indian religion is teaching *about* religion. It is but a part of a secular, historical course of study approved by the District as part of the curriculum for fifth grade students. The students' exposure to Roberts' religious books and Bible cannot be deemed teaching about religion in the same way. We find that exposure to the tenets of a little known religion, such as those followed in American Indian culture, is far less influential on young students than exposure to a modern day, widely observed religion which is a recognizable part of our society. *Roberts v. Madigan*, 702 F.Supp. 1505, 1517 (D.Colo. 1989).

Another example appeared in the 1995 *Rosenberger* case before the U.S. Supreme Court. The University of Virginia funded newsletters for a Muslim and a Jewish student publication, but refused to fund an evangelical Christian publication because it was religious. The difference? The University stated that the Christian publication was religious; the Jewish and Muslim ones were only cultural. (See Brief of Petitioners, *Rosenberger v. Rector and Friends of the University of Virginia*, 1994 WL 704081, pp. 5–6.)

In another case, disgruntled taxpayers challenged an expenditure by the City of San Jose, California, to build a statue of Quetzecoatl, the Aztec god, to honor the Hispanic residents of the city and the city's Hispanic heritage. The taxpayers claimed that using government money to build a statue of a god violated the Establishment Clause. The Ninth Circuit bent over backwards to explain away this problem in that San Jose was promoting its cultural heritage and not a religion:

> Plaintiffs also cite the speech given by Luis Valdez at the unveiling ceremony and to statements of Councilmember Blanca Alvarado, attesting to her own spiritual response to the piece and sharing her impressions of Aztec culture. Review of these statements reveals that they were made not in a religious spirit, but in homage to the City's Mexican heritage, and to affect someone on an emotional or spiritual level, or even "move [her] to tears." This does not imbue the work with religious content. *Alvarado v. City of San Jose*, 94 F.3d 1223, 1231 (9th Cir. 1996).

The Ninth Circuit probably reached the right conclusion in this case, but I doubt that it would have reached the same conclusion ("no Establishment Clause violation") if the City of San Jose had honored its Mexican heritage by expending tax money to erect a statue of the Virgin of Guadalupe or of Jesus Christ. This case shows the tendency to treat non-Christian religious things as "cultural," and not violating the Establishment Clause, and Christian things as "religious" and violating the Establishment Clause.

7. The Establishment Clause Does Not Require Courts to Invalidate Laws When Lawmakers Enact Them with Religious Motives.

People of faith have entered the public square to argue against injustices and advance various reforms. For example, a monk named Temelecus urged his fellow Romans that the Roman

Empire should abolish the bloody gladiator games. He paid with his life. Christian abolitionists in England and the United States such as William Wilberforce fought against slavery. Martin Luther King, Jr. opposed segregation of blacks in the South in the 1950s and 60s because of biblical commands for equality.

However, with the rise of conservative Catholics and evangelical Christians participating in the public political realm, many have raised questions about "separation of church and state." They claim that if the government were to enact the legislation proposed by the conservative Christians, like restricting abortion or banning same-sex "marriage," it would violate the Establishment Clause. This argument is raised by those who oppose the political goals of conservative Christians. They impune the "religious" motives of their legislative proposals, rather than look to whether their proposal actually has the government advance religion or not.

For example, in 2006 the Washington State Supreme Court refused to strike down the state's marriage law challenged by activists because it did not allow same-sex couples to marry. The Washington Supreme Court correctly and properly left this matter to the people and their elected representatives to decide.

However, one dissenting justice, Bobbe Bridge, who wanted to find a state constitutional right to same-sex "marriage," said the state's marriage law violated the Establishment Clause because many people of faith believe God designed marriage to consist of one man and one woman:

> [W]hat we have done is permit the religious and moral strains of the Defense of Marriage Act (DOMA) to justify the State's intrusion. As succinctly put by amici the Libertarian Party of Washington State and the Log Cabin Republicans of Washington: "To ban gay civil marriage because some, but not all, religions disfavor it, reflects an impermissible State religious establishment." (Amicus Curiae Br. of the Libertarian Party of Washington State et al. at 11) After all, we permit civil divorce though many religions prohibit it—why such fierce protection of marriage at its beginning but not its end?

This Establishment Clause argument really offers no help to a court in deciding a case because religious groups come down on both sides of this issue and others, such as abortion, the death penalty, welfare reform, taxes, etc. A state legislature would "violate" the Establishment Clause by enacting legislation on either side of the issue. For example, if a state were to enact or abolish the death penalty for murder, a court would have to invalidate that legislation because the lawmakers codified a "religious viewpoint."

If both sides of an issue can cite religion to defend it, they have effectively neutralized any value of an "Establishment Clause" analysis for deciding a case. Government would have only a few laws or maybe none at all, if it could not legislate in areas where a religious group has taken a stand on a certain law or public policy position. Also, many laws overwhelmingly accepted by the people are ones with which religious groups agree. No one would (or should) seriously argue that laws against bank robbery violate the Establishment Clause because Christians, Jews, Muslims, etc., prohibit stealing in their respective religions.

That is what the Supreme Court ruled in a case challenging the Hyde Amendment, which limits federal funding of abortions for poor women. Those who brought the lawsuit argued that it violated the Establishment Clause because it aligned with Roman Catholic doctrine. The Supreme Court rejected that argument, stating,

> ...it does not follow that a statute violates the Establishment Clause because it "happens to coincide or harmonize with the tenets of some or all religions." *McGowan v. Maryland*, 366 U.S. 420, 442. That the Judaeo-Christian religions oppose stealing does not mean that a State or the Federal Government may not, consistent with the Establishment Clause, enact laws prohibiting larceny. (*Ibid.*) The Hyde Amendment, as the District Court noted, is as much a reflection of "traditionalist" values towards abortion, as it is an embodiment of the views of any particular religion. (491 F.Supp., at 741. See also *Roe v. Wade*, 410 U.S., at 138 141) In sum, we are convinced that the fact that the funding restrictions in the Hyde Amendment may coincide with the religious tenets of the Roman Catholic Church does not, without more, contravene the Establishment Clause. *Harris v. McRae*, 448 U.S. 297, 319–320 (1980).

A recent federal district court opinion made the same point:

> It may very well be true that those who participate in the abortion debate on the pro-life side are members of religious organizations whose religious beliefs form the basis for their views. However, that does not transform the pro-life stance into one that is religious in nature, nor does it transform the phrase "Choose Life" into religious speech. Nothing in constitutional jurisprudence supports the conclusion that political speech which is derived from one's ethical or religious beliefs or background

transforms it into religious speech. Many religious persons and organizations may be opposed to capital punishment, or perhaps in favor of gun control. Those political issues are not therefore automatically transformed into religious issues simply by virtue of the religious beliefs of their supporters. The same is true for the abortion debate. *Children First Foundation, Inc. v. Martinez*, 2007 WL 4618524, *11 (N.D.N.Y, 2007).

Interestingly, one of the plaintiffs who brought the lawsuit challenging the Hyde Amendment as codifying Roman Catholic doctrine was the Women's Division of the Board of Global Ministries of the United Methodist Church. So, under this theory of the Establishment Clause, the Supreme Court could not win. If it upheld the law, it codified Roman Catholic doctrine into law. If it struck down the law, it codified United Methodist theology into law.

More amazingly, those who want the law books expunged of statutes agreeing with the religious doctrines of conservative groups ignore huge examples done by religious groups that advocate non-conservative views. For example, The National Council of Churches, a consortium of churches holding liberal theological views, submitted an amicus brief in a 2007 case before the Supreme Court called *Commonwealth of Massachusetts v. Environmental Protection Agency*, No. 05–1120. This is a case challenging the EPA's decision that it lacks authority under the Clean Air Act to regulate carbon dioxide as a hazardous air pollutant because of its alleged role in global warming.

I do not express any opinion one way or the other on the merits of this case. But note how the National Council of Churches defended its interpretation of the federal Clean Air Act:

> Followers of the Judeo-Christian tradition are called to be responsible, just stewards of the Earth and the abundant resources that it makes available, today and for future generations. See Genesis 2:15, 9:12. Also, the NCC tells us that the EPA should regulate CO2 emissions because Christian ethics preaches love of our fellow humans as ourselves, (Matthew 22:39 and Mark 12:31–33), and more particularly, care and compassion for those who are the most vulnerable and needy. See, e.g., Matthew 19:21, 25:34–40; Luke 14:13–14.

Well...a whole lot of Bible quoting going on here. The National Council of Churches is telling the Supreme Court that it should interpret the Clean Air Act a certain way because of what the Bible says. Wow! Why aren't the strict separationists pouncing on this NCC brief and screaming that the Supreme Court may not rule this way without running afoul of the Establishment Clause?

I would be amazed if people like Justice Bobbe Bridge would apply the standard she used in the Washington marriage case to find that the EPA would violate the Establishment Clause if it regulated carbon dioxide emissions under the Clean Air Act just because some group of churches happens to agree with that position. Of course, there is no Establishment Clause violation in that situation. And neither do states violate the Establishment Clause when they define marriage as one man and one woman.

Conclusion

Justice Brennan summarized well the foundational error of the extreme separation position: "The Establishment Clause does not license government to treat religion and those who teach or practice it, simply by virtue of their status as such, as subversive of American ideals and therefore subject to unique disabilities." *McDaniel v. Paty,* 435 U.S. 618, 641 (1978). Under the Establishment Clause, there should be no coercion, no censorship of religion, and no violation of individual conscience.

CHAPTER FOUR

Religion, Identity, and Morality in Public Schools

T. Jeremy Gunn, American Civil Liberties Union

The role of religion in public schools is one of the most sensitive and volatile topics on the political and legal landscape. Along with other controversial issues that arise in the culture wars—particularly abortion and homosexuality—it raises not only public policy questions, but triggers deep emotions as well as questions of identity: *"who are we* as a people?"

I once had the occasion to compare public school textbooks from France and the United States that were used in the last quarter of the nineteenth century, the period when universal, compulsory education was becoming the norm in both countries. While the textbooks understandably offered illuminating examples of major cultural differences between the two countries, they also had an interesting similarity. The authors of the history textbooks, whether French or American, thought of their mission as one of helping to mold "our youngest citizens." The textbooks did not simply teach history, they taught *moral* lessons about what it means to be French or to be an American. Similarly, the original proponents of flag ceremonies and the Pledge of Allegiance, also at the end of the nineteenth century, self-consciously acknowledged—indeed prided themselves on—their efforts to promote common ideas about citizenship.[1] Education is designed to help mold children into the kind of people parents and adults want them to be.

Many parents believe, understandably enough, that religion is not simply one subject among others about which their children should learn a thing or two, but rather that it is fundamental to their identity as Christians, as Evangelicals, as Muslims, as Jews, or as nonbelievers. While some (perhaps many) parents like the idea of public schools reinforcing the appropriate religious education of their children, almost all parents presumably would object to public schools promoting any religious beliefs that they reject. Those who might strongly favor public schools promoting "the Christian Bible" would be strongly opposed to their children attending a school that was promoting the Quran.

One story that best illustrates this point for me occurred a few years ago. I had just been in Kazakhstan to help with some issues regarding government suppression of religious freedom. Both national and local government officials of that country had engaged in practices that discriminated against some minority religious groups, particularly Evangelical Christians and Protestant missionaries coming from the United States. After making my return flight connection in Frankfurt, Germany, I sat next to a woman who immediately introduced herself as an "Evangelical Christian from Texas." She volunteered to me that she had just spent some time speaking to the "wives" of U.S. Army Chaplains in Germany. (Apparently no chaplains had husbands.) After telling me this about herself, she asked in a friendly way about what I had been doing. Though briefly debating in my mind whether this would be a productive conversation, I responded to her that I had been working on religious freedom issues in Central Asia. While I half expected her to respond with something like "that's nice," she took an unexpected tack and said in a somewhat accusatory tone: "Well, we don't have religious freedom in our country." It was as if I should first resolve abuses in the United States before traveling overseas.

I asked her what she meant. She offered a single example to illustrate the lack of religious freedom in the United States: "We are not allowed to pray before high school football games." She was, I assumed, referring to the case *Santa Fe Independent School District v. Doe*, 530 U.S. 290 (2000), where the U.S. Supreme Court held that a school in Texas had impermissibly been involved in promoting prayer before football games. (In fact no one said that people could not pray before the game; only that the school should not be promoting it.) Against my better judgment, I responded by saying that "it is curious that you should say this, because in Kazakhstan, from where I have just come, Evangelical Christians would *not* want the government or public schools to be involved in promoting prayer—because that would mean having Islamic prayers." My fanciful hope was that she would tap her forehead and say: "You know, I never thought of it that way. That wouldn't be right for Evangelicals to be pressured to offer Islamic prayers in Kazakhstan, and I can now see why it wouldn't be fair to pressure others into the kind of prayers that I would want in Texas." That was not her response. Rather, with some feeling she said, "But this is *our* country."

"*Our* country?" Whom does she include—and exclude—in the word "our"? Does "our" country believe that it is right for Baptist prayers but not Muslim prayers to be offered in public schools? Though we did not pursue the conversation further, and I did not ask such questions, I imagined that for her "our country" referred not only to a place where public schools can and should promote prayers at football games, but where each day of school would open with prayer. Public schools would offer Bible courses, and the Ten Commandments might be proudly displayed.

Though my fellow passenger said nothing herself about nostalgia or the 1950s, I inferred that she would—like many others—think of the 1950s as a golden age before the "Supreme Court took prayers and Bibles out of schools," as is so often lamented. It is sometimes said, though less frequently than a few years ago, that the moral breakdown in the 1960s followed from secularization of the schools. Whether or not my traveling companion believed this I do not know. But it is part of a mythical version of American history that quickly assumes a causal link between "removal of God from schools" and "decline of the country." Variations of this broadly appear on websites urging that religion be put back in public schools where it belongs. But how accurate is this causality?

I will propose a counter-causality that I acknowledge up front is offered tongue-in-cheek. But I think it illustrates why the popular "removed God" causality is nonsense rather than something that should be taken seriously.

Let's start with the youth rebellion beginning in 1967–68. At first blush, the causality chronology looks pretty compelling. The Supreme Court ruled in 1962 in *Engel v. Vitale* that public schools could not write an official prayer—though importantly it allows children themselves to offer prayers provided that the schools were not promoting them. The following year in *Abington v. Schempp*, it ruled against devotional Bible reading in public schools. Many figures associated with the religious right—Pat Robertson, Jerry Falwell, Billy James Hargis (father and son) and others—have dated their conversion to political activism from these two court decisions.

So did these decisions have anything to do with the youth rebellion, Haight-Ashbury, drugs, promiscuity, or demonstrations? College students who were 20 years old in 1967 would have been fifteen-years old at the time of the prayer decision, perhaps a little old for the Supreme Court's decisions to have had much effect on their education. But now let's look at some real people. The following lists the ages in 1962–63 of some people who became prominent later in the decade:

> Angela Davis – 18
> Jimi Hendrix – 20
> Huey Newton – 20
> Jim Morrison – 21
> Janis Joplin – 21
> Charles Manson – 28
> James Earl Ray – 34
> Timothy Leary – 42

Obviously the formative years had long since passed by the time of the Supreme Court decisions. But this leads us to ask what *was* happening in the United States when these rebellious youths of the sixties were in elementary schools? The twenty-year old of 1967 would have been five-years old in 1952. Angela Davis would have been 10. In the 1950s, America was awash in official public statements supporting God. The first Presidential Prayer Breakfast took place in 1953. "Under God" was added to the Pledge of Allegiance in 1954. A law was adopted requiring "In God We Trust" to be placed on currency in 1955. In 1956, "In God We Trust" became the national motto. Stone monuments of the Ten Commandments began appearing at government buildings in 1955 and 1956 in conjunction with the release of the Cecil B. DeMille movie of the same name. Presidents Truman and Eisenhower frequently issued proclamations promoting prayer. Many schools began the day with prayer and Bible reading. America was filled with official, public, generic religion. And with what effect on the next generation? Rebellion?

I do not suggest for a moment that the rebellions of the late 1960s actually had anything to do with official religion in society and public schools in the 1950s. There is no evidence of causality. The claim would be an after-the-fact—*post hoc ergo propter hoc*—logical fallacy. *But if* someone wants to argue that public school practices are indicators of public morality and that we should put religion in the schools in order to promote public morality, then they have a whole lot of explaining to do when it comes to the most "pious" of years and the most "rebellious" of generations. Ultimately these "causality" arguments say less about the actual influence of public schools on public morality, and more about how people make such associations in their own minds regarding public schools and the moral direction of the country.

Like the textbook writers in France and the United States in the late nineteenth century, there is an understandable wish by many to use public schools to mold their idealized moral image of the next generation. But efforts to do so are not likely to be particularly effective in the absence of strong parental guidance, and they are likely to provoke arguments about *whose* religious beliefs "our" schools should be teaching.

NOTES

1. This was not all innocent. Among recurring themes of those promoting a common nationality were their dislike of immigrant cultures, foreign accents, foreign religions, and unusual facial features.

CHAPTER FIVE

Metaphysics, Metaphor, and Meaningfulness: How to "Teach the Controversy" in Science Class

Steve Broidy, Wittenberg University

There is irony in my State Department of Education's position on the controversies surrounding the teaching of evolution in science classes. The State Department urges teachers to "teach the controversy." What the Department seems to intend by that position is that science teachers should discuss, as legitimate and parallel approaches for explaining the origins of and changes in the physical world, both evolutionary arguments and creationist or "design" accounts.

I want to argue here that although taking this approach would be logically problematic and pedagogically confusing, another interpretation of the phrase "teach the controversy" can be the basis of an approach that has real merit. Though the approach I will advocate takes issue with some of the State Department's assumptions, I do want to thank the Department for supplying the key phrase.

I take the view here that one of the most valuable things that science teachers (and others) can do is to help students to understand both the logic and the importance of this controversy. Teaching the controversy, in other words, can be the occasion for learning that will help future citizens to understand more deeply and judge more reasonably the positions involved—not just in science class, but on a range of questions and disputes that mirror this one.

I will explore, first, the important logical distinctions that students (and faculty) must learn in order to recognize why empirical scientific claims and arguments are not direct competitors of faith-based metaphysical beliefs, for the issues involved here. Confusion on this point accounts for a great deal of the heat that the evolution/design controversy has generated. Next, I consider the role that metaphorical thinking plays in connecting both empirical theorizing and metaphysical speculation. The "as if" of metaphor provides branches for our thinking that outline both the common origins of and the clear differences between the processes of empirical investigation and the formation of principles of religious faith.

However, "teaching the controversy" should not merely be an occasion for exploring the logical roots of belief. What is equally important in teaching this controversy is the lesson it should provide for educators and students alike in the crucial importance of the meaningfulness of what is learned. I argue that much of what gives the creationist/design positions their political and emotional power is just what is often missing from the manner in which science is taught in our schools. The key factor here is the need for coherence in what we learn and how we live. Creationist/design positions provide their adherents with a world that makes larger sense to them than the compartmentalized realms of the various specialties and sub-specialties of empirical science. It makes learning meaningful to individuals—as all teaching must do, if learning is to be long-lived, accessible to our thinking, and useful. Interestingly, even as scientists in a number of fields search for a "theory of everything" (for examples from different perspectives, see Hawking, 1988; and Wilson, 1998), faith-based accounts of "everything," though leading to logical category mistakes when applied to the current controversy, have always offered such coherence.

The Logic of Empirical and Metaphysical Truth Claims

The Evolution vs. Intelligent Design controversy currently playing out not only in courtrooms and editorial pages, but also in schools, churches, science organizations and think tanks around the world, frustrates science teachers and agitates parents and students. Advocates of various agendas are all maneuvering to get into position to "name the issue." Is the question really one of "facts versus superstition," "who gets to control the curriculum," "fairness to competing theories," "faith versus science," or some other provocative characterization? Such formulations are likely to feed the partisan fires, but an overarching responsibility of educating is to help students to find clearer and more useful ways of naming the problems and decisions they and their communities face. Making personal choices that succeed in contributing to a community consensus depends, among other things, on such a starting point.

Rethinking the controversy in educationally useful terms begins by recognizing the ways that various versions of the question are not only provocative, but also unclear. One general principle we can help students to absorb is that it's hard to reasonably respond to a question when we don't know what the question is. The current controversy is in part founded in talk that—unwittingly or by design—is troublesomely ambiguous.

A prime example is the term "theory." We argue about whether to accept the *theory* of evolution or intelligent design *theory*. We wonder if it's fair to teach one theory but not the other, or to give more time to one theory rather than another: after all, they're all *theories*. We take up positions on whether "evolution" is a theory at all.

As it happens, we recognize in ordinary speech several meanings of "theory." Sometimes we use "theory" to apply to claims that require conclusive evidence to be available and understood before we accept them as true. If we're reluctant to agree that such evidence is currently at hand, we can call the claim a "theory." Scientists are traditionally very cautious about concluding that a given empirical hypothesis is supported by conclusive evidence; and this may account for many well-established scientific claims still being termed "theories." Many of the claims that make up the (also ambiguous) "theory of *evolution*" are themselves conclusively supported; others are not. The point is that one ordinary sense of "theory" has this meaning.

But in a second sense of the term, a claim or set of claims is a theory if it is of the logical variety that neither is susceptible to nor requires "evidence." This sense of the term articulates an article of faith. I remember a dispute among members of a small independent church in my part of the country about whether God approved of women as ministers in the church. The debate came to a head when a leader of the congregation fell deathly ill. Church members prayed at his bedside in the hospital for hours. Finally, all save one of the church members went home. One woman (a candidate, she insisted, for the ministry) remained and prayed throughout the night. In the morning, the church leader began what became a complete recovery. "You see?" the ministerial candidate's supporters in the church proclaimed, "That's evidence that God wants women to be ministers!" But the other side replied, "No. That's your *theory;* but what happened has no relation to what God wants in this matter."

What can "really" count as "evidence" in this situation? What if someone had claimed that the recovery was evidence that Satan wanted church members to be deceived about what God really wants—what really counts as "evidence" here? We can't seem to decide these questions in the way we do for theoretical claims of the first sort, above. It's puzzling to consider what, if anything, can count as evidence at all, in the usual sense. The key lesson here is that some kinds of theory, by their very terms, are about factual issues that are outside of the reach of what we ordinarily call evidence.

Our claims about the nature of God are of this sort: that God is without extension in time and space, yet omnipresent, to cite several. Our claims about what God is and wants will always represent theories in this second sense. It is not that we don't have the conclusive evidence we need. It is that our acceptance or rejection of such claims is subject to commitments of faith, for which we have reasons for belief that are causes of belief, but not evidence. Philosophers sometimes call such claims "metaphysical"—claims about facts that are outside of or independent of the physical. That doesn't make such theories either superior or inferior to "empirical" theories about physical facts. It just makes them logically different; and it helps our thinking to keep the differences in mind when we tackle a decision about what's true, and about what theory to accept.

A third sense of "theory" is the one that gets used by scholars in particular fields when they want to talk about ways of looking at things that help us to explain what we're seeing, and sometimes to predict what will happen. A good theory in this sense is one that explains a lot and results in many accurate predictions. For example, it matters less whether Sigmund Freud's or Erik Erikson's theory of human social development is "true," in this sense, than which one explains more of the findings in that area and proves more helpful in predicting what else we'll find.

We can look at both "theory of evolution" and "intelligent design theory," in *this* sense, as theories whose fruitfulness and explanatory powers may be discussed. Interestingly, since they are theories of different logical kinds, it doesn't really make sense to think of them as competing alternatives. They may both be good theories of their kind, in this third sense of the term. Moreover, it is not (at least not logically) inconsistent to assimilate one of these theories to the other.

But the current debates are plagued by our inability to keep these kinds of theories distinct. If some scientists and teachers insist that "intelligent design" claims are wrong because the "evidence" is in favor of what the philosopher Alvin Plantinga disapprovingly calls "unguided evolution" (Plantinga, 2007), they should realize that such a claim assumes what can only be accepted by a commitment of faith: that there is no supernatural "Guide" to the process. No evidence, even in theory, can be brought to bear on such a question, since it's a metaphysical issue.

The other side of that confusion comes from those who insist that there is evidence to support the view that there is a "Designer." This comes in the form of purported inconsistencies and gaps in scientific explanation of old and modern observation of the natural record, or else as an intuitive leap expressing the view that the human intellect can readily and clearly discern purpose and design in the natural world (as an Austrian Cardinal recently put it).

But unless the "Designer" in this position is a *physical* rather than a metaphysical being, no "evidence" of this or other kinds can count. If the relevance of any such "evidence" is challenged, the only defense available to its advocates is to make another commitment of faith connecting the "evidence" and the claim it purportedly supports.

In fact, "design" arguments such as the one above have been around since at least biblical times. Psalm 19 claims that "the heavens declare the glory of God." St. Thomas Aquinas, in the

Summa Theologica's "Fifth Way" support for God's existence (Article 3, Q. 2), introduced one of the earlier formal design arguments. The perception of design in the universe was offered as evidence that there is a God. But not only does such a connection blur the distinction between empirical and metaphysical issues—a "category mistake"—but the argument is circular and subject to infinite regress (as was noted by some philosophers at least as early as the 18th Century. See Hume, 1748/1999). To conclude there is a "Designer" on the grounds that you perceive a "design" is to include the thing you're trying to prove in the very language of the "evidence" with which you support your conclusion! Moreover, was there a designer for the designer?

If teachers can help students to understand and apply this fundamental logical distinction, perhaps this rising generation of citizens will know how to conduct a more reasonable public debate over the place of faith and science in education. A *New York Times* account of a July 2005 poll by the Pew Forum on Religion and Public Life and the Pew Research Center (Goldstein, 2005) found that many Americans today seem confused about this logical difference. In the poll, 42% of respondents said that humans and other living things have always existed in their present form. Only 26% said that living things have evolved over time through natural selection. It's possible that many respondents were simply unaware of the tremendous volume of empirical evidence pointing to continual and ongoing changes in living species. It seems equally likely that many Americans judge the truth of such empirical claims by drawing on their religious metaphysical beliefs, rather than on the evidence that is relevant to deciding empirical questions.

Schools and teachers don't do students any favors by allowing gaps in their knowledge and fundamental confusions of reason to persist. I still keep in mind a story I heard from a health teacher years ago about how her principal, in the name of "compromise" and "keeping the customer happy," had forced her to change the grade on two siblings' anatomy tests, though the students had given an incorrect answer to a question about how many ribs a human being has. The students had answered that men have one less rib than women, since their religion said that was the case. No amount of empirical observation had any effect on this belief, and when the test scores came back, the students' parents had angrily complained to the principal that the teacher had discriminated against them as religious believers. Changing that grade was an easy way out, but I wonder what the long-term effect of that decision has been on the students' abilities to understand and deal with the physical world around them—as well as their ability to understand the sources and implications of their religious commitments.

It is not "fairness" that should guide public decision making on whether either or both "evolution" and "intelligent design" should be "taught" in biology classes. Such attempts at fairness overlook the nature of the issues involved. Speaking to a Rotary Club meeting in Nashville in August 2005, then Senate Majority Leader Bill Frist said that "I think today a pluralistic society should have access to a broad range of fact, of science, including faith"; and "I think in a pluralistic society that is the fairest way to go about education and training people for the future." The appeal to fairness explicit in these remarks is compelling—unless we notice that "pluralism" is oddly irrelevant to the question of what should be the role of empirical or metaphysical accounts of the progress of life, in science instruction. We are not *either* empiricists or metaphysicians, as we are either Christians or Jews or of Swedish or English ancestry. We deal with issues of both empirical and metaphysical fact all the time, every day of our lives. What would be fair to our children, in the long run, is to make them competent in seeing the differences between the two kinds of questions, the different obligations they place on us in making decisions about them, and in recognizing that—despite protestations to the contrary by partisans—there is no way to show any logical incompatibility between claims of the two logical types.

From Metaphor to Metaphysics, and Other Turnings

Metaphysical issues and empirical issues are of differing logical sorts, but the origins of the claims we create in both categories may have important things in common. It is tempting, and usual, to say, at this point, that the origins of pronouncements about the origins and progress of the universe around us lie in a search for truth. But it seems to me more valuable to shift the field a bit by noting, as writers such as John Dewey have suggested, that our concern with such pronouncements originates in a "quest for certainty" (Dewey, 1929, ch. 1). That is, the origin of such claims lies as much in our own emotional and intellectual needs as in any "objective" reality. Indeed, the upshot and perhaps the major value in deciding questions of truth is arguably the level of certainty we may have as a basis for our beliefs and, indirectly, our actions.

The path to truth claims, however, and to levels of certainty, is a branched one. I want to argue that the path begins with a state of wondering and possibility, as we try out alternative answers to questions for which we do not have answers. In hope, fear, curiosity, wonderment, or other emotional states, we ask, in effect, "What If?"

"What if?" is the language of speculation, of dreams, of active searches for alternatives, and of hypothesizing. And "What If?" may take us in several directions regarding investigation and belief formation. But all such activity runs through metaphorical thinking and speech:

1. *"What If?"* to *"As If."* Metaphorical thinking plays with, and metaphorical pronouncement invites us to act "as if." Within limits or without them, metaphor involves playing out the consequences of treating something as if it were something else. When we face what we do not know, metaphorical thinking offers us a way, within our experience and current knowledge, to consider answers to our questions.

The move from What If to As If—the metaphorical move, as it were—is what characterizes diverse activities such as creating fiction and fantasy, and also many forms of play. It can describe the activity that informs theorizing—in the third sense of the term that speaks to applying a particular perspective or "lens" to phenomena in order to describe, interpret, and predict features of those phenomena; and it can include modeling. We should note that sometimes we, instead, make an opposite metaphorical move from the direction of belief—"No Ifs!"—to As If. An example might be the distancing from actual belief that characterizes ontological studies, as contrasted with ontological beliefs.

There is a long tradition in epistemology and philosophy of language, from St. Augustine to modern day writers (for example, Belth, 1977) that holds that we advance our knowledge primarily by connecting it to what we already know. Human development theorists from Piaget to the present have argued that we often assimilate new information to established patterns of knowledge, in order to make sense of that new information; and the newer neurological and brain studies appear to support versions of that theory. That process also connects things we already know in new ways, as a means of looking at our knowledge with fresh eyes, as theorists of creative thinking have demonstrated. Metaphorical thinking takes us from considering possibilities to actively, if tentatively, treating something as though it were something else. It is a form of play-acting or pretending. To speak metaphorically, then, is in speech-act terms to invite an audience to pretend as well (Broidy, 1977).

It is important to note that thinking and speaking metaphorically do not imply belief. To pretend is, among other things, to keep a conscious distance from belief; and when we think or speak of one thing as something else—that is, metaphorically—we must recognize that we do not actually believe that it is that something else. When we lose awareness of that point, or when we choose to abandon it in favor of truth claims, we have commenced to believe.

2. *"What If?" to "As If" to "No Ifs!."* The move from metaphorical thinking and speech to actual belief and the language of truth has several branchings. Scientific claims (though, of course, not all the claims of scientists) are empirical in nature; that is, they raise issues of what the physical facts may be. As such, they go—however reluctantly and belatedly sometimes—from hypothesizing and theorizing—As If—to truth claims, when the presence of conclusive physical evidence warrants such a move.

Within the empirical domain, the move from What If to As If to No Ifs is also, arguably, one that we make when we leap to conclusions, when we demonstrate paranoia, when we develop "conspiracy theories," or superstitious beliefs. What we do not require, in these instances, is the conclusive physical evidence that characterizes belief in empirical claims generally accepted as true. We may be attracted to all of the above, for various reasons, but in naming them as we do we signify that, in our view, their move to No Ifs is not warranted.

On the other hand, we often make the move to actual belief concerning issues of metaphysical fact, that is, questions about what is or isn't the case outside of the physical world (including the question of whether there is anything at all "outside of the physical world"). Though the progress of our thinking may follow the same paths as with a progression to a belief in an empirical claim, that progress occurs on a different logical plane, as I argued earlier. Despite the different stance with regard to the possibility and quality of evidence that distinguishes empirical from metaphysical issues, however, my point here is to observe the similar patterns of thinking and speaking that characterize the progress of both sorts of beliefs. It is indeed important to notice that God-based claims about the origins and development of the universe are not, as such, superstition, since superstition deals with empirical issues. Scientific claims on the subject are not, as such, erroneous or incomplete. But it is also crucial to notice that both sets of beliefs are branchings of the same intellectual processes. Intellectually, they are first cousins, once removed. Moreover, though they represent different paths to the coherence, meaningfulness, and even certainty for which we search, the existence of that search makes both empirical and metaphysical quests for "truth" emotional relatives as well—and liable to equal effectiveness in that regard.

Teaching the Controversy & Making Learning Meaningful

As valuable as teaching the logical sources and tests of belief may be, in the course of "teaching the controversy," the disputes over teaching evolution enable educators to highlight a more general and more profound concern. This concern is perhaps implicit in the numerous demands brought by advocates of creationism and intelligent design to schools across the nation. I would like to interpret this movement, whether it is spontaneous or organized, as indicating a deeper need than establishing a religious basis for education. Though it is rarely articulated, I prefer to see in this advocacy a thirst for coherence in our children's education.

There is considerable precedent for such a perspective. William James, for example, in his early 20th century work *The Varieties of Religious Experience* (1904), notes the effect religious metaphysical commitment can have in achieving "inner unity and peace" that is characterized by "a firmness, stability and equilibrium…" (pp. 175–76). Here James is speaking of conversion or counter-conversion experiences in which disparate and incompatible beliefs and feelings are resolved in a new formulation, a sort of accommodation, to use a Piagetian term (cf. "paradigm shift"). The experiences James describes are often anguished ones for those who undergo them, but they culminate in a sense of integration, of

The Role of Religion in 21st–Century Public Schools

coherence. A new "model" of experience is formed. Such an experience engages entirely, and out of it comes learning, new knowledge, understanding—the ability to place things in relation to one another, within an encompassing whole.

We should note, too, that the equilibration this "religious attitude," as James characterized it (p. 53), provides can be threatened by plausible alternatives. Competing cognitive and emotional structures can be rejected, assimilated, or result in distancing the existing and the competing structures from belief—re-metaphorizing them. The first two responses preserve equilibrium; but the third upsets it—an occasion for anxiety, but also, as cognitive developmental theorists argue, an occasion for energizing learning and re-animating the quest for coherence (Marcia, 1980).

There is considerable evidence that a search for coherent purpose, for ways to make learning and living meaningful, is a feature of adolescent and young adult students in particular. Indeed, it would be surprising if it were not, given adolescents' growing capabilities in what Piaget called "formal operational thinking." Importantly for our purposes here, formal operational thinking is characterized, among other features, by adolescents' increasing ability to imagine and consider alternative possibilities, including possibilities for future events. A particular interest of many younger adolescents is in recognizing ideal possibilities, and in recognizing discrepancies between ideal situations and reality (Piaget, 1972).

Given the growing preference that many adolescents display for these ways of making intellectual sense of the world around them, and their places in it, there should be little surprise at the results of recent national studies of college students' views on meaningful lives, spiritual quest, and religious practice. A 2005 study by the Higher Education Research Institute at UCLA, titled "The Spiritual Life of College Students," under the leadership of Alexander and Helen Astin, for example, found more than half of the 112,000 students at 236 colleges it surveyed scoring high in a set of attitudes the study called "Spiritual Quest." Spiritual Quest, in this study, referred to students' interest in the meaning/purpose of life, and developing a meaningful philosophy of life. Similarly, the study found that more than half of the students surveyed scored high in "Spirituality," defined as "believing in the sacredness of life, seeking out opportunities to grow spiritually, and believing that we are all spiritual beings." (rather than levels of religious observance, or "religiosity") (p. 8).

While the study revealed clear differences among students of various religions and denominations, between religious students and nonreligious students, and between politically conservative and liberal students, the clear inference to be drawn from the study is that older adolescents, at least, have a strong commitment to seeking and living by overarching narratives of meaningful life.

We should expect this quest for coherence and direction in the world around them to extend to parts of their lives in which they invest considerable time and effort, and that includes schooling.

Educating for coherence means teaching students to see what they learn in any discipline, any day, as part of a larger picture, as fitting into a growing awareness of how the living world of which we and our learning are parts carries on. Specialized learning can create knowledge and interest; but only a coherent learning creates meaningfulness. It is in the meaningfulness of what we learn that its value is founded. The greatest favor we can do our students is teach them—in science class and in every class—that learning without meaningfulness is wasted; because the point of learning is as part of building a coherent, valued life for individuals and their communities. This is to animate learning with spiritual quest and even spirituality—with a search for and a sense of how what we come to know about the world uncovers some coherent and overarching meaning.

The late Neil Postman wrote in *The End of Education: Redefining the Value of School* (1996) that "there is no surer way to bring an end to schooling than for it to have no end." (p. 4). That is to say, long-term learning requires a relation to long-term aims—to the emotional commitments we have made or seek to make to ideals that make learning meaningful and give it direction. "Teaching the controversy," carried out as careful, logical distinction making and honoring fully the quest for meaningfulness in what students bring to study of scientific investigation, is the best way to approach resolution of the controversy. But if educators are not prepared or competent to work toward that coherent education, then the creationist/intelligent design movement, despite its confusions and political agenda, will continue to present itself to many students, and their families, as a preferable alternative.

BIBLIOGRAPHY

Aquinas, T. (1947). *Summa theologica* (Fathers of the English Dominican Province, Trans.). Benziger Brothers.

Augustine. (1947) *The confessions of St. Augustine.* Transl. Rex Warner. New York: New American Library.

Astin, A., and Astin, H. (2005). *The spiritual life of college students.* Los Angeles, CA: Higher Education Research Institute, UCLA.

Belth, M. (1977). *The process of thinking.* New York: David McKay Company.

Broidy, S.J. (1977). *Understanding and misunderstanding educational metaphor: A speech-act theory.* The Ohio State University, Ph.D. dissertation.

Dewey, J. (1929). *The quest for certainty: A study of the relation of knowledge and action.* New York: Minton, Balch & Company.

Goldstein, L. (2005, August 31). Teaching of creationism is endorsed in new survey. *New York Times,* p. A7.

Hawking, S. (1988). *A brief history of time: From the big bang to black holes.* New York: Bantam Books.

Hume, D. (1748/1999). *An enquiry concerning human understanding* (Tom Beauchamp, Ed.). Oxford: Oxford University Press.

James, W. (1904). *The varieties of religious experience.* New York; Longman's, Green, and Co.

Marcia, J.E. (1980). Identity in adolescence. In J.Adelson (Ed.), *Handbook of adolescence.* New York: John Wiley & Sons.

Paley, W. (1867). *Natural theology: Or evidence of the existence and attributes of the deity collected from the appearances of nature.* Boston: Gould & Lincoln.

Piaget, J. (1972). Intellectual evolution from adolescence to adulthood. *Human Development, 15, 1012.*

Plantinga, A. (2007, March/April). The Dawkins confusion. *Books and culture: A Christian review.*

Postman, Neil. (1996). *The end of education: Redefining the value of school.* New York: Vintage Books.

Wilson, E.O. (1998). *Consilience: The unity of knowledge.* New York: Borzoi Books.

CHAPTER SIX

College Fraternities and Expressive Association: Discrimination, Diversity, and Education

Daniel Cohen, University of Missouri–Columbia

Religious Fraternities and University Recognition: The Case of BYX

Early in the winter of 2006, I was intrigued by a potential legal matter that had occurred at the University of Missouri–Columbia, the state-funded public university where I teach religious studies. In the local paper I noticed a report about an overtly Christian fraternity called *Beta Upsilon Chi*, known by the acronym "*BYX*." This fraternity explicitly requires all its members and officers to be Christians and to share the group's Christian beliefs. According to the newspaper report, this Christian fraternity had now been approved for formal recognition by this state-funded public university.

Initially, I wondered if this represented a possible violation of the Establishment Clause of the First Amendment, which prohibits the government from promoting or endorsing religion explicitly, for the University of Missouri is a public educational institution receiving public funding. In addition, was the official acceptance of a fraternity, such as BYX, whose membership was restricted by choice and said to be based on religious precepts, at odds with university and state anti-discrimination policies? The matter was far more complicated from a legal perspective than it first appeared.

Interestingly, the BYX fraternity's initial application for full recognition at the University of Missouri–Columbia campus (MU) had been approved. However, as the newspaper article noted, MU officials had later determined that the fraternity's charter and its by-laws actually violated University policy and campus rules directly as these forbid discrimination based on race, color, religion, national origin, ancestry, age, gender, sexual orientation, disability, and status as a Vietnam War veteran. Thus, after BYX's initial endorsement for recognition as a student organization by the University, its recognition was subsequently slated to be rescinded because the fraternity's explicit policy of religious discrimination was not in compliance with University requirements for student organizations and because of BYX's unwillingness to modify its charter. It was at this point that a prominent legal aid group from Virginia, the Christian Legal Society, took up the cause of this Christian fraternity. Surprisingly, all it took was a letter sent by a lawyer from this out-of-state legal aid association for MU to reverse its position once again and now grant BYX, the avowed Christian fraternity, official recognition as a registered student group on campus.

What appeared odd in this situation was that not only established university policies on non-discrimination, but also U.S. constitutional requirements connected specifically to the Establishment Clauses of the First Amendment (which extends to states though the Fourteenth Amendment), would seem to prohibit the recognition of an explicitly religious affiliated fraternity at a state-funded public institution. In common parlance, MU's sanction of BYX seemed to be a violation of the separation between church and state, in addition to the plain promotion of discriminatory practices. Why did pre-existing legal guidelines not clarify the matter? Were there other legal issues that were more compelling in this situation? As it turned out, rights of expressive association, a constitutionally guaranteed right—although not one spelled out explicitly in the wording of the Constitution or its amendments—became the deciding factor here. But this summary of the matter renders a far too superficial understanding of the complexity of this issue legally, politically, and socially.

Notably, the issue of formally recognizing avowed religious affiliated fraternities (and sororities) at public institutions is a topic of increasing national significance. I argue that the endorsement of such groups and similar organizations may represent a worrying trend, namely the erosion of the constitutional separation of matters of religion from the secular affairs of the state as mandated at the founding of the nation. This issue is a growing national concern as the U.S. grapples with its role as one of the world's most religiously diverse nations. Religious diversity is increasing in America and becoming more complex to mediate, especially in the legal arena. The implications both for religious rights and the foundations of religious freedom are affected directly by court decisions and legislative policies.

This paper will examine certain recent legal cases involving official university recognition of campus fraternities that require specific religious affiliations (and often oaths or declarations of faith) for membership. In addition, other important legal cases that illuminate this matter and contain relevant legal concepts, issues, and precedents, but that do not necessarily deal with precisely the same concerns, will be discussed. Although this discussion will not be exhaustive, my intention is to explore some of the legal precedents that are advising institutional policies and decisions currently and to look at this complicated issue in terms of the tension it identifies between competing constitutional rights and legal concerns with respect to interpretation of the religious rights of individuals and student organizations.

Religious Clubs and Constitutional Rights: A Shift in Legal Orientation

The core legal issue in the BYX fraternity matter revolves around the interplay between their rights of freedom of association and the degree of discrimination permitted to them on the basis of religious affiliation (and belief). There is both a legal and a social tension developing here that deserves some discussion from a variety of perspectives.

On the one hand, we can examine this issue in terms of U.S. tax codes and the rights of nonprofit organizations. Generally, sororities and fraternities register themselves as nonprofit 501(c)(7) organizations with the IRS. This tax status classifies fraternities and sororities as "social and recreation clubs," and it is clearly indicated by the IRS that any charters, by-laws or written policies, etc. of such organizations must not provide for "discrimination against any person on the basis of race, color, or religion"

(IRS Publication 557). But there is also a disclaimer regarding religion in the very next paragraph of the IRS publication expanding on this matter. The IRS publication goes on to state:

> However, a club that in good faith limits its membership to the members of a particular religion to further the teachings or principles of that religion...will not be considered as discriminating on the basis of religion. (p. 49)

Is the reason for this qualification tied to the federal government's requirement, via the Free Exercise Clause of the First Amendment, to avoid interfering with the practice of religion whenever (legally) possible? No, the central constitutional issue here involves implied rights of expressive association under freedom of speech and association that could allow religiously based student organizations, such as religious fraternities, to restrict their memberships in order to protect the expression of their religious beliefs and viewpoints. Included here is the right of student groups to restrict their membership on discriminatory bases (e.g., religion, sexual orientation) despite University and state anti-discrimination policies and applicable laws, because the Court sees the membership of a group as constituting an expression of the group's ideals and beliefs and therefore this form of discrimination is protected under freedom of expressive association.

Interestingly, important legal discussions revolving around the religious expressions and the rights of student groups including fraternities have usually not ultimately focused on either the establishment or the free exercise clauses of the First Amendment—the centerpieces of religious freedom in the U.S Constitution. While it is true that some legal cases have included arguments about religious fraternities or universities in terms of First Amendment issues that pertain to religion explicitly, these concerns have not typically been central in the legal decisions rendered.

In fact, concerns related to the First Amendment clauses protecting the freedom of religion are often dismissed as legally inconsequential during the progress of a case. For example, the important U.S. Supreme Court decision in *Widmar* in 1981 involved a previously recognized student organization (an evangelical Christian club) that lost its campus recognition as a student group and was told that it could no longer use University buildings at a public university for meeting space. Due to the religious orientation of their meetings, the University was concerned that its sanction and support of the group might be in violation of the Establishment Clause by allowing public resources to be used to promote religion. The group countered that the University's restriction represented a violation of its free exercise of religion and free speech rights. In many ways, the case initially appeared to be shaping up as "a classic conflict between the establishment and free-exercise principles" (Flowers, 2005, p. 122). However, it was the free speech issues that predominated in the Court's decision and not concerns about the religion clauses of the First Amendment. Largely ignoring the free exercise concerns of the student group and the establishment concerns of the University, the Court refocused the case on whether the University could exclude groups based on the content of their speech (Malanga, 2007, p. 768). Here the Court was directly and explicitly reflecting on its earlier *Healy* decision from 1972 where a radical student group (the SDS) was determined to have been wrongly prohibited from university recognition and the use of university facilities on the basis of its expressed views and ideals. Student groups cannot be limited access to university facilities based on the expressed beliefs of their message.

In the matter of the BYX fraternity at the University of Missouri, the problem with its recognition at MU was connected to its requirement that all members and officers must share the group's (version of) Christian beliefs. Since the University of Missouri's by-laws explicitly prohibit any form of discrimination on the basis of religion (etc.) by sponsored student organizations, BYX was found to be in noncompliance and thereby became ineligible for recognition as a registered student organization. Either BYX had to amend its charter by-laws or else it would no longer be recognized (i.e., derecognized) by the University, thereby losing the associated rights and privileges, including the receipt of student activity funds, which accompany such recognition. In this regard, a letter was sent to the University on behalf of BYX by an attorney from the Center for Law & Religious Freedom, which asserted that BYX's rights of association were being threatened, and, furthermore, that the University's policies "systematically punished" religious viewpoints (Tracey, 2006). Although related, these two issues need to be addressed separately.

The issue of the recognition or nonrecognition of Christian (or for that matter any religious-denomination-restricting) fraternities has erupted at a number of both private and public colleges and universities quite recently. Tufts, Middlebury, Grinnell, Williams College, Ball State, Rutgers, the Universities of North Carolina, Washington, California, Illinois, Missouri, and many other schools, have wrestled with this issue. Why is this issue surfacing only more recently? How come it did not become a developed point of legal contention long ago, as college fraternities have been in existence since the founding of the nation?[1]

The issue of racial and religious discrimination in college social fraternities has a long history. As James notes, "[b]y the early twentieth century many social fraternities adopted written clauses that specifically required whiteness and Christian affiliation for membership" (James, 2000, p. 304). However, this situation begins to change after World War II, induced in part by a rising sense of social justice that postwar veterans had just gone to war to protect. In addition, servicemen of any race, religion, or economic background had the opportunity to get a college education through the GI bill. Accordingly, "[c]ollege enrollment in the United States skyrocketed at the end of world War II" and at the same time "[c]ollege social fraternities that restricted membership to white Protestants received increased scrutiny from a number of students who found fraternity life undemocratic" (James, 2000, p. 303). Later, the civil rights movement in the 1960s would create increased pressure and momentum for social and legal changes. After the 1950s "fraternity discrimination continue to be debated, but the controversy gradually moved out of student control and into the realm of legal and administrative authority" (James, 2000, p. 324). Today, this is the domain of such controversies, whether they involve race, religion, sexual orientation, etc. The question remains, however, why the issue of religious discrimination with respect to fraternities and other student organizations received virtually no attention until recently.

The answer lies in the shifting focus of the Supreme Court illuminated by successive decisions that reflect on the tension between rights of association versus institutional, state, and federal policies of nondiscrimination based on the U.S. Civil Rights Act. While the Court has attempted to develop a logical and legally applicable response to address this tension, the results generated have not always been consistent. Despite inconsistencies in its rulings, a significant shift in the orientation of the Supreme Court in terms of the balance between nondiscrimination policies and the rights of expressive association has occurred.

While it is increasingly apparent in a legal sense that a student group does not need to sacrifice its freedom of expressive association rights simply because the content of its beliefs are religious, this does raise certain concerns. In the *Widmar* decision in 1981 the Supreme Court had indicated that the University (UMKC) must not discriminate against the religious content of the student groups' speech even though some of their meeting time is spent in religious worship (i.e., no violation of the Establishment Clause). The University was determined to have created a "limited open forum" by just allowing student organizations to form and be recognized, and thereby all forms of speech connected with these groups, including religious, must be protected. One serious problem with this legal logic, as Justice White's dissent to the *Widmar* decision pointed out, is that now religious speech produced during devotional practices becomes like any other form of speech protected by the freedom of speech and thereby "the Religion Clauses would be emptied of any independent meaning in circumstances in which religious practices took the form of speech" (Flowers, 2005, p. 123). On this basis, constitutional rights of the freedom of speech will always overpower freedom of religion and often at the expense of the Establishment Clause in particular.

Since the Supreme Court struck down the test of compelling state interest in determining the application of religious rights and eliminated many of the safeguards of the separation of church and state in its *Smith* decision in 1990, there has been a scramble to reassert legislation and legal remedies (e.g., the *Religious Freedom and Restoration Act* ands its ongoing modifications). In the *Smith* decision, laws of general applicability overran First Amendment rights of religious freedom. Here the compelling state interest test (regarding interference with religious freedom) was deemed invalid in terms of the legal tension between laws of general applicability and the Free Exercise Clauses of the First Amendment. The Court's ruling indicated that the Free Exercise Clause did not apply to laws aimed at general behavior except in limited circumstances *or* if it was used in combination with another constitutionally protected right—such as free speech. Thus, the

Free Exercise Clause becomes weakened greatly, unless supported or propped up by another constitutionally guaranteed right (Flowers, 2005, p. 159). Are constitutional rights of religious freedom now becoming subsumed increasingly by freedom of speech (and its variants)?[2]

This development is potentially problematic for a number of reasons. According to some observers, there is a "general understanding with respect to other constitutional rights that each is independent of the others and protected by itself" (McBride, 1997, p. 136). However, increasingly with respect to religion this no longer seems to be the situation. Pertinent here is how different aspects of constitutional guarantees insuring freedom in regard to religion specifically are becoming trumped increasingly by other constitutional rights and legal concerns. Are we creating competing hierarchies of constitutional privilege and in the process emptying the religion clauses of the First Amendment from any independent meaning, or are we acting to preserve the best intent of the law? It is a legal and social question of significant concern. In my view constitutional rights should usually work in a complementary and reinforcing manner and not be viewed as operating in direct competition with one another.

The Problem of Competing Constitutional Rights

What has become the central focus, increasingly, in cases involving the rights of religiously oriented fraternities (or other explicitly religiously oriented student groups), and more recently, particularly groups with explicit Christian orientations, are constitutionally guaranteed rights of expressive association, which have been legally derived from associated constitutional aspects of freedom of speech, and, to a lesser extent, assembly. To better understand why this change has occurred, some additional background will be useful.

Notably, legal rights pertaining to the freedom of association are not expressly included or even addressed in the First Amendment. However, the U.S. Supreme Court has recognized the importance of the freedom of association and regards it as a right that is implicit in the First Amendment. In a 1958 landmark case involving the NAACP, the U.S. Supreme Court expressly recognized the right of association as correlative to explicit First Amendment rights of freedom of speech and freedom of assembly.

An Alabama federal court had found previously that the NAACP was in contempt for not supplying a full list of its members as ordered, but the U.S. Supreme Court agreed with the NAACP that the lower court's injunction represented a breech of the NAACP's First Amendment rights of free speech and assembly. This decision is important because group association, the Court indicated, was found to be inseparable from freedom of speech (Smart, 2001, p. 390).

Carrying the important legal issue of the relationship of antidiscrimination statutes and associational rights further, in its 1984 decision in the *Roberts* case the U.S. Supreme Court, in a case involving the rights of women to become members of the Jaycees, ruled in favor of admitting women and indicated that there was a compelling state interest to prohibiting *invidious discrimination*. The Court determined that the admission of women would not impair the ability of the Jaycees to impart their message and also adhere to Minnesota's nondiscrimination laws. Its position on associational freedom in respect to state nondiscrimination statutes is clear:

> We are persuaded that Minnesota's compelling interest in eradicating discrimination against its female citizens justifies the impact that application of the statute to the Jaycees may have on the male members' associational freedoms. In prohibiting such practices, the Minnesota Act therefore "responds precisely to the substantive problem [i.e., discrimination] which legitimately concerns" the State and abridges no more speech or associational freedom than is necessary to accomplish that purpose (1984, *Roberts v. United States Jaycees*).

One important question to ask in the specific context of the rights of religiously oriented college fraternities is precisely when does religious (or other forms of) discrimination that is required for membership become invidious? This beckons us to examine the implications of educational codes in relation to state and federal law, and the legal point that emerges is that while some actions may constitute a form of discrimination based on religious affiliation, those that do not do so *excessively* thereby avoid falling into the prohibited category of invidious discrimination, and therefore are permitted.

However, to explore this concern further, first we need to see how the Supreme Court further developed its position in the

Roberts decision (involving women's membership in the Jaycees). In its decision, the Court articulated a framework for examining associational rights by delineating two specific, but separate, domains of the freedom of association. Specifically, constitutional rights of association were delineated by the Court into those involving "intimate association" and those dealing with "expressive association" (1984, *Roberts v. United States Jaycees*).

Intimate association rights act to protect close human relationships such as those between husband and wife or more broadly the bonds existing among family members, but they may extend beyond family ties as well. Until recently, legal cases invoking intimate association were not directly relevant to the issue of the institutional recognition of religious-oriented fraternities. However, this has changed recently, and I will discuss this issue and some of its developments below.

On the other hand, rights of expressive association pertain to activities covered in the First Amendment such as association for purposes of speech, assembly, petition (for the redress of grievances), and would also include the exercise of political, social, economic, educational, cultural, and religious ends (1984, *Roberts v. United States Jaycees*). The rights of expressive association surrounding this wide range of interests are constitutionally guaranteed according to the Court and are centrally pertinent to the legal concerns of most religiously oriented college organizations, including fraternities.

In its 1984 *Roberts* decision, however, the Supreme Court acknowledged that there are limits to the rights of expressive association in relation to states' compelling interest in abolishing invidious discrimination. Thus, the Court made it clear that the right of expressive association is not absolute, as there may at times be compelling and overriding reasons that justify a curtailment or limitation of rights of expressive association, and which are unrelated to the suppression of a group's beliefs. The focal point for the Supreme Court's decision was that the admission of women as full members of the Jaycees did not impair the Jaycees' ability to express its views, nor did it force it to alter its explicit message of enhancing the interests of young men. Here the Court was deferring to anti-discrimination concerns for the public good (i.e., public accommodation laws) and using the precedent of "compelling interest" to justify its decision.[3] In legal and social terms, however, the need to enforce nondiscrimination rules versus a group's right to expressive association has come increasingly into direct confrontation. This tension is expressing itself repeatedly in conflicts between many religiously prescribed fraternities and public (as well as private) colleges.

Prior to 1995, the Court more narrowly defined the circumstances in which expressive association rights were impinged and suggested that antidiscrimination laws were always representative of compelling government interests (Bernstein, 2004, p. 196). However, since 1995 the Supreme Court has addressed increasingly the associational rights of groups and organizations in terms of their ability to restrict membership, even in a discriminatory manner, in order to protect the expression of their beliefs and values. The change began with the *Hurley* decision in 1995 where the expressive rights of (private) organizations were addressed and their right to restrict their message even in a discriminatory way was allowed. Here the Court recognized "parades" as "forms of expression" subject to freedom of speech and associated constitutional protections. Because the Court determined that parades constitute forms of expression, even state antidiscrimination laws could not force parade organizers to include groups they found undesirable, (such as the Irish-American Gay, Lesbian and Bisexual Group of Boston), in a St. Patrick's Day Parade. The organizers were entitled to refuse any group that communicated a message which the parade organizers did not wish to express, where even the demonstrated presence of an objectionable group in the parade represented a counter-message.

The *Hurley* decision indicated that a private organization, here the veterans group that organized the parade, had the right to control the speech content and thereby the statement the parade expressed. It was successfully argued that a gay and lesbian group's participation and the display of their banner would alter the organizers' intended message.[4] Further reiterating this position, the *Dale* decision in 2000 made it clear that, according to the Supreme Court, private groups, such as the Boy Scouts of America, can use the constitutional protection of the expression of their beliefs to restrict their membership, even in discriminatory ways. In the *Dale* decision, the right of expressive association was dramatically revived (Bernstein, 2004, p. 196). Here some background information and qualifying remarks will be helpful.

Until the year 2000, expressive association cases were analyzed under a legal framework established by the Supreme Court that began with *Roberts* (decided in 1982), and later included associated decisions (specifically, *Rotary Club of Duarte* in 1987 and *New York State Club Association* in 1988). These cases are often referred to collectively as the "*Roberts* trilogy" (Malanga, 2007, p. 759). Under this emerging legal framework, any organization making a claim of expressive association was required to show convincingly that if nondiscrimination policies were applied to the organization it would "significantly burden the organization's expressive activities " (Malanga, 2007, p. 760). At this point, it was the state's interest in eliminating discrimination that was seen as the compelling issue. The legal orientation was that state antidiscrimination laws were not motivated by the suppression of ideas and beliefs and were therefore constitutional and should be explored.

However, even as far back as 1958, in the *NAACP* decision, the Court had asserted that group association enhances the propagation of points of view and is therefore inseparable from freedom of speech, a powerful and inalienable constitutional right (Smart, 2001, p. 390). The *Dale* decision in 2000, however, represented a major legal turning point. Here the Court moved explicitly towards deference to a group's beliefs and views over its discriminatory policies, in a case involving the Boy Scouts of America.

The *Dale* dispute revolved around an unwanted troop member, an avowed homosexual, who was also a recognized community spokesperson for gay and lesbian rights, and who had been removed as assistant scoutmaster. Here the Court was dealing with the forced inclusion of an unwanted person whose presence was deemed detrimental to the moral message the Boy Scouts believed was appropriate for them to portray. In this way the *Dale* decision connects legally with that of *Hurley*, as both matters involved the right to exclude undesirable members tied to rights of expressive association.

While the Boy Scouts were successful in the case, it must be noted that the Court's decision was not based solely on the fact of "Dale's identity as a homosexual, but, significantly, on his status as an active gay rights leader" who was recognized publically in his community in this capacity (Malanga, 2007, p. 778). In spite of its deference to expressive association in this case, the Court also explicitly indicated in its decision that regardless of the high priority of the issues of freedom of speech and the associated freedom of expressive association, this leaning does not shield a group against antidiscrimination laws just because a group is forced to accept an unwanted member (Smart, 2001, p. 394). In addition, as Justice Stevens' dissent to the decision pointed out, the Court had previously been consistent in favoring state antidiscrimination laws over claims of First Amendment freedom of expressive association (Smart, 2001, p. 394). However, the *Dale* decision "substantially altered the balance" between these two competing concerns, but it failed to establish a rule or procedure for dealing with this rising conflict (Smart, 2001, p. 394).

One problem emerging after *Dale* is that now practically any case of potential discrimination could be transformed into a matter of potential freedom of speech and expressive association. Even commentators who hold opposing views on the efficacy of the Supreme Court's *Dale* decision ("did not go far enough" versus "sheer lunacy") agree on this aspect of its outcome:

> Almost any organization is eligible for protection from antidiscrimination laws that the Court provides...an expressive association claim is available to any entity that wants to discriminate at any time for any purpose. (Koppelman, 2002, as Cited in Bernstein, pp. 207–208)

There is a bigger problem that develops here with the *Dale* decision in that:

> ...it produces perverse results: a group that is stridently prejudiced will receive more protection than one that is quieter about its views, and thus the rule creates an incentive to disseminate the very prejudices that antidiscrimination laws aim to temper. (Koppelman, 2004, p. 28)

This represents a dangerous legal territory to enter in terms of the social and moral betterment of society achieved traditionally (since the Civil Rights Act) on the basis of antidiscrimination laws. Problematically, the legal assertion of associational rights suggests that discrimination must not only be tolerated but perhaps encouraged as well: "An association is more likely to win immunity from an antidiscrimination law, the more clearly its message is a discriminatory one" (Koppelman, 2004, p. 57). Furthermore, by treating individuals as symbols and groups as legal instruments of expressive association, it now becomes potentially possible to reinterpret or turn what were previously viewed as acts of invidious discrimination into the exercise of constitutionally protected rights (Smart, 2001, p. 397).

In regard to the tension between rights of expressive association and permissible discrimination the questions is where are the limits or safeguards to prevent abuses. This concern immediately presents a number of related concerns that must be briefly addressed.

Related Concerns: Group Rights and Individual Rights: Are They the Same?

The matter of the BYX fraternity is a direct reflection of this emerging controversy. In the letter from the Center for Law & Religious Freedom to MU, the writer refers to the *Roberts* decision in asserting the rights of association of BYX. However, there is no single decision by the Supreme Court that has defined this complex territory. Many important cases are relevant in mapping out the legal issues incorporated within this debate.

The *Dale* decision of the Court, as well as others previous to it (e.g., *Roberts, Duarte, NY State Club Assn.*), have shown that a tension can manifest between upholding state public accommodation laws and the freedom of expressive association. Such legal decisions raise some worthy considerations about the distinction between a group's expression of its beliefs and those of the individuals who comprise it. While there are certainly excellent legal, political, social, economic, and religious reasons for protecting the rights of expression of minority groups from being overrun by the majority, it is important to explore whether the constitutionally protected message a group expresses as its beliefs is the same qualitatively as that expressed by its various individual members. One might ask in a broader sense whether protecting the set of beliefs of the group is the same as protecting individuals' personal and constitutionally protected liberties. As Volokh (2006) has commented recently:

> What a group's beliefs are is potentially a more complex question than what an individual's beliefs are, since a group's members may well disagree among each other on certain matters (even matters that are important to the group's philosophy). Nonetheless, courts have generally not

been troubled by this and have usually accepted that groups do indeed have beliefs that can qualify for religious accommodation. (p. 1951)

This issue may be especially relevant in matters that reflect religious views. Not only the experience of religion or expressions of religious devotion and sentiment, but also religious beliefs and ideals held can vary significantly among individuals even within a single religious group, and this could make ascertaining a group's core message problematic as there may be a wide range of beliefs and views expressed. What if a wide range of opinions (e.g., about appropriate group membership policies) exists within the group concerning the best way to express its ideals? A legal determination of the boundaries of a group's expressed beliefs may become increasingly necessary as internal disagreements arise over the very characterization of what constitutes proper and appropriate group criteria determining which applicants are unacceptable to the group. What if these criteria change over time? If discrimination is permitted on the basis of religion, then it could also be allowed on the basis of sexual orientation, or race, or ethnicity, etc. There is an additional issue that arises from this discussion. If the group's beliefs are not coherent, homogenous, and consistent in terms of an expressed message, this state of affairs could make it difficult to identify the beliefs that unify a group if there is sufficient consensus about the expressed message that needs to be protected.

Related Concerns: Commerce, Equal Access, and University Funding

Obviously, the government or a university has the right to restrict free speech and the activities surrounding expressive association if an activity is harmful and disruptive to the functioning of society, but not merely on the basis of the ideas it conveys or the message it portrays. One proposed solution to reconcile the tension between rights of expressive association with attendant discriminatory practices that may be detrimental to the interests of society is by viewing these often competing concerns more clearly in terms of commerce (Smart, 2001; Volokh, 2006). In other words, "the stronger a group's relationship to commerce, the less expectation it should have of inviolable freedom of expressive association"

(Smart, 2001, pp. 397–398). This idea is not as farfetched as it may initially sound for a number of reasons.

First, a focal point of many state antidiscriminatory laws revolves around providing equal access to business goods and services, especially in places of public accommodation. Equal opportunity is certainly a concern for the nation, and historically overt discrimination and discriminatory policies based on race (etc.) have been used to limit the social good of society by disenfranchising millions of people unjustly. Because colleges and universities are offering educational goods and services, the allowance of discriminatory practices in terms of social club memberships might be seen as a way of denying equal access. What type of social message should our public universities convey? Do we want religious affiliation or sexual orientation, for example, to become markers of socially acceptable forms of discrimination? There is also a problem, from the educational perspective, in permitting student (social) groups to restrict their access to preserve their message. An important purpose for the existence of student social groups is to promote the experience of diversity for students within the University environment. Accommodating this pursuit is part of a university's institutional mission. Certainly, in a globalizing world, in a country rapidly diversifying religiously, racially, ethnically, etc., part of the responsibility of the University (and especially the public university) is to better equip students not only to accept but also to productively engage with the experience of social and cultural diversity.[5] By allowing religious fraternities to discriminate, however, part of the message that is transmitted at the University is that practicing different forms of discrimination is justified morally, protected legally, and an acceptable part of the American way of life.[6]

It has been suggested that part of the issue in situations such as those involving the BYX fraternity is the right of access to student activity funds at universities and colleges. Does this mean a student group can be discriminatory and gain university recognition as long as it does not request access to such funds? This approach is not a viable alternative, and it is unnecessary to explore such a potentially complicated solution. The legal concern has been addressed by the Supreme Court in both the *Widmar* (1981) and *Rosenberger* (1995) decisions. However, the underlying issue of contention is viewpoint neutrality versus viewpoint discrimination.

Viewpoint Neutrality, Religion, and Discrimination

In *Widmar* (1981) the Supreme Court found no sufficient constitutional justification for permitting the University of Missouri at Kansas City to discriminate against student religious groups that sought to use school facilities for religious meetings and worship. This decision was based largely on the determination that the University, by allowing the existence of student organizations, had created a limited public forum for student organizations' speech, changing the University's status (vis-à-vis to the student organizations) to a state actor and thereby triggering guarantees against viewpoint and content discrimination. Additionally, the Court "found allowing religious speech within university forums did not violate the Establishment Clause of the First Amendment" (Snider, 2004, p. 854). Excluding religious speech while permitting other forms of speech was deemed content-based discrimination by the Court (1981, *Widmar v. Vincent*). I have already commented on a potential problem this allowance creates by privileging speech rights in such a way that these will always outweigh concerns for religious rights. However, another important legal concern is whether student religious organizations that are funded entities of a state university, and thereby considered as limited public forums, "are sufficiently public in nature that more exacting nondiscrimination rules [should] apply to them" (Snider, 2004, p. 860).

The *Rosenberger* (1995) decision involved a religiously oriented student newspaper at the University of Virginia that lost its student activities funding. In *Rosenberger*, a student group had sued the University claiming that its refusal to fund their newspaper was viewpoint discrimination specifically against the newspaper's religious viewpoint. One of the important aspects of this case is that the Court determined that the University, by merely allowing student groups, had created a "limited public forum" making it a state actor that may not engage in viewpoint discrimination, even if the forum is its own creation. The *Rosenberger* decision against the University was based on the Court's determination that the University's actions were a form of impermissible viewpoint discrimination. The link between the *Widmar* and *Rosenberger* rulings is that both involved legal determinations of viewpoint discrimination that were deemed by the Court to be a breech of student groups' associational rights. In addition, "[t]hose two rulings put an end to the argument that the constitutional separation of church and state prevented public institutions from recognizing or supporting religious student groups" (Bullag, 2005, p. 4).

Despite these rulings, it is difficult to see how a student religious fraternity could ever claim infringement of its free exercise rights of religion as part of the basis of any denial of recognition as a student organization. As a student organization the religious fraternity is established as a social club (not a religious congregation), and while it may hold and espouse specific religious beliefs and views, its identity as a student organization should not be based on the group's identity as a practicing religious congregation for the purposes of recognition as a valid student organization. The problem here is that any student group's claim of breaches of constitutional free exercise within this context creates a logical conundrum. Simply stated, the legal protection afforded to a student organization's right of *expression* of its religious ideas and beliefs is not the same as protecting its rights to *practice* religion—at least not in terms of legal and constitutional stipulations.

Belief Versus Conduct: The Line Between Rights of Association and Invidious Discrimination

An analogy exists within the distinction found in the professional study of religion between two basic types of approaches: theological and academic. One approach involves the pursuit of theological training, often to become a minister, rabbi, priest, or other form of religious leader or expert, while the other approach involves the historical study of religion as an academic and intellectual pursuit. Certainly, these two endeavors may overlap, but the point is that the government does not, and in my view rightfully should not, allow the use of public education funds to promote the *theological* study of religion. For example, in 2004 a Washington state college student was denied state government scholarship funds that he wanted to use to pursue a degree in pastoral ministries (2004, *Locke v. Davie*). Just as the theological and the academic pursuits of religion are seen differently through the lens of constitutional reasoning, so too many of the protections afforded to religious practice and worship are qualitatively different from the study and discussion of ideas regarding the tenets, beliefs, and practices of religions.

One significant legal problem that remains is that the U.S. Supreme Court itself has failed to create any compelling rules test to resolve the tension that increasingly exists between the concern both for achieving nondiscrimination and at the same time protecting rights of association. If student groups do present educational opportunities (through the potential for social and economic benefits), then this generates potent reasons for asserting the public message of the positive value of society-wide nondiscrimination and the need to follow nondiscriminatory policies, as long as schools are clear that such policies will apply only to recognized student groups without either endorsing or not endorsing any particular religious point of view.

This tension between nondiscrimination and rights of association brings us back to the issue of BYX and whether it can legally discriminate against those whom it deems to be inappropriate for membership based on their religious disposition. The legal argument is that the forced inclusion of unwanted members into the fraternity would represent a significantly greater legal burden than conditioning the benefits of University recognition upon the relinquishment of certain association rights (Malanga, 2007, p. 781). Here one might argue that the University is forcing its point of view on the student group, but this perspective would be erroneous, for while belief may not be regulated or restricted, conduct can.

Schools have no right to force groups to act in nondiscriminatory ways in terms of their expressed *beliefs*; however, they are required to manage and regulate discriminatory *conduct*, which is precisely what nondiscrimination policies are meant to do. Sometimes part of the problem is that the wording of many schools' nondiscrimination policies is too restrictive in terms of protecting student groups' rights of freedom of belief, but if wording is corrected, then this may often solve the problem, e.g., as it did in the AIO decision recently rendered in Federal District Court, which is discussed below. First, let me clarify that schools cannot (and should not) regulate expressions and their associated beliefs, whether they regard them as discriminatory or not. However, according to the Court, and here I would agree, conduct is another matter, and a school's nondiscrimination policies must work in this arena to prevent immediate harms. In other words, groups such as BYX may hold whatever views they like, whether informed by religious beliefs or from any other sources or platforms of insight. The school's policies cannot aim to replace any group's viewpoints but merely to prohibit discriminatory membership policies (i.e., conduct) that could deny concrete economic and social benefits to those affected categories of persons—for if this occurred it would constitute invidious discrimination.[7]

What is important, and has at times been misunderstood, is that universities and colleges are not forcing student organizations to accept unwanted members, who these organizations see as harming their ability to convey their beliefs, through their nondiscrimination policies. The legal concern is not about "[t]he forced inclusion of dissonant voices into the group" (Snider, 2004, p. 877). The point of university nondiscrimination policies is not to impose an adverse impact upon a student organization's view, for example, that religiously unqualified individuals or persons of inappropriate sexual orientation are unacceptable as group members. Rather, the intent of university antidiscrimination policies is simply to prevent the act of discrimination (Malanga, 2007, p. 795).

In one sense, since schools create a limited public forum by encouraging and accommodating student associations and groups, does this automatically mean that school policies should be dictated by matters of public accommodation? Does this mean that a university or college should be able to force inclusion into student groups, for public accommodation laws often force inclusion even upon private entities? The clear answer is "no" because public accommodation laws are categorically different from legally based nondiscrimination policies. These two operate differently; nondiscrimination policies simply place conditions on the sought-after benefits of university recognition while also helping to ensure that all students have equal access to the tangible economic and social benefits that may be derived from membership in a recognized social group or club.

Belief, Conduct, and Status: The Developing Legal Landscape of Viewpoint Neutrality

In May 2006, the Federal District Court ruled against the Alpha Iota Omega (AIO) fraternity in its claim that the University of North Carolina (UNC) had transgressed its rights of association, etc. AIO objected to portions of the University's nondiscrimination policy concerning religion and sexual orientation. The legal dispute was ruled officially moot by the District Court because, since the time of the original lawsuit, UNC had both acknowledged certain problems and changed its written policy on the recognition of student organizations.[8] In this decision an important distinction in regard to religion was made by the Court: "religion as a set of beliefs" is separate "from religion as a status." According to the District Court, while religious belief and religious status "often overlap" they represent "two distinct concepts." This distinction is highly significant in terms of the tension between issues of nondiscrimination and rights of association connected to freedom of speech. It means that a university may not prohibit discrimination on the basis of a group's religious beliefs, but it may restrict its official acknowledgement of groups that discriminate on the basis of religious status—and this would include a person's religious label and religious ancestry as well.

Not surprisingly, the Court's *AIO* decision, although already rendered, was not cited in the letter by the attorney from CLS on behalf of BYX. However, this Court decision was clear that a University "must protect all students' First Amendments rights by maintaining 'viewpoint neutrality in the allocation of funding support' and 'may not prefer some viewpoints to others.'" This legal position represents the other side of the coin. In other words, a more nuanced recent view of the tension between nondiscrimination rules and rights of association is that universities are to protect the engagement of their nondiscrimination policies by making them apply equally to all groups without regard to viewpoints expressed by the groups themselves.

Notably, the letter sent to the University of Missouri on behalf of BYX from the Center for Law & Religious Freedom had used as a precedent case, *Christian Legal Society v. Walker* decided in the 7th Circuit Court in July 2006. As indicated by the attorney for the Center, in this case Southern Illinois University's (SIU) application of an antidiscrimination policy to force a religious student organization (i.e., the Christian Legal Society [CLS])[9] to open its membership to persons who rejected its religious beliefs was rejected by the Court as a violation of the group's rights of association. This case reveals many of the insufficiencies of the current legal status regarding the tension between nondiscrimination and rights of association as here it must be asked whether the Court was specifically regulating belief or conduct in its decision. As detailed in some length in a recent edition of the *Harvard Law Review*, in the SIU case the Circuit Court erroneously assumed that de-recognition by the university was a tool of forced inclusion (*Harvard Law Review* 120, 2007). However, as the law review article makes clear, by using this approach the Court's further "reasoning on the merits of the [plaintiff's] expressive association claim was flawed" (p. 1116). The problem with the Court's decision was that the University (SIU) "did not force" the religiously oriented student organization (CLS) "to accept homosexual members into its private organization...[i]t merely conditioned funding [and thereby recognition] on compliance with its nondiscrimination policy" (p. 1117).[10] Thus, the University had no intention of targeting CLS's conduct on the basis of its expressive viewpoint, and as the Supreme Court has made clear in other contexts, "acts are not shielded from regulation merely because they express a discriminatory idea or philosophy" (Malanga, 2007, p. 795). Overall, the case represented the loss of "an important opportunity to support a public university's decision to expend resources only on those student organizations that are open to all *students*" (*Harvard Law Review* 120, p. 1119).

This observation leads specifically to the greater issue raised by the attorney from the Center for Law & Religious Freedom in his letter on behalf of BYX, namely, whether the University of Missouri's policies regarding student organizations "systematically punished" religious viewpoints and were therefore not value neutral. University legal policies must protect all students' First Amendment rights by maintaining value neutrality in the allocation of recognition and thereby funding support to student organizations. However, if membership distinctions are made on the basis of religious status (rather than belief) these remain as discriminatory actions and the University would be legally correct to prohibit such activities even if it meant the curtailment of specific rights of expressive association. Nondiscrimination policies regulate conduct, not belief, and they must apply to all student organizations seeking recognition and also must be applied without regard for the message or expressed beliefs of such groups (whether religiously based or otherwise). This is viewpoint neutrality (Malanga, 2007, p. 795).

Finally, it is important to determine whether a university's nondiscrimination policies are tailored so as to be as narrowly drawn as possible in order to achieve nondiscrimination while having the least impact on the rights of student groups. The point here is that a university's nondiscrimination policies need only apply to those groups that seek university recognition, and in this way they effectively remain narrowly tailored and constitutional.[11] But more directly, this aspect highlights the problems that remain as the U. S. Supreme Court has yet to weigh in directly on "whether the stronger interest is that of a university's students to be free from discrimination, or that of the members of an official student organization to exercise their freedoms under the First Amendment" (Hamilton and Bentley, 2005, p. 625).

Conclusion: Emerging Legal Frameworks

Prior to 2006, virtually all universities and colleges challenged by these developments granted exceptions or waivers to affected student groups. However, there are some notable exceptions. Two law schools, Hastings College Law School (Hastings) and the University of Southern Illinois Carbondale School of Law (SIU), as well as the College of Staten Island (CSI) that is part of the CUNY system, have gone to court. All these schools are public institutions and receive public funding, which likely influenced their decisions to litigate.

In the CSI matter, an orthodox Jewish fraternity was not allowed to restrict women from its membership based on gender discrimination violations of the College's nondiscrimination policy. Notably, the initial decision, prior to the appeal, is cited by the attorney writing on behalf of BYX to the University of Missouri. However, subsequent to the attorney's letter, the initial court ruling in favor of the fraternity at CSI was reversed by the U.S. Court of Appeals (2nd Cir.) in September 2007. The Court of Appeals determined that "the district court applied the wrong test and, as a result, reached an incorrect conclusion." As the Court pointed out:

> The mere fact that the associational interest asserted is recognized by the First Amendment does not necessarily mean that a regulation which burdens that interest must satisfy strict scrutiny. In assessing a First Amendment associational-rights claim, a court must balance the associational interest asserted against the conflicting regulatory interest (*Chi Iota Colony of Alpha Epsilon Pi Fraternity v. City Univ. of N.Y.*, U.S. Court of Appeals, 2nd Cir. p. 3, line# 13–16).

Here the Court rightly pushes back against the use of rights of association to allow and promote discriminatory practices (and importantly, without infringing on the beliefs that may underlay a group's position). Interestingly, the fraternity at CSI had sought protection primarily under its rights of intimate association, not of expressive association. It was not the first time a fraternity had gone to court over asserted rights of intimate association, although in the earlier fraternity lawsuit concerns over the expression of religious beliefs was not at issue. However, in both cases the litigating fraternities were not successful with their claim of breeches of their rights of intimate association. Determinations of violations of rights of intimate association are based on measures of an organization's associational strengths examined through court-established parameters, which include size, selectivity, purpose, and exclusion of members.

Two other recent court decisions are intriguing. Both decisions involved the Christian Legal Society, which was suing for breeches of its associational rights as a student organization. Interestingly, while the factual circumstances of *Hastings* (in California) and *SIU* (in Illinois) are similar, the decisions reached went in opposite directions. In *Hastings* the Court classified Hastings' antidiscrimination policy as conduct, rather than speech, and thereby concluded that the law school's nondiscrimination regulation was applicable to the fraternity. In contrast, in the *SIU* decision the Court found that antidiscrimination policies of SIU regulated speech and therefore they violated the student organization's (i.e., CLS's) First Amendment right to free speech and expressive association.

The polarity expressed by these recent decisions (and of *Walker* and *CSI*) reflect the ongoing tension existing between rights of association and nondiscrimination policies. Recognition of the extent of this tension between associational rights and nondiscrimination policies is revealed increasingly in a variety of law reviews and in many other articles discussing these matters. I highlight just a few examples to show this developing area of discussion.

In a 1995 article entitled, "The Clash between the First Amendment and Civil Rights: Public University Nondiscrimination Clauses" (Paul and Rose, p. 889) in regard to "the right of university religious organizations to discriminate on the basis of sexual orientation" (Paul and Rose, 1995, p. 890), the authors note:

> Thus, the real issues are whether protecting homosexuals from discrimination is a compelling state interest, and whether forcing student religious groups to sign nondiscrimination clauses constitutes the suppression of ideas. (p. 909)

Here the idea of a contest between competing legal and constitutional rights and the "trumping" of one constitutional right by another is highly prevalent: "The ultimate question is which of the conflicting civil liberties existing in this context will trump the other" (Paul and Rose, 1995, p. 890).[12] By 2001 the matter had broadened considerably, with the explicit legal tension developing between different constitutional rights clearly evident:

> The Court's consistent refusal to permit the government to endorse the beliefs or practices of religious groups creates some constitutional complications. Some of the most vexing issues raised by these cases involve the relationship between the Establishment Clause of separation and the principle of free association implicit in the First Amendment's free expression clauses. (Gey, 2001, p. 1887)

In 2005, in an edition of the *Harvard Law Review* addressing "public university antidiscrimination policies and religious student organizations," the growing tension between antidiscrimination rules and the right of expressive association is addressed directly:

> Although the Supreme Court has shown a strong commitment to protecting expressive association, the concept remains perennially plagued by a seemingly intractable definitional problem, namely, how the elements of an expressive association claim can genuinely protect expressive organizations, yet be restrictively defined so as not to completely undermine sometime conflicting government rules such as anti-discrimination re-

quirements. This concern, because it is fundamental to any expressive association analysis, warrants much more consideration than is possible in this Note. (*Harvard Law Review* 118, p. 2882)

A 2007 law review article, reviewing expressive association and the rights of student organizations to discriminate, notes how this issue remains unresolved, giving a sense of the need for additional Supreme Court rulings to clarify and mitigate the existing legal tensions:

> The Supreme Court has not yet weighed in on "whether the stronger legal interest is that of a university's students to be free from discrimination, or that of the members of an official student organization to exercise their freedoms under the First Amendment." (Hamilton and Bentley, 2005, p. 625)

However, when seen through the lens of the Court's distinction between religious belief versus conduct, the practice of actively discriminating against certain statuses of students is very different from a group holding the view that such discrimination is religiously (or otherwise) sanctioned.

It is apparent that a general shift in the focus of the Supreme Court from the civil rights of different categories of persons to the constitutional rights of individuals and groups has occurred (Smart, 2001, p. 398). Examining the various legal decisions the courts have rendered recently, opportunities both to preserve the protections of state antidiscrimination laws and to extend their provisions to an even wider range of people,[13] while at the same time protecting associational rights, have been missed, which is regrettable. Thus, the internal interests and differing orientations of these two important legal realms are becoming increasingly pitted against one another creating an unfortunate potential not only for escalating legal and social abuses, but also for turning the freedom of religion (and of nonreligion) increasingly into a political and social battleground.

NOTES

1. The first college social fraternity was established prior to the adoption of the nation's Constitution. It was established at the College of William and Mary in December 1776 (see McBride, 1997:134).

2. I have omitted a discussion of the "hybrid rights doctrine" as it contains a number of difficulties and problems. See: Paul and Rose (1995:919) for a favorable view, and Volokh (2006:1922, footnote #10) for a more pessimistic perspective including additional references.

3. One ongoing problem that taints this procedure is that the "Court has never set forth a rule defining what makes an interest compelling" (Volokh, 2006:1963).

4. Perhaps it could also be argued that the organizers, by creating an open public forum (i.e., the parade activity itself) must then allow any group that wished to participate to not have their views, ideas, or beliefs suppressed, by virtue of each groups' rights of expressive association to have their message heard in a public forum in which they otherwise fully qualify for participation.

5. It has been argued, at times, that if Christian fraternities are not allowed to discriminate in their membership then the experience of diversity in the university setting would actually be decreased. However, repeated evidence does not support such the contention that a group's ability to express its views is hampered by the inclusion of members who hold beliefs inconsistent with the group's message (see e.g., *Christian Legal Soc'y Chapter of Univ. of Cal. v. Ka*ne, 2006 U.S. Dist. Ct. (N.D. Cal., Apr. 17, 2006). Even in the *Dale* decision, the Supreme Court expressly noted that a group engaged in expressive association is not entitled to "erect a shield against antidiscrimination laws simply by asserting that mere acceptance of a member from a particular group would impair its message" (*Boy Scouts of Am. v. Dale* 530 U.S. 653 (2000); also cited in *Christian Legal Soc'y Chapter of Univ. of Cal. v. Kane*, 2006 U.S. Dist. Ct. (N.D. Cal., Apr. 17, 2006) at 68).

6. In addition, recent legal decisions suggest that Universities themselves are organizations that have rights of expressive association in terms of their projected image and message. Does this create a conflict over whose message, that of the student group or that of the University, should be protected legally?

7. When we begin to consider the size of some of the national organizations of fraternities and sororities, the potential for wide-scale campus discrimination and the exploitation of university student group funding sources for select groups, who perhaps also represent the religious majority at a university or college, creates an issue of considerable concern.

8. The defendants (AIO) argued unsuccessfully that the new policies were no different than the old ones.

9. The Center for Law & Religious Freedom is an offshoot of the Christian Legal Society.

10. One problem SIO encountered was that while the court found SIO's policy viewpoint neutral on its face, there was strong evidence that it was not being applied in a viewpoint neutral and consistent manner (see Malanga 2007: 795, footnote #289; *Christian Legal Soc'y v. Walker*, 453 F.3d 853, 866 (2006).

11. As the Supreme Court has additionally pointed out, "[f]reedom of association [also] plainly presupposes a freedom not to associate" (*Roberts v. United States Jaycees*, 468 U.S. 623 (1984)).

12. Here the authors are talking about whether a student religious organization can discriminate against "homosexual conduct."

13. Especially in a world that is globalizing, where countries like the U.S. are becoming much more diversified religiously, ethnically, linguistically, socially, and culturally.

BIBLIOGRAPHY

Bernstein, David E. 2004. Expressive Association After Dale. *Social Philosophy and Policy* 21, 195–214.

Bullag, Burton. 2005. Choosing Their Flock. *Chronicle of Higher Education*, January 28, 2005.

Center for Law & Religious Freedom. Letter from Timothy J. Tracey, Litigation Counsel, Center for Law & Religious Freedom to Taylor McKinney, Vice Chair of Administration, University of Missouri, dated December 14, 2006.

Columbia Daily Tribune, Columbia, MO. 2006, December 28. "Christian Frat Wins Blessing: MU Drops Demand on Discrimination" by Alan Scher Zagier (Associated Press).

Flowers, Ronald B. 2005. *That Godless Court? Supreme Court Decisions on Church-State Relationships* (2nd ed.). Louisville, Kentucky: Westminster John Knox Press.

Gey, Steven G. 2001. The No Religion Zone: Constitutional Limitations on Religious Association in the Public Sphere. *Minn. L. Rev.* 85, 1885–1916.

Hamilton, Dona and Eric Bentley. 2005. Enforcing a University's Non-Discrimination Provision for a Student Organization's Selection of it Members and Officers. *J. Law & Educ.* 34, 615–626.

Harvard Law Review. 2005. Leaving Religious Students Speechless: Public University Antidiscrimination Policies and Religious Student Organizations. *Harv. Law Rev.* 118, 2882–2904.

Harvard Law Review. 2007. Constitutional Law - First Amendment - Seventh Circuit Holds That Public University Cannot Refuse to Recognize Student Group Based on Group's Violation of School Nondiscrimination Policy - *Christian Legal Society v. Walker. Harv. Law Rev.* 120, 1112–1119.

Internal Revenue Service (IRS), *Publication 557* (rev. March 2005). "Tax Exempt Status for Your Organization" U.S. Department of the Treasury. Document available at: http://www.irs.gov/pub/irs-pdf/p557.pdf

James, Anthony W. 2000. The College Social Fraternity Antidiscrimination Debate, 1945. *Historian*, 62(2), 303–324.

Koppelman, Andrew. 2002. Sign of the Times: *Dale v. Boy Scouts of America* and the Changing Meaning of Nondiscrimination. *Cardozo Law Review* 2, 1819–1838.

Koppelman, Andrew. 2004. Should Noncommercial Associations Have an Absolute Right to Discriminate? *Law and Contemp. Probs.* 67(4), 27–57.

Malanga, Christina A. 2007. Notes: Expressive Association—Student Organizations' Right to Discriminate: A Look at Public Law Schools' Nondiscrimination Policies and their Application to Christian Legal Society Student Chapters. *New Eng. Law Rev.* 29(3), 757–799.

McBride, Scott Patrick. 1997. Freedom of Association in the Public University Setting: How Broad is the Right to Freely Participate in Greek Life? *U. Dayton Law Rev.* 23(1), 133–168.

Paul, Richard and Derek Rose. 1995. Comment: The Clash between the First Amendment and Civil Rights: Public University Nondiscrimination Clauses. *Mo. Law Rev.* 60, 889–929.

Smart, Christopher W. 2001. Case Comments: The First Amendment: Expressive Association of Invidious Discrimination? *Florida Law Rev.* 53, 389–398.

Snider, Mark Andrew. 2004. Viewpoint Discrimination by Public Universities: Student Religious Organizations and Violations of University Nondiscrimination Policies. *Wash. & Lee Law Rev.* 61, 841–882.

Tracey Letter from Timothy J. Tracey, Litigation Counsel, Center for Law & Religious Freedom to Taylor McKinney, Vice Chair of Administration, University of Missouri, dated December 14, 2006.

University of Missouri. *Rules and Regulations of the University of Missouri-Columbia: M-Book 2006-07.* http://web.missouri.edu/~umcstudentlifembook/

Volokh, Eugene. 2006. Freedom of Expressive Association and Government Subsidies. *Stanford Law Rev.* 58(6), 1919–1968.

U.S. COURT CASES CITED

1958 *NAACP v. Alabama ex rel. Patterson,* 357 U.S. 449 (1958).

1972 *Healy v. James,* 408 U.S. 169 (1972).

1981 *Widmar v. Vincent,* 454, U.S. 263 (1981).

1984 *Roberts v. United States Jaycees,* 468 U.S. 609 (1984).

1987 *Bd. of Dirs. of Rotary Int'l v. Rotary Club of Duarte,* 481 U.S. 537 (1987).

1988 *N.Y. State Club Ass'n. v. City of N.Y.,* 487 U.S. 1 (1988).

1990 *Employment Div. of Oregon v. Smith,* 494 U.S. 872 (1990).

1992 *R.A.V. v. City of St. Paul,* 505 U.S. 377, 390 (1992),

1995 *Hurley v. Irish-Am. Gay, Lesbian, & Bisexual Group of Boston, Inc.,* 515 U.S. 557 (1995).

1995 *Rosenberger v. Rector and Visitors of Univ. of Va.,* 515 U.S. 819 (1995).

2000 *Boy Scouts of Am. v. Dale,* 530 U.S. 640 (2000).

2000 *Pi Lambda Fraternity, Inc. v. Univ. of Pittsburgh,* U.S. Court of Appeals, 3rd Cir. (amended November 29, 2000).

2004 *Locke v. Davey,* 540 U.S. 712 (2004).

2006 *Christian Legal Soc'y Chapter of Univ. of Cal. v. Kane,* 2006 U.S. Dist. Ct. (N.D. Cal., Apr. 17, 2006).

2006 *Alpha Iota Omega Christian Fraternity v. Moeser,* U.S. Dist. Ct. for the Mid. Dist. of NC, May 4, 2006.

2006   *Christian Legal Soc'y v. Walker*, 453 F.3d 853 (7th Cir., July 10, 2006).

2007   *Chi Iota Colony of Alpha Epsilon Pi Fraternity v. City Univ. of N.Y.*, U.S. Court of Appeals, 2nd Cir. (September 13, 2007).

CHAPTER SEVEN

Prayer in Public Schools: Forming a More Perfect Union?

Susan E. Waters, Auburn University

The Preamble to the Constitution of the United States affirms, "We the people of the United States, in order to form a more perfect union, establish justice, insure domestic tranquility, provide for the common defense, promote the general welfare, and secure the blessings of liberty to ourselves and our posterity, do ordain and establish this Constitution for the United States of America" (ratified 1787).

There are Americans who think it necessary "in order to form a more perfect union" that the Christian religion be an integral part of the public school curriculum—not just the Christian faith in general but a specific form of it. There are other Americans, both Christians and non-believers, who do not support prayer in the public schools, but for very different reasons. Regardless of what side one is on, most Americans agree there is an underlying tension. This tension is usually seen as a struggle between two extremes: those who mix church and state and those who simply want to erase the Christian faith completely from American public life. The first group, the "mixers," seek to turn public schools into an extension of "their" church, and the second, the "erasers," are hostile to religion, and not only want to kick God out of the classroom, but off of the planet. Yet there is a middle ground, a third group of Americans, persons of faith, who prefer to view the issue not so much in terms of a separation of church and state, but in terms of not "mixing" church and state. Their concern is not the elimination of religion from American public life, but *whose* religion is going to be represented in the public schools. In terms of the prayer debate, the latter would not be concerned with simply the outward act of praying, but with the content of the prayers.

This study intends to trace the origins of this debate and court rulings regarding religion in public schools, especially school prayer, which reached a watershed with the Supreme Court's involvement in the 1960s. Many Americans anathematized the 1962 landmark decision by the United States Supreme Court as a ruling that kicked God out of the schools. It was branded as a pro-Communist establishment of atheism in public schools—a canard that persists to this day. The Court, however, specified that it was not striking down prayer, but the government's power "to *prescribe by law* any particular form of prayer which is to be used as an official prayer in carrying on any program of *governmentally sponsored* religious activity" (emphasis added, *Engle v. Vitale,* 1962, p. 1262).

Critics of the ruling claimed that state-sponsored school prayer had been trouble free for over 170 years until the Supreme Court trespassed into that sacred territory. Senator Strom Thurmond (R – South Carolina), a spokesman for this viewpoint, said in a 1983 hearing on the subject of prayer in the public schools that before the 1962 Supreme Court ruling "no one raised the point, no one tested it, no one went to the Supreme Court" (Voluntary school prayer, 1983, p. 419). The historical record, however, reveals just the opposite. Disputes and conflict over prayer and religion in public schools have raged as long as public schools have existed in America.

Setting the Theological Stage: A Brief History

Before we cross that historical bridge, it is necessary to look further back in time and briefly trace the theological path that led to the founding of our nation, especially the path that involves the relationship of church and state. There is a persistent human tendency to blur the distinction between church and state, which at times has resulted in a tyranny of the state, at other times in a tyranny of the church. For the Christian Church it has gone back at least to 313 A.D., when Emperor Constantine legalized the Christian faith in the Roman Empire. Constantine used the power of his office to support and promote the church, using government funds to build churches (e.g., the Church of the Holy Sepulcher).

Constantine established Christianity as the official religion of his empire and appointed himself head of both state and church. Even though Constantine permitted the bishops to determine doctrine, he understood his role to be the enforcer of doctrine, to root out all heresy, to uphold church unity and to ensure God was properly worshiped in his empire (Richards, 1979).

That scenario reversed in medieval times, with papal authority overtaking temporal authority. Already for years the popes had claimed it as a right inherent in their office that they not only rule the church, but also secular government. Finally, in 1075 A.D., Pope Gregory VII formalized papal dominance in the document known as *Dictatus Papae* (Papal Dictation). Among the twenty-seven claims of power, the most notable are:

> That the Pope has the power to depose emperors, that his decree can be annulled by no one, and that he alone may annul decrees of any one; that he can be judged by no man; that he has the power to absolve the subjects of unjust rulers from their oath of fidelity, and that all princes shall kiss his feet. (Henderson, 1910, pp. 366–367)

This state of affairs lasted for several centuries, until the Protestant Reformation of the sixteenth century, at which time two major models of church and state would emerge, one of them having a significant influence on the issue of prayer in public schools in America. It is commonly thought that the Reformation had two main players—Roman Catholicism and Protestantism. In reality there were three, Roman Catholicism, Reformed Protestantism, and Lutheranism. At first, two distinct and independent movements existed within the Reformed Protestant camps, one in the German part of Switzerland, led by Ulrich Zwingli and the other in French Switzerland, spearheaded by John Calvin (Mayer, 1961). For a while it seemed that the two movements would remain separate and distinct until Calvin forged a union between the two by authoring a doctrinal statement with which both could agree known as the *Consensus Tigurinus* of 1549 (Klotsche, 1945; Mueller, 1949). While not all reformed church bodies that emerged from the Reformation were in unanimous agreement with John Calvin, he did more to shape reformed theology than any other individual. He is in that exclusive group of people in history who have influenced not only their own age but also future generations.

He inspired the Puritan revolution of the seventeenth century and may be called the spiritual father of the American republic:

> Calvinism, in its various modifications and applications, was the controlling agent in the early history of our leading colonies; and Calvinism is, to this day, the most powerful element in the religious and ecclesiastical life of the Western world (Mayer, 1961, p. 205).

England did not colonize America until the seventeenth century, at a time when Calvinism had been firmly established in England. Unlike Canada, which was colonized by French Roman Catholics, and Central and South America, which were colonized by Spanish and Portuguese Roman Catholics, English Calvinists colonized America. A basic understanding of Calvin's theology, especially as it impacts the doctrine of church and state, is indispensable for a clear and accurate evaluation of the early American theological scene. The other participant in the Reformation was Lutheranism, led by Martin Luther. While Calvin and Luther had much in common, they differed greatly on certain articles of the Christian faith, with one in particular being the doctrine of Church and State. While Luther and Calvin agreed that God instituted both church and state, their agreement ends with the relationship between the two and their respective duties.

Martin Luther. Luther understood the Christian to be living in two spheres at the same time, one a heavenly spiritual kingdom, the church, the other an earthly civil kingdom, the state. Because of this dual citizenship, a Christian has dual obligations and loyalties, different and separate. Each sphere has its own task and authority: the task of the church is to create faith in the Gospel of Christ for the justification of the sinner leading to eternal life, its authority being the Word of God; the state is given the task of keeping law and order on earth, punishing evil and rewarding good, its authority being human reason and the sword. For Luther, God created both spheres, which means the Christian responds to God in both spheres, yet in very different and distinct ways. The Christian responds in the church as a justified child of God through faith in Christ, and in the state as a law-abiding citizen, even if the state is a heathen republic with Caesar as its god, as the first Christians experienced in Rome. There were limits for Luther to what Christian good works can accomplish, and the church was not to be preoccupied with transforming the civil order.

This is one of the issues that divided Luther from Calvin, who praised Luther for reforming the church, but thought Luther did not go far enough. Therefore, Calvin reasoned it was his mission to reform the state, transforming it into a handmaiden of the church. Luther, however, maintained there is no command in the New Testament given to the church to transform civil governments into Christian governments. He challenged those who thought that it was the church's mission to make the state its handmaiden in his treatise, *Temporal Authority: To What Extent It Should Be Obeyed*:

> Again you say, "The temporal power is not forcing men to believe; it is simply seeing to it externally that no one deceives the people by false doctrine; how could heretics otherwise be restrained?" I answer: This the bishops should do; it is a function entrusted to them and not to the princes. Heresy can never be restrained by force. One will have to tackle the problem in some other way, for heresy must be opposed and dealt with otherwise than with the sword. Here God's word must do the fighting. If it does not succeed, certainly the temporal power will not succeed either, even if it were to drench the world in blood. Heresy is a spiritual matter which you cannot hack to pieces with iron. (Brandt, 1962, p.114)

John Calvin. On the other hand, Calvin viewed church and state as a symbiosis, a relationship with mutual benefit. He stated in his definitive theological work, *Institutes of the Christian Religion*:

> The church, in some measure, begins the heavenly kingdom in us, even now upon earth, and in this mortal and evanescent life commences immortal and incorruptible blessedness, while to the state it is assigned, so long as we live among men, to foster and maintain the external worship of God, to defend sound doctrine and the condition of the Church, to adapt our conduct to human society, to form our manners to civil justice, to conciliate us to each other, to cherish common peace and tranquility. (1962, IV, xx, 2)

Even though state and church function together, Calvin assured followers that the state never controls what the church teaches; instead, the state aids the church. In theory, Calvin identified the difference between the two realms, although in his practice they overlapped. As a result, Calvin wrote about the church as the conscience of the state, and he saw the state as the enforcer of the church and the Bible. His model led him to set up a theocratic state in Geneva, an arrangement that seemed to differ little from what the Popes had tried to do for centuries.

It was out of this confused amalgamation of church and state that Western Europe, especially England, began to colonize America. United States history reveals considerable confusion of church and state, and before the Revolution America had state churches, all rooted in Calvin's model. Law in Massachusetts, New Hampshire and Connecticut established the Congregational Church. The Dutch Reformed was the legal church in New Amsterdam; the Anglican Church was the established religion in Maryland, Georgia, and the Carolinas. On the eve of the Revolution only three colonies had no provision for an established church: Rhode Island, Pennsylvania, and Delaware. At the time of the American Revolution, a majority of the population had grown up in families exposed to some form of Puritanism. The Puritans' Massachusetts Bay Colony was a Geneva-style Calvinist theocracy, with the Bible being the source and norm of church and civil law. It is ironic that the Puritans left England to seek religious freedom, only to establish a colony devoid of religious toleration. They sought to establish their religion, while prohibiting and shunning all others.

The spiritual Great Awakening, begun in 1734 by Jonathan Edwards and continued by George Whitfield, laid the foundation of the American Revolution (Tracy, 1997). In this Calvinist revival, the colonists came to believe that their mission first required political independence, and pursuit of political liberty was literally a religious crusade, being convinced that America, like Israel, was a God-chosen nation (Reichley, 1985). Against this perplexing backdrop, we enter the paradox of the founding of our nation, which would form the foundation for the subsequent disputes over prayer in the public schools. While the various colonies had adopted constitutions based on Calvin's model that wedded church and state, the Constitution that would unite the states into one nation, especially the First Amendment, would separate and not mix church and state. At first some of the states continued to have established state churches, although that quickly faded in the new republic.

Another facet of the paradox is the diversity of religious beliefs among the founding Fathers. Arguably, the majority of the people living in the colonies were Calvinist Christians, as demonstrated by their constitutions. However, many of the founding fathers, who comprised the intelligentsia of the day, were not Christians, but were Deists or Unitarians, substituting a rational God of nature for the God revealed in the Bible. They rejected God as Trinity, the deity of Christ, and many other foundational doctrines of the historic Christian faith.

Thomas Jefferson. Two examples of notable Deists are the brilliant statesmen, Thomas Jefferson and George Washington. Jefferson, third president of the United States and author of the Declaration of Independence, rejected the Anglican faith in which he had been raised and declared himself as "a sect by myself as far as I know" (Greely, 1995, p. 42.). He denounced Calvin's Christian theology as "blasphemous" (p. 50), and went so far as to write in a fiery letter to John Adams that Calvin "was indeed an atheist, which I can never be," that his religion was demonic, and "if ever man worshipped a false god, he did" (Adams, 1983, p. 7).

Jefferson rejected the historic Christian doctrine of the Trinity as absurd (p. 5) and scoffed at it as the "hocus pocus phantasm of a god like another Cerberus with one body and three heads" (Greely, 1995, p. 49). Even though Jefferson held Jesus in high regard as a moral teacher, he rejected him as the Savior God. In a letter to William Short in 1819, he clarified his view that most of what the Bible says about Jesus is myth: "The immaculate conception of Jesus, his deification…his miraculous powers, his resurrection and visible ascension…the Trinity, original sin, atonement, regeneration, etc. have resulted from artificial systems" (p. 42).

While tossing much of the historic Christian faith overboard, Jefferson often identified himself as a Christian, which uninformed people today point to as proof that he was a Christian. Jefferson could comfortably refer to himself as a Christian, as long as his redefined version applied. Heavily influenced by the writings of Unitarian Dr. Joseph Priestly, Jefferson concluded that the Bible contained so many distortions and errors the first Christians actually were not Trinitarians, but had a Unitarian concept of God, and therefore, he could be a true Christian without being a Trinitarian (Adams, 1983, p.15). While serving as President of the United States, Jefferson embarked on the task of editing the New Testament in order to demonstrate what he considered to be the true Christian faith and the real Jesus. He purged all the 'distortions and errors' he found, (e.g., the divinity of Christ, the virgin birth, the miracles, the resurrection, and any references to a

Triune God) and retained what he judged to be the authentic sayings of Jesus, an exercise he considered as easy as finding "diamonds in a dunghill" (Adams, 1983, p. 352).

George Washington. The faith of the other notable founding father, George Washington, has been debated, because he said very little publicly or privately about the precise nature of his beliefs. However, like Jefferson, he distanced himself from his boyhood Anglican faith, and spoke of God in generic terms, such as the Supreme Being, the Grand Architect, and the Great Ruler of Events, evoking the assertion that his letters and speeches "clearly display the outlook of a Deist" (Holmes, 2003, p. 84). Washington occasionally attended the Episcopal Church wherever he happened to be residing at the time. The Rector of the church in Philadelphia, Dr. Abercrombie, observed that every Sunday the Lord's Supper was celebrated; it was Washington's custom "to arise just before the ceremony commenced, and walk out of the church. This became a subject of remark in the congregation as setting a bad example." When asked in an interview why Washington did this, Abercrombie responded, "Sir, Washington was a Deist" (Smith, 2006, pp. 27-28; Steiner, 1995, pp. 26–27).

Other Deists or Unitarians among the founding fathers were Benjamin Franklin (Franklin, n.d., p. 27), James Madison, fourth president and father of the Constitution and Bill of Rights (Hutson, n.d.; Steiner, 1995), and John Adams, second president of the United States, who hypothesized "that this would be the best of all possible worlds if there were no religion in it" (Greely, 1995, p. 41). Adams also supported and signed into law the Treaty with Tripoli, which declared, "The government of the United States of America is not, in any sense, founded on the Christian Religion" (Library of Congress, 1797).

From the amalgam of the founding fathers, Jefferson and Madison moved to the forefront in the movement that eliminated special ties between the state and all religious denominations. Their principle was written into the First Amendment of the Constitution: "Congress shall make no law respecting an establishment of religion, or prohibiting the free exercise thereof." Later, in 1802, in a well-known letter to the Connecticut Baptists, Jefferson described the First Amendment as "building a wall of separation between church and state" (Greeley, 1995, p. 134), clarifying the intent that it was not to be understood as being hostile to religion, but as guaranteeing the freedom of all religions by not favoring any particular one.

The Debate Begins: First in the Streets, Then in the Courts

It is into that crucible, molded by a paradox, that we enter the beginning of the conflict over prayer in the public schools, which did not begin during the social unrest of 1960s as many assume, but began a few decades after the American Revolution and the birth of our nation. This centuries-long debate over religion in the public schools is framed by the most sacred principles upon which America is based: majority rule and individual rights. The courts have had to grapple with the difficulty of balancing these competing principles, with each subsequent court case moving incrementally from majority rule to the rights of the individual.

However, before the debate entered the courts, it was first fought in the streets of America in the early 1800s. The Reformed Protestant majority who followed Calvin's model, which blended church and state, dominated the new nation. Calvinists held to a strong belief that everyone should be able to read the Bible, and religious teaching was essential to promoting morality. The educational process in the public schools included readings from the King James Version of the Bible (KJV), hymns, and prayers on a daily basis, all of the content in line with their particular brand of Protestantism.

With the arrival of large numbers of Catholic immigrants, the issue of religion in the schools took on a whole new dimension. The number of American Roman Catholics rose from 35,000 in 1790 to over 3,000,000 in 1860 (Greenawalt, 2005). The first serious conflict over religion in public school was not between Christians and agnostics or atheists, as many assume, but between Protestants and Catholics, with Catholics being viewed as outsiders and a threat to democracy by the Protestant majority (DelFattore, 2004).

The Roman Catholic protest. The school prayer crisis began in the late 1830s when Catholic Bishop John Hughes requested from the Public School Society (PSS) in New York City access to the same public funding that the Protestant schools were receiving (Lannie, 1968). It is somewhat ironic that the school prayer debate began, not over religion *per se*, but over funding. The Calvinist

Reformed Protestants banded together and adopted the approach of identifying their schools as "nonsectarian," which meant they promoted no specific religion. On the other hand, Calvinists labeled the Catholic schools as "sectarian," because they promoted the specific religion of the Roman Catholic Church. Understanding how this double standard could even be considered possible by rational people is dependent upon recognizing that the nation was founded not simply as a Christian nation, but by those who followed, to one extent or another, John Calvin's model of church and state, which allowed them to view the public schools simply as a natural extension of their church. All other Christians were considered to be outside of the circle and identified as a sect.

In response to Bishop Hughes' request for public funding from the PSS, the New York city council decided that Catholic schools were sectarian and therefore not eligible. Predictably, Hughes rejected their decision, and maintained that by denying funds to Catholic schools on the basis of sectarianism, the city council should also withhold funding to schools that observed Protestant beliefs and practices, because to a Catholic, their faith is also sectarian. In his response, Hughes argued, "There could be no Christianity without sectarianism, for if Roman Catholicism, Methodism, Episcopalianism, Presbyterianism, Lutheranism, *et al.* were removed from the schools, then Christianity would cease to exist in them. Sectarianism and Christianity were one and the same" (Lannie, 1968, p. 54). His opponents responded with the vitriol that would mark the prayer debate from this point forward, that "the Catholic Church was a devious, equivocating, untruthful enemy of God's word as presented in the KJB, and thus a threat to freedom, democracy, morality, and Americanism" (DelFattore, 2004, p. 18).

This standard established by the Calvinist majority became the official policy in New York whereby "nonsectarian" schools would be eligible for public funding, but not "sectarian" schools. The beginning of the use of the terms "sectarian" and "nonsectarian" in the debate over religion in the public schools would prove to be very important, because it would become the benchmark for later court decisions well into the twentieth century. The Calvinist Protestant majority was bent on viewing *their* religion in the public schools as essential to realizing the U.S. Constitution's goal of "a more perfect union" (Preamble). Their religion in the public schools was linked with American patriotism, moral and ethical values, and the preservation of a peaceful society. They argued that their religion in the public schools was not sectarian, but generic; it was actually a display of patriotism and not religious in nature, and therefore could not lawfully be excluded from the schools. This view would form the basis of their argument in the courts for decades until the courts began to shift their decisions from favoring the majority to deciding in favor of the rights of the individual.

Philadelphia riots. Not surprisingly, Roman Catholic Bishop Hughes did not receive the requested funding. The controversy was contentious, but basically only a war of words, unlike the one that erupted in Philadelphia about the same time in 1844, in which the city school board enacted a policy giving themselves final say over the content of any religious program in the public schools. The board was definitively Calvinist, and they mandated the daily reading of the King James Bible by all public school students, as well as their version of prayers and hymns. The Roman Catholic bishop of Philadelphia responded to the school board that Catholic students could not in good conscience take part and asked the board to either excuse them from the religious devotions or allow them to use the Catholic version of the Bible, the Douay Version. He also asked that they be excused from participation in singing the hymns and the prayers.

The school board gave assurance to the bishop that no student would be forced to listen to readings from the King James Bible, but they did not allow the Catholic Douay Bible to be used in the daily readings. Even though that became the official policy, Catholic parents were soon protesting that their children were being humiliated, beaten, suspended, and expelled for refusing to participate. Like their counterparts in New York, the Protestant majority continued to believe that immigrant children could not be truly Americanized unless they learned to revere the King James Bible and Reformed theology. Anti-Catholic rallies were appearing throughout Philadelphia, escalating into mob violence, shootings, and the destruction of homes, churches and businesses. Countless people were injured and twenty lost their lives. The rioting became so violent that heavily armed troops had to be stationed in the city for weeks (Feldberg, 1975). When the rioting was quelled and peace returned to Philadelphia, grand juries were appointed to examine the events, and they found that the violence was caused by "the efforts of a portion of the community to exclude the Bible from public schools" (Scharf & Wescott, 1884, p. 668). Obviously, the "portion of the community" referred to were the Roman Catholics and "the Bible" was the King James Version. However, Catholics did not try to exclude the Bible from public schools, they were only requesting their version, the Douay, be included. The Calvinist Protestant majority, which continued to keep a tight-fisted control of the nation's public schools, repeatedly denied their requests.

When our nation was in its infancy, the daily religious education in the public schools consisted of Bible reading, hymns, and prayers, all in one package. Early in the conflict involving religion in the public schools, the focus was on which version of the Bible would be read, arising from the nature of the participants, (i.e., Protestant versus Catholic). The rest of the package, the hymns and prayers, were always on the table, but were not in the forefront. As the debate progressed over time, the focus was on the praying part of the package.

Into the courts. Not long after the events in New York City and Philadelphia, the debate involving religion in the public schools would leave the streets and for the first time enter the courtroom. In 1854 Roman Catholic Lawrence Donohoe told his daughter Bridget not to read the King James Bible in class, and subsequently she was expelled from school. He enrolled her in a private school and sued the State of Maine for reimbursement. His lawyer tried to convince an American court that the majority should not rule in matters of religion and that the religious views of the Reformed Protestant majority were, in fact, sectarian, and a violation of Catholics' religious freedom. He argued:

> As Protestants regard instruction in Protestant Christianity as the most essential branch of education, therefore, if the majority of the school be Protestant, the committee may enforce such a system of instruction on all; and Mahomedans (Muslims), Catholics, or Mormons may follow their example if they get the power. "The greatest good of the greatest number." This tyrannical doctrine of pure democracy, we generally hear only from the lips of demagogues. (*Donohoe v. Richards,* 1854, p. 387)

This court case, at the state level, was not only the first of its kind, but also the first to test the prevailing doctrine of majority rule. The nation, not yet a century old, began its journey of balancing the two sacred pillars upon which America is based: majority rule and individual rights. Still firmly entrenched in a majority rule environment, the state court ruled against Donohoe and declared that the King James Bible was nonsectarian and their request to use the Catholic Douay Bible was a ploy intended to remove the Bible from the public schools. In addition, the court observed that if Catholics did not want to read the King James Version, they should not defy the school committee but seek to elect members who would grant them their wishes (DelFattore, 2004). The Calvinist Protestant majority had the power, and it was their religion that was going to be in the public schools and all students were required to participate.

Today most school prayer lawsuits are heard in federal courts, but in the nineteenth and early twentieth century these cases were only heard in state courts. Federal courts did not become involved until mid-twentieth century, with the Supreme Court entering the scene in the 1960s. The reason that federal courts did not get involved was the very wording of the First Amendment, which stated, "Congress shall make no law respecting an establishment of religion, or prohibiting the free exercise thereof." The First Amendment specifically applied to Congress and not to the states. Congress (i.e., the federal government) could not establish a national church or interfere with a citizen's free exercise of religion. However, each state could determine the religious practice allowed within its territory. The New Jersey constitution of 1776, for example, limited the civil rights of Roman Catholics. It stated, "No Protestant inhabitant of this colony shall be denied the enjoyment of any civil right, merely on account of his religious principles." North Carolina's 1776 constitution was more to the point, "no person who shall deny the being of God or the truth of the Protestant religion...shall be capable of holding any office or place of trust." And again, South Carolina's 1778 constitution had a clause that read, "The Christian Protestant church shall be deemed, and is hereby constituted and declared to be, the established religion of the state" (Evans, 2007, p. 22). In every instance, the Protestant religion referred to was Calvinism or some form of it.

The Catalyst for the Shift to the Federal Courts: The Fourteenth Amendment

Eventually, the states dissolved their official churches and relaxed requirements for public office, but continued to mandate religion in the public schools. This meant that school prayer became the focal point at a time when federal courts began to gain authority over the states in the debate of religion in schools. What gave the federal courts the legal authority to intervene was the ratification of the Fourteenth Amendment in 1868, which stated in part, "No State shall make or enforce any law which shall abridge the privileges or immunities of citizens of the United States; nor shall any State deprive any person of life, liberty, or property, without due process of law; nor deny to any person within its jurisdiction the equal protection of the laws."

It may not be readily apparent what the Fourteenth Amendment has to do with school prayer, since it does not mention religion at all; moreover, this post-Civil War amendment was directed at racial equality and not necessarily religious freedom. However, its "equal protection under the law" clause came to be interpreted by the Supreme Court in the mid-twentieth century to mean that states, like the federal government, must respect the religious liberties protected by the First Amendment of the U. S. Constitution. Consequently, the states were no longer legally able, as they once were, to enforce or mandate certain religious beliefs and practices, especially in the public schools. The application of the Fourteenth Amendment to the First Amendment did not happen immediately. As the nation's population became more diverse, the Calvinist Protestant majority began to lose their grip on the public schools, and an increasing number began to think that the only equitable solution would be to exclude all religion from the public schools. In 1876 one of the first to do so was a Presbyterian minister who observed that it was not fair that the Protestant supporters of school prayer denied the very same thing to Catholics (Spear, 1876).

From majority rule to individual rights. The state court cases lead up to the Supreme Court's intervention in the 1960s, setting the stage for a shift from majority rule to individual rights. In 1872, the Protestant majority filed one of the earliest of these cases challenging a Cincinnati, Ohio, school board policy that excluded all religious activities from the public schools. They used the same argument that marked all of the earlier ones, namely that Christianity was part of the nation's heritage and is essential to good citizenship and morality and cannot lawfully be excluded from the public schools. Once again, Christianity was to be understood as Calvinist Protestantism and not Catholicism. The Superior Court of Cincinnati agreed; however, the Ohio Supreme Court reversed the ruling, essentially deciding that the only equitable solution was to let each religious group teach its religion in their churches and not in the public schools (*Board of Education v. Minor,* 1872). This was the first case of its kind at the state level that began to recognize that the Reformed Protestant majority could not lay exclusive claim to public schools in a nation of diverse religions.

Subsequent cases at the state level leaned toward an "opt out" policy, whereby the student, if he/she did not want to participate, could opt out and leave the classroom, attempting to pacify both sides. But this left much to be desired, because opting out led to intimidation and degradation at the hands of the majority toward those students who left the classroom, and kept in place a sectarian form of religion in the public schools. The "opt out" model met a roadblock in a 1910 Illinois case, involving a challenge from Catholic parents that the Protestant Bible readings, prayers, and hymns were discriminatory and violated the state constitution. Not surprisingly, as seen often in past cases, the local school board claimed those activities were nonsectarian and not discriminatory, and they simply promoted morality, good citizenship and would unite the entire school (DelFattore, 2004). Nevertheless, the Illinois Supreme Court found these activities did violate the Constitution and observed that even though the majority of the Illinois citizens were Protestant, "the law knows no distinction between the Christian and the Pagan, the Protestant and the Catholic. All are citizens. Their civil rights are equal...there can be no distinction based on religion" (*Ring v. Board of Education of District 24,* 1910, p. 349).

The Supreme Court Enters the Fray

This set the stage for the Supreme Court's involvement in the school prayer debate. The principle at issue was whether the "establishment clause" of the First Amendment applied not only to the federal government via the Congress, but also to the states by virtue of the "due process" clause of the Fourteenth Amendment. The Supreme Court solidified this principle in several decisions, some early ones being *Cantwell v. Connecticut* (1940) and *Everson v. Board of Education of Ewing Township* (1947), even though neither of these cases directly involved religion in the public schools. They addressed conflicts of a religious nature outside of the classroom. Up to this time, most cases involved disputes between Roman Catholics and Reformed Protestants. In *Cantwell v. Connecticut* (1940), several Jehovah's Witnesses were arrested for distributing anti-Catholic literature in a Catholic neighborhood. The Court ruled in favor of the Jehovah's Witnesses because their conduct was orderly and lawful, and "the fundamental concept of liberty embodied in the Fourteenth Amendment embraces the liberties guaranteed by the First Amendment" (*Cantwell v. Connecticut,* 1940, p. 903). The Supreme Court reiterated that principle in *Everson v. Board of Education of Ewing Township* (1947), which involved school bus subsidies for parochial school children. The local school board reimbursed families for bus fares regardless of which school the child attended, public or parochial. Everson, a local taxpayer, challenged the use of public funds for transportation to parochial schools. The Court ruled that offering free transportation to all students is similar to making police and fire department services available to all. Paramount in the decision was the Court's reiteration that the First Amendment applies to the states as well as to Congress:

> The "establishment of religion" clause of the First Amendment means at least this: Neither a state nor the Federal Government can set up a church. Neither can pass laws which aid one religion, aid all religions, or prefer one religion over another (*Everson v. Board of Education of Ewing Township*, 1947, p. 511).

The first case directly involving religion in the public schools to be heard by the Supreme Court was in 1948. It began in 1945, when an unusual mix of participants made a request of the school board in Champaign, Illinois. No longer were the Roman Catholics and Calvinists squaring off; this time a group of Protestant, Catholic, and Jewish clergy joined together to request permission to conduct voluntary religious instruction in the public school during school hours. The school board agreed, and the voluntary program of religious education commenced. Not surprisingly, it was fraught with problems from the beginning. The Jehovah's Witnesses were excluded from offering classes, leading to allegations of discrimination. The Jewish community became disillusioned, because separating the Jewish students from the Reformed Protestant majority led to anti-Semitic slurs. Also, students who refused to participate had to sit in the hallway during the religion classes as if being punished (DelFattore, 2004).

Mrs. McCollum, a student's mother and atheist, filed a complaint. The school board responded that it was only offering the classes to those who chose to attend, and no student would be forced to participate. The Illinois state courts agreed with the school board, but the Supreme Court did not. The Court observed, "This is beyond all question a utilization of the tax-established and tax-supported public school system to aid religious groups to spread their faith. And it falls squarely under the ban of the First Amendment (made applicable to the States by the Fourteenth) as we interpreted it in *Everson*" (*McCollum v. Board of Education of School District No. 71,* 1948, p. 209).

The Regent's Prayer. More than a decade would pass before the Supreme Court would hear another case dealing with religion in the public schools. This time it would be a landmark decision specifically affecting prayer in the schools. It began when the New York State Board of Regents, whose responsibility it was to oversee the local school boards and the educational process in their state, appointed a committee to write a prayer that would be used in the public schools. The committee consisted of Protestant, Catholic and Jewish clergy, who were instructed by the Regents to create a prayer that was nonsectarian and would not offend anyone. The prayer came to be known as the Regents' Prayer: "Almighty God, we acknowledge our dependence upon Thee, and we beg Thy blessings upon us, our parents, our teachers and our Country" (DelFattore, 2004, p. 69). The Regents' Prayer was to be prayed at the beginning of every school day along with readings from the Bible, followed by the Pledge of Allegiance. Students who did not want to participate were allowed to leave the classroom each morning, but as in the other opt-out situations, became targets for insults and intimidation.

Several Jewish parents, people of faith, from a northern New York school district objected to the Regents' Prayer and in 1958, filed a lawsuit in the state court to have it removed. The political climate in America during the 1950s was different than the climate in all the other court cases dealing with religion in the public schools. Communism had become a formidable enemy of the American way of life, and the cold war was a daily fact of life. To many Americans the best defense against it was not economic or political, but religious. Therefore, like their nineteenth-century Calvinist predecessors, religion in the public schools was deemed necessary in order to promote patriotism and moral values, only this time the threat was not from the Vatican, but from atheistic Communism, which also prompted the addition of the words "under God" to the Pledge of Allegiance. However, some religious groups criticized the Regents' Prayer as sectarian, favoring monotheism over other religions that are polytheistic or agnostic. Others, because of its lack of doctrinal content, labeled it as "mealy-mouthed mush" and totally useless as a prayer (DelFattore, 2004, p. 71). This double-edged sword of criticism would weigh heavily on the future of the Regents' Prayer all the way to the Supreme Court.

The Jewish parents contended that the state laws requiring or permitting use of the Regents' Prayer must be struck down as a violation of the Establishment Clause of the First Amendment, because that prayer was composed by governmental officials as a part of a governmental program to further religious beliefs. As most state courts had ruled since the Civil War, the New York courts ruled that the Regents' Prayer could be used in the public schools only if those who did not want to participate were excused. They also found that this prayer was not sectarian because it was accepted by the majority of people and did not constitute any "formal religion" (DelFattore, 2004, p. 73).

Engel v. Vitale. The case now entered the realm of the Supreme Court, with the Court's landmark decision in 1962. The long standing paradigm of majority rule trumping the rights of the individual shifted with the Supreme Court's 6–1 ruling that government-directed prayer in public schools was an unconstitutional violation of the Establishment Clause (*Engel v. Vitale,* 1962). The Supreme Court's view of the relationship between American history and school prayer also differed greatly from the

New York state courts. The Supreme Court stated in its decision, "It is a matter of history that this very practice of establishing governmentally composed prayers for religious services was one of the reasons which caused many of our early colonists to leave England and seek religious freedom in America" (p. 1264). The Court added the reminder that early colonists knew "one of the greatest dangers to the *freedom of the individual* to worship in his own way lay in the Government's placing its official stamp of approval upon one particular kind of prayer or one particular form of religious services" (p. 1266). The shift from majority rule to the rights of the individual concerning prayer in the public schools was now official and the law of the land. The courts had struggled for centuries over the tension between these two pillars of our republic, because of the paradox that existed at the founding of our nation. While the majority of the people who colonized America were Christian, the majority of the Founding Fathers who crafted the founding documents were not. The main authors of the Constitution, Diests Madison and Jefferson, in order to prevent the religious tyranny in England from being exported to America, crafted the First Amendment to read: "Congress shall make no law respecting an establishment of religion, or prohibiting the free exercise thereof."

The paradox revisited. The Supreme Court made mention of this paradox by pointing out in their decision, "It is an unfortunate fact of history, that when some of the very groups which had most strenuously opposed the established Church of England found themselves sufficiently in control of colonial governments in this country to write their own prayers into law, they passed laws making their own religion the official religion of their respective colonies" (*Engel v. Vitale,* 1962, p. 1265). The vast majority of Christians who colonized America were followers of the theology of John Calvin, whose model of church and state essentially combined them into one, with the state aiding the church. As a result of enjoying the power their majority status gave them, and because they viewed the state, especially the public school system, as an extension of their church, Calvinists were able to control the schools as their personal parochial school system. What resulted, however, was centuries of butting their heads against the wall of the First Amendment, which separated church and state.

The majority rule principle as it applied to prayer in the public schools ended with the 1962 Supreme Court decision. For the first time in American history the Supreme Court told state officials what they could and could not do with regard to prayer in the public schools. From that time on the federal government, upholding the Establishment Clause of the First Amendment, as applied to the states through the Fourteenth Amendment, would be a major factor regarding religious expression in public education. In its 1962 decision, the Court was quick to point out that it did not ban all references to religion from the public schools. Students could continue to read historical documents and sing patriotic songs that mention God, and teachers could continue to teach *about* religion without promoting any one sect. When the decision was announced, public opinion went against the Court denouncing *Engel v. Vitale* as a pro-Communist establishment of atheism in the public schools. However, the Court had addressed that issue defending the decision: "It is neither sacrilegious nor antireligious to say that each separate government in this country should stay out of the business of writing or sanctioning official prayers and leave that purely religious function to the people themselves and to those the people choose to look to for religious guidance" (p. 1269). In other words, let the churches do their duty, which is to teach and practice their faith, and the government do their duty, which is to take care of civil matters. On the day the decision was announced, several members of Congress lashed out against the Court. Senator Herman Talmadge (D-Georgia) said, "The ruling was an outrageous edict which has numbed the conscience and shocked the highest sensibilities of the Nation. If it is not corrected, it will do incalcuable damage to the fundamental faith in Almighty God which is the foundation upon which our civilization, our freedom, and our form of government rest" (*Congressional Record,* as cited in DelFattore, 2004, p. 78).

Correcting the Inconsistency

In a perfect example of the impossibility of trying to reconcile Calvin's model with the U.S. Constitution, Representative Horace Kornegay (D-North Carolina) said, "This decision should be disturbing to all God-fearing people in that it appears to foster and advance the cause of atheism. I am a staunch believer in the separation of church and state, but not in the separation of God and government" (p. 78). Alternatively, Senator Jacob Javits (R-New York) offered the view that *Engel v. Vitale* did not eliminate student prayer, but "merely forbade state endorsement of any particular religion" (p. 81). This is also the view of those who consider prayer a very important aspect of their faith, who are concerned more with the *content* of the prayers instead of just the *act* of praying. These people of faith know their children do not need the public schools to tell them when and what to pray because they can pray to God anytime they want to. They also do not want their children in a public school classroom to be exposed to someone else's religion, especially in today's religious climate, where there is much more plurality than in the 1960's. The paradigm shift that occurred in the 1962 Supreme Court decision put the rights of the individual ahead of the majority when dealing with religion in the public schools. If school prayer were to be reinstated, then all religions in America, and not just the majority religion, would have the right to be heard, creating a cacophony of mass confusion.

Removing government sponsored prayer and religious instruction from the public schools was not a result of activism of atheists, like Madalyn Murray O'Hair, nor did it begin in the 1960s, as many assume. The controversy about prayer in the public schools has raged as long as public schools have been in existence. The question was not whether to have religion in the schools, but *whose* religion. For centuries the answer to that question was provided by the majority religion of early colonists who followed the Reformed Protestant theology of John Calvin. Accordingly, the majority then believed a "more perfect union" would be formed by their religion being the one observed in the schools. The problem was twofold. First, no other religion, whether Christian or not, would be tolerated; and second, the Calvinist model of church and state was inconsistent with the First Amendment of the Constitution. The Supreme Court decision of 1962 corrected that inconsistency by protecting the religious rights of the individual from domination by the majority. If religion is to be part of the public school curriculum, then all religions must be permitted access to that venue. The better solution, chosen by the Court, in order to truly "form a more perfect union" and retain freedom for all, is to have *no* religious activities in the public schools, leaving religious instruction and prayers to the churches and families where they belong.

John F. Kennedy, the sitting president at the time of the landmark Supreme Court decision, best summarized the solution for the controversy, saying,

> In the efforts we're making to maintain our Constitutional principles, we will have to abide by what the Supreme Court says. We have a very easy remedy here, and that is to pray ourselves. We can pray a good deal more at home and attend our churches with fidelity and emphasize the true meaning of prayer in the lives of our children. (*John Fitzgerald Kennedy*, as cited in Sherrow, 1992, p. 50)

BIBLIOGRAPHY

Adams, D. W. (Ed.). (1983). *Jefferson's extracts from the gospels*. Princeton, NJ: Princeton University Press.

Board of Education v. Minor, 23 Ohio St. 211 (1872).

Brandt, W. I. (Ed.). (1962). *Luther's works: The Christian in society* (American ed., Vol. 45). Philadelphia: Muhlenberg Press.

Calvin, J. (1962). *Institutes of the Christian religion*. (H. Beveridge, Trans.). (Vol. 2). Grand Rapids, MI: Eerdmans. (Original work published 1536) *Cantwell v. Connecticut*, 310 U.S. 296 (1940).

DelFattore, J. (2004). *The fourth R: Conflicts over religion in America's public schools*. New Haven, CT: Yale University Press.

Donohoe v. Richards, 38 Me. 379 (1854).

Engle v. Vitale, 370 U.S. 421 (1962).

Evans, M. S. (2007). The custom of the country. *American Spectator, 40*(2), 20–24.

Everson v. Board of Education of Ewing Township, 330 U.S. 1 (1947).
Franklin, B. (n.d.). *The autobiography of Benjamin Franklin*.

Greely, R. E. (1995). *Thomas Jefferson's freethought legacy: A saying per day by the sage of Monticello*. Amherst, NY: Prometheus Books.

Greenawalt, K. (2005). *Does God belong in the public schools?* Princeton, NJ: Princeton University Press.

Henderson, E. F. (1910). *Select historical documents of the middle ages.* London: George Bell and Sons.

Holmes, D. L. (2003). *The religion of the founding fathers.* Charlottesville, VA: Ash Lawn-Highland.

Hutson, J. (n.d.) James Madison and the social utility of religion: Risks vs. rewards. In *James Madison: Philosopher and practitioner of liberal democracy.* Retrieved Sept. 2, 2007, from http://www.loc.gov/loc/madison/hutson-paper.html

Klotsche, E. H. (1945). *The history of Christian doctrine* (Rev. ed.). Grand Rapids, MI: Baker Book House.

Lannie, V. P. (1968). *Public money and parochial education: Bishop Hughes, Governor Seward, and the New York school controversy.* Cleveland, OH: Press of Case Western Reserve University.

Library of Congress. (1797). *Treaty of Peace and Friendship between The United States and the Bey and Subjects of Tripoli of Barbary* (archives #122). Retrieved September 28, 2007, from http://memory.loc.gov/cgi-bin/ampage?collId=llsp&fileName=002/llsp002.db&recNum=23

Mayer, F. E. (1961). *The religious bodies of America.* St. Louis, MO: Concordia Publishing House.

McCollum v. Board of Education of School District No. 71, 333 U.S. 203 (1948).

Mueller, J. T. (1949). Notes on the Consensus Tigurinus. *Concordia Theological Monthly, 20,* 894–909.

Reichley, J. A. (1985). *Religion in American public life.* Washington, D.C.: The Brookings Institution.

Richards, J. (1970). *The popes and the papacy in the early middle ages 476–752.* London: Routledge & Kegan Paul.

Ring v. Board of Education of District 24, 245 Illinois 334 (1910).
Scharf, T. J., & Wescott, T. (1884). *History of Philadelphia, 1609–1884.* Philadelphia: L. H. Everts.

Sherrow, V. (1992). *Separation of church and state.* New York: F. Watts.

Smith, G. S. (2006). *Faith and presidency: From George Washington to George W. Bush.* New York: Oxford University Press.

Spear, S. T. (1876). *Religion and the state.* New York: Dodd & Mead.

Steiner, F. (1995). *The religious beliefs of our presidents: From Washington to F.D.R.* Amherst, NY: Prometheus Books.

Tracy, J. (1997). *The great awakening: A history of the revival of religion in the time of Edwards and Whitefield.* Carlisle, PA: The Banner of Truth.

Voluntary school prayer Constitutional amendment: Hearings before the Subcommittee on the Constitution of the Committee on the Judiciary of the U. S. Senate (1983).

CHAPTER EIGHT

Thwarting the Court: A Historical Perspective on Efforts to Undermine the Supreme Court's School Prayer Decisions and the Effects on Religious Minorities

Craig A. Smith, California University of Pennsylvania

When considering the question, "What *should* the role of religion be in 21st–century public schools," we should remember what role religion *has* played recently in public schools. It has been now over four decades since the Supreme Court's historic decision in *Engel v. Vitale* (1962), where the Court banned state-sponsored devotional prayer in public school classrooms, but that does not mean that the issue of school prayer nor its advocates have been silenced. Ever since the *Engel* decision was handed down, strenuous efforts have been undertaken to undermine or reverse the decision and return organized, devotional prayer to public schools. More significant, however, the effects of these efforts have led to hostility and abuse against those opposed to a return to school prayer, creating a climate of fear and intimidation. In a 1999 book focusing on the harassment that occurs when dissenters object to religious exercises in public schools, Ravitch found, "Unfortunately, today we see terrible instances of discrimination occurring as the result of public school religious exercises and the divisiveness those exercises breed" (p. 2). Similarly, in a 1996 account decrying the "tyranny" of those who threaten fellow citizens in the name of school prayer, Alley observed, "[We] find citizens who sought to implement the Bill of Rights in public schools against the prevailing cultural mores continue to suffer discrimination. The most egregious abuses against fellow citizens occurred in those communities where the overwhelming number of residents belonged to a single religious tradition" (p. 18).

This essay will provide a historical perspective on the relationship between religion and public schooling by examining peoples' reactions to the Supreme Court's school prayer decisions and subsequent efforts to thwart those decisions. Also highlighted will be the kinds of harassment and persecution suffered by dissenters who sought to enforce the Court's rulings. For simplicity, the use of the terms "majority" and "minority" throughout this essay will denote either the numerically greater or fewer members of a given community and should not be construed to mean any particular religious denomination or its adherents. The purpose of this essay is twofold: to show how past public perceptions of the Supreme Court's school prayer decisions have oftentimes been intemperate and misleading, creating excessive hostility for the sake of religious expression, and to emphasize the need for greater tolerance and respect for dissenting religious views while acknowledging at the same time that prayer does have a place—a constitutionally acceptable place—in public schools.

Background: Before *Engel v. Vitale*

It was not until the mid-twentieth century that the Supreme Court first gave attention to religious expression and the Establishment Clause of the First Amendment as applied to the states through the Fourteenth Amendment (*Cantwell v. Connecticut*, 1940), a doctrine known as incorporation of the Bill of Rights against state action, although hostility toward religious dissenters had been practiced for a century beforehand.[1] In the late nineteenth century the Supreme Court first borrowed the phrase "separation of church and state" from the writings of Thomas Jefferson (*Reynolds v. U.S.*, 1879),[2] but it was not until *Everson v. Board of Education* (1947) that the expression came into common parlance when

Justice Hugo Black wrote, "The 'establishment of religion' clause of the First Amendment means at least this: Neither a state nor the Federal Government can set up a church. Neither can pass laws which aid one religion, aid all religions, or prefer one religion over another. Neither can force nor influence a person to go to or remain away from church against his will or force him to profess belief or disbelief in any religion. No person can be punished for entertaining or professing religious beliefs or disbeliefs....In the words of Jefferson, the clause against establishment of religion by law was indeed to erect 'a wall of separation between Church and State'" (p. 15–16).

This "wall" as designed by the Court in *Everson* was meant to be high and impenetrable, but over the ensuing half century its parapets were continually assailed. The year following *Everson* the Court decided *McCollum v. Board of Education* (1948), a case challenging a noncompulsory release–time program for religious instruction; the Methodist minister who started the program, Clifford Northcutt, stated flatly he would fight for it even if it were unconstitutional. Even before the Court ruled against the program, the family involved in the suit was subjected to "vitriolic harassment." They received thousands of hateful letters, which included comments such as, "you slimy bastard" and "[y]our filthy rotten body produced three children so that you can pilot them all safely to hell." Other equally malicious statements included, "Rats like you should be put on the firing line to be shot," and "We will make some lovely incisions in your filthy bellies and pull out those nervy Guts one by one, slow and easy." The child in the case, James Terry McCollum, was regularly beaten up by other students as a form of punishment and called a "godless Communist" (Alley, 1996; Ravitch, 1999).

This was just the beginning salvo against the "wall of separation." For a decade afterwards public uproar over school religious exercises subsided. A few years after *McCollum* the Court backed away from controversy when it supported a release–time program for religious instruction if the students were transported off the school campus (*Zorach v. Clauson*, 1952); the majority of justices contended that extending *McCollum* any further might be viewed as "hostility to religion" (p. 315).

Throughout its history the United States has been regarded as a "Christian nation," and although Protestant hegemony waned in the twentieth century, Christian hegemony did not (Feldman, 1997; Ravitch, 1999). By the time of the *Engel* decision twenty-four states required or permitted prayer in the public schools. A national survey of public school superintendents taken the year before *Engel* was decided revealed that 76% of public schools provided their teachers with materials to help in teaching about religion; Gideon Bibles were distributed or Bible reading was conducted in 42% of the schools; about half of the schools had homeroom devotionals; and chapel exercises were held in 22% of the schools (Fenwick, 1989). According to Justice Potter Stewart, who authored the only dissenting opinion in *Engel*, prayer in American public schools had become one of the "deeply entrenched and highly cherished spiritual traditions of our Nation" (p. 450).

Public Reaction to the *Engel* Decision

When the Supreme Court declared the nondenominational school prayer of the Board of Regents of New York unconstitutional in *Engel v. Vitale*, public reaction was immediate and loud. One Atlanta clergyman (who later admitted he had not read the decision) claimed it was "the most terrible thing that's ever happened to us." A Connecticut minister called Chief Justice of the United States, Earl Warren, the anti-Christ and urged his impeachment. In the two weeks following the decision, the *New York Times* recorded a series of negative reactions: Representative George Andrews of Alabama said, "They put the Negroes in the schools and now they've driven God out," and Congressman John Rooney of New York warned "that the ruling could put the United States schools on the same basis as Russian schools." An editorial in *The Pilot*, the oldest Catholic paper in the country, called the decision "a stupid decision, a doctrinaire decision, an unrealistic decision, a decision that spits in the face of our history, our tradition and our heritage as a religious people." Episcopal Bishop James A. Pike declared that the Court had "just deconsecrated the nation" (as cited in Fenwick, 1989, p. 130–32).

Unsurprisingly, *Engel* prompted consideration of a "Christian amendment" to the Constitution; indeed, the 1964 platform of the Republican Party called for such an amendment. On the day after the announcement of *Engel*, two amendments were submitted in Congress, and in the days that followed nearly one hundred fifty were proposed. After a week had passed state governors urged

Congressional action, but Congress ultimately failed to affect the Court's decision. To demonstrate its disapproval, though, the House of Representatives voted unanimously to replace the stars on the wall above the speaker's desk with the motto "In God We Trust."

Congressional disappointment was not the least reaction to *Engel*. The plaintiffs in the case received numerous hate letters, one erroneously surmising, "This looks like Jews trying to grab America as Jews grab everything they want in any nation. America is a Christian nation." Another bitter letter declared, "If you don't like our God, then go behind the Iron Curtain where you belong, Kike, Hebe, Filth." Not all of the plaintiffs in *Engel* were Jewish, but, because of Jewish support for the decision, an editorial in the Catholic journal *America* warned that there had been "disturbing hints of heightened anti-Semitism." The editorial asked, "What will have been accomplished if our Jewish friends win all the legal immunities they seek" and bring upon themselves "social and cultural alienation?" In response, the American Jewish Congress replied, "[I]t is a sorry day for religious liberty in the United States when an effort to protect the guarantees of the First Amendment should evoke thinly veiled threats of anti-Semitism" (as cited in Feldman, 1997, p. 233).

Outraged at the Court's intrusion into what was regarded as a local issue, many schools vowed to defy the ruling; in Long Island, New York, where *Engel* originated, eight school district superintendents stated their intention to ignore the Court. In Atlanta, Georgia, the deputy superintendent of public schools said, "We will not pay any attention to the Supreme Court ruling." At the start of the next school term the Religious News Service surveyed several states concerning school prayer and concluded, "[F]irst samplings of schools in 15 states indicates that they will continue their former practices of prayer and Bible reading without change" (as cited in Fenwick, 1989, p. 135). Most state officials interviewed drew a distinction between the New York State Board of Regents' prescribed prayer and the practice of Bible reading and reciting the Lord's Prayer.

The issues of Bible reading and recitation of the Lord's Prayer were addressed by the Supreme Court the very next term in *School District of Abington Township v. Schempp* (1963), but by then the general mood of the country had softened. Most Protestant denominations, including the leaders of the American Baptist and Presbyterian churches, and Jewish groups were favorable to the Court's *Schempp* decision. The greatest objections remained with the Roman Catholic Church and Protestant groups in the south. Following *Schempp*, the Reverend Billy Graham stated, "At a time when moral decadence is evident on every hand, when race tension is mounting, when the threat of communism is growing, when terrifying new weapons of destruction are being created, we need more religion, not less." He called the decision a penalty for the 80 percent of Americans who "want Bible reading and prayer in the schools." Governor George Wallace of Alabama declared that he would personally go into schools and read from the Bible; instructing the state board of education to ignore the Supreme Court opinion, he stated, "I don't care what they say in Washington, we are going to keep right on praying and reading the Bible in the public schools" (as cited in Fenwick, 1989, p. 140). In neighboring Mississippi, Governor Ross Barnett planned to advise teachers to ignore the Supreme Court, and to a certain extent this position prevailed; one year after the decision six states required religious services in the public schools by state law and nine others continued Bible reading as a matter of tradition.[3]

Public reaction to *Engel* and *Schempp* provoked numerous attempts over the next three decades to reverse or devise ways around the Court's decisions. In one such attempt, an Illinois kindergarten teacher deleted the single reference to God but continued to pray: "We thank you for the flowers so sweet; we thank you for the food we eat; we thank you for the birds that sing; we thank you for everything." A federal appeals court admitted that the ensuing lawsuit seemed to be making an issue out of something of little real significance but still found the verse unconstitutional. Quoting from *Schempp*, the appeals court concluded, "[I]t is no defense to urge that the religious practices here may be relatively minor encroachments on the First Amendment. The breach of neutrality that is today a trickling stream may all too soon become a raging torrent."[4]

Congressional Attempts to Introduce Prayer in Schools

The proverbial floodgates opened on the Court's rulings when Congress sought to undermine them. Of all the cases decided by the Supreme Court in the twentieth century, none has sparked more action in Congress than *Engel* (Alley, 1994). Due to the large number of separate constitutional amendments all competing for legislative attention and the political maneuverings to prevent any such action, Congress initially struggled to bring any amendment out of committee.[5] In 1966 an amendment introduced by Senator Everett Dirksen of Illinois fell just 17 votes short of passing the full Senate, and in 1971 a resolution sponsored by Representative Chalmers Wylie of Ohio gained enough votes to bypass committee consideration but failed a floor vote by 48 votes. Unwilling to yield, the House and Senate attempted again in the early 1980s to restrict the Court's jurisdiction in school prayer cases but ultimately failed. A bill sponsored by Senator Jesse Helms of North Carolina initially succeeded in passing the Senate but failed in the House. When the Senate tried to revive the bill a few years later, a successful filibuster prevented it after a move for cloture failed on seven occasions. The best chance Congress ever had of proposing a constitutional school prayer amendment came in 1984 when a majority of the Senate voted in favor of an amendment offered by President Ronald Reagan, but the vote of 56 to 44 still fell short of the two-thirds vote required. In 1992 the Senate tried again but wound up 12 votes short of the required number. The House took its turn in 1999 with a proposal sponsored by Representative Ernest Istook of Oklahoma, gaining a majority vote but similarly failing to reach the two-thirds majority required.

The one enduring success of Congress's repeated attempts to protect prayer in the public schools came in 1984 following defeat of the "Reagan Amendment." Congress successfully passed a legislative bill that became known as the Equal Access Act, which allows religious and Bible study clubs to meet in public schools during noninstructional time if other noncurricular student groups are also permitted.[6] There are numerous safeguards built into the act to ensure that the religious activities are voluntary and student initiated. The ostensible purpose of the act was to protect school prayer advocates from perceived discrimination in public schools, but the effect of the act at one Salt Lake City school was to prevent any student clubs from meeting—including religious clubs—in an effort to stop gay student clubs from meeting on equal terms (Alley, 1996; Ravitch, 1999).

Lower Federal Courts Respond to School Prayer

Although Congressional efforts to reverse the Supreme Court's school prayer decisions have proven less than successful, actions by lower federal courts have done far more to undermine the Court's rulings and to encourage school prayer advocates. Soon after the Supreme Court decided *Lee v. Weisman* (1992), a case involving a middle school graduation prayer, a ruling by the Fifth Circuit Court of Appeals, which comprises the states of Texas, Louisiana, and Mississippi, appeared to defy the Supreme Court's authority. The *Lee* case originated when the school principal, Robert E. Lee, invited a Baptist minister to officiate at graduation. One Jewish student, Merith Weisman, objected when the minister thanked Jesus Christ for the students' accomplishments. In an effort to appease the parents' complaint, the principal arranged to have a Jewish rabbi deliver the prayer when Merith's sister, Deborah, prepared to graduate. This was beside the point, though, since for the Weismans it was not a question of *which prayer* was more acceptable but whether *any prayer* should be permitted. The Supreme Court found the graduation prayer in *Lee* impermissible as a kind of "indirect coercion," meaning students were compelled to participate in a religious exercise not of their choosing even though it was their choice to attend graduation. In a surprising argument, lawyers for the Justice Department favoring school prayer went so far as to admit that classroom prayers had *always been coercive*, but since attendance at graduation was not required there was no First Amendment violation. The Supreme Court disagreed (Alley, 1996; Greenburg, 2007).

The Fifth Circuit Court of Appeals, on the other hand, used the particular facts of *Lee*—namely, the school district had chosen members of the clergy to deliver the prayers, and school district officials maintained control over the content of the prayers—to reach a different conclusion. As a result, school boards all across the country received a letter from the American Center for Law and Justice (ACLJ) suggesting that organized "student-initiated" prayer would be acceptable at school graduations if it were voluntary and if a majority of the graduating class voted for it (Ravitch, 1999). The basis for this assertion came from the Fifth Circuit Court of Appeals, which upheld such a practice provided the prayer was voluntary, nonsectarian, and nonproselytizing[7] (*Jones v. Clear Creek Independent School District*, 1991).

Difficulties were soon encountered with the Fifth Circuit's acceptance of "student-initiated" graduation prayer. Strossen (1995), a law professor and president of the American Civil Liberties Union (ACLU), argued that because of peer pressure, religiously dissenting students would feel especially excluded by a student-led prayer approved by a majority of their classmates. "A majority vote can never justify a constitutional violation," she wrote. "After all, constitutional guarantees are designed precisely to protect the rights of individuals or members of minority groups from the tyranny of the majority" (p. 626). Another difficulty with nonsectarian prayer is that the term itself presents an oxymoron. If a statement is nonsectarian, it cannot be a prayer; conversely, if it is a genuine prayer, it cannot be nonsectarian. An example of such a dilemma involved a student from Texas who sued his local school for mental anguish because he was not permitted to use the words "Jesus" or "God" in a nonsectarian, nonproselytizing prayer. The student, the son of a Baptist minister, complained that he did not know how to pray without saying "Jesus" (Coyle, 1995).

Further difficulties over the Fifth Circuit's endorsement of "student-initiated" graduation prayer presented themselves when other Circuit courts reached opposite results. Both the Third Circuit (*ACLU v. Black Horse Pike Board of Education*, 1996) and the Ninth Circuit (*Harris v. Joint School District No. 241*, 1994) ruled "student-initiated" graduation prayers unconstitutional, leaving the country in a quandary over which circuit court to follow. Objecting to the majoritarian rule prescribed by student-led prayer, the Ninth Circuit stated, "[S]chool officials cannot divest themselves of constitutional responsibility by allowing the students to make crucial decisions....Elected officials cannot avoid constitutional mandates by putting them to majority vote."

Support from the ACLJ for the Fifth Circuit's endorsement of "student-initiated" graduation prayer has led to further controversy and greater confusion. The ACLJ has encouraged school boards across the nation to engage in the exercise, claiming in their literature that the Supreme Court's denial of an appeal "let stand" the Fifth Circuit's decision and that the decision is legally valid "across the nation." These claims, especially that the Supreme Court "let stand" the Fifth Circuit's decision, have been criticized as misleading, even plainly wrong. The assertion that the Fifth Circuit's opinion is applicable to any part of the nation outside the Fifth Circuit would extend the decision beyond that court's jurisdiction, something impossible to do. More important, though, claiming that the Supreme Court "let stand" the Fifth Circuit's decision suggests that the Supreme Court "approved of" the Fifth Circuit's ruling. Nothing could be further from the truth. Any denial to review an appeal from a lower circuit court carries no implications whatsoever of the justices' views regarding the lower court ruling or how the Supreme Court would decide the case. Justice Felix Frankfurter reminded the country in *Maryland v. Baltimore Radio Show* (1950): "This Court has rigorously insisted that such a denial carries with it no implication whatever regarding the Court's views on the merits of a case which it has declined to review. The Court has said this again and again; again and again it has to be repeated." Another justice, William Brennan (1960), who was arguably diametrically opposed to much of Frankfurter's jurisprudence, similarly stated, "A denial of *certiorari* is not an affirmance of the lower court judgment as some erroneously think. ... The denial does not mean that the Court agrees with the result reached by the lower court. ... The Court may well take the very next case raising the same question and reach a different result on the merits" (p. 402).

To make matters worse, when the Supreme Court denied the appeal from the Fifth Circuit, the ACLJ considered it a victory for "student-initiated" graduation prayer, but when the Supreme Court denied a similar appeal from the Ninth Circuit the ACLJ did not consider it a defeat. Instead, the ACLJ claimed that the Fifth Circuit's decision was then "the only federal appeals court decision on the issue." Acknowledging that the Ninth Circuit's decision "directly conflicted" with the Fifth Circuit's, the ACLJ still viewed a denial to review the Fifth Circuit's opinion as endorsement of "student-initiated" graduation prayer while at the same time saw a denial to review the Ninth Circuit's opinion as *further endorsement*. The ACLJ cannot have it both ways.[8]

The Harmful Effects of School Prayer Decisions

When one considers the many different approaches—or tests—the Supreme Court has used over the years to define constitutionally permitted religious expression in public schools, you arrive at a legal morass of overlapping, oftentimes confusing rationales for how the Court explains the prohibitions and possibilities of the First Amendment religion clauses. Frequently cited is the "Lemon" test, a three-part criterion named for *Lemon v. Kurtzman* (1971). In it, the law has to have a clear secular legislative purpose, neither advancing nor inhibiting religion, and should not foster "an excessive government entanglement with religion." The Court has also devised the "Coercion" test as found in *Lee v. Weisman* (1992), which would render a state practice unconstitutional without consideration of any part of the "Lemon" test. Finally, what some regard as a separate test altogether, the "Endorsement" test asks whether the government's endorsement of religious belief is relevant to a person's standing in the political community (*Allegheny v. ACLU*, 1989; *Lynch v. Donnelly*, 1984). These legal definitions, so important in setting the boundaries for what is constitutionally permissible, unfortunately ignore the harmful effects that the Court's rulings have had on individuals who opposed the religious exercises taking place in their schools. Because of the potential for violence and harassment, when civil liberty violations occur few people dare to oppose them. According to Strossen (1995), "[V]ictims of religious liberty violations do not want even to file a claim in court, even when we [the ACLU] assure them they would win because of the hostility, enmity, persecution, and attacks they would face. I fully sympathize with their reluctance to make themselves into pariahs or even martyrs" (p. 610).

Incidents of violence against religious dissenters have not lessened since the Court's *Engel* and *Schempp* decisions; in fact, what were once considered unintended "threats" against religious dissenters are now more often being carried out. In 1999 Ravitch asked, "Harassment, discrimination, beatings, death threats, bomb threats, hate mail, destruction of property, and school prayer—what is out of place on this list?" "Ironically," he replied, "a frequently correct answer would be 'nothing'" (p. ix). In 1991 the ACLU found that "[of] all the issues the ACLU takes on—reproductive rights, discrimination, jail and prison conditions, abuse of kids in the public schools, police brutality, to name a few—by far the most volatile issue is that of school prayer. Aside from our efforts to abolish the death penalty, it is the only issue that elicits death threats" (Strossen, 1995, p. 615). Significantly, many of these incidents did not pit the numerically greater Christian faiths against Jewish, Muslim, Hindu, or Buddhist; just as often one Christian denomination discriminated against another Christian view.

One example from the early 1980s of the ferocity evident between conflicting Christian views involved two families in Little Axe, Oklahoma. Joann Bell, who belonged to the Church of the Nazarene, and Lucille McCord, who belonged to the Church of Christ, were both devout Christians who believed that religious devotion belonged to their own church and individual consciences. In 1980 they objected to the distribution of Gideon Bibles and to teacher-led religious meetings held on school property before the start of the school day. As a result, their families were subjected to vicious reprisals because their children chose not to attend the meetings. Teachers and fellow students led the assault; when the children were asked why they would not attend the meetings, many assumed they did not believe in God. Some teachers gave Fundamentalist-oriented quizzes, and one of the children failed a test based on the King James Bible because he refused to take it. An upside-down cross was taped to the children's lockers, and a prize-winning goat belonging to one of the children active in the school's Future Farmers of America chapter had its throat slit. Another child needed emergency surgery when his arm was fractured in a playground accident while the school superintendent delayed medical treatment and parent notification for much of the school day.

From there attacks against the families became more hostile, extending to the entire community. At one school board meeting Joann and Lucille were trapped in the bathroom by board members who shouted, "We are going to do what we want here," with the board vice president distributing signs reading "Atheists Go Home." The families received hate mail and threatening phone calls, with one caller repeatedly telling them that he was going to break into their house, tie up the children, rape the mother in front of them, and then "bring her to Jesus." Another caller threatened to blow up the school, killing the children inside. When the parents rushed to school to retrieve their children, Joann Bell was physically assaulted by a school employee who threatened to kill her. Following the assault, the Bells' home was burned to the ground, destroying everything in it because the Little Axe Volunteer Fire Department arrived at the scene with no water in their tanks. The McCords moved out of the district when Lucille received her own obituary in the mail (Alley, 1996; Ravitch, 1999; Strossen, 1995).

Another example of religious intolerance between different Christian denominations occurred a decade later in Ecru, Mississippi, where Lisa Herdahl and her family faced ostracism and intimidation from the entire community. In an area that was predominantly Southern Baptist, the Herdahl's attended a Pentecostal church because neither Lisa's religion, Christian Scientists, nor her husband's, Lutheran, were represented in the town. When one local Baptist minister learned that the family attended Pentecostal services, he reportedly told them they would burn in hell. At the children's school, daily activities included regular Bible reading and prayers broadcast over the school intercom. Lisa told her six children, who were all baptized as Lutherans, not to attend the Bible readings, but there was little she could do about the broadcasts. She had taught her children to pray directly to God, but the broadcasts prayed in the name of Jesus. The children were consequently ridiculed and harassed by their peers for their nonattendance at the Bible study; they were referred to as "devil worshippers" and atheists for not believing in God. One child had to wear headphones in class to avoid hearing the broadcasts, and another child worried that a classmate would suffer physical abuse at home if they played together. The family received death threats and bomb threats, and when the harassment became unbearable one child informed his parents that he did not want to be a Christian any longer if this was how they acted (Alley, 1996; Ravitch, 1999; Strossen, 1995).

These two extreme examples of intolerance and persecution are not, at first glance, what one might expect from a school prayer incident. Typically, the assumption is that dissenters of religious expression in public schools are either non-Christians or non-religious and that these incidents involve at most taunting and derision. Not so for the Bell, McCord, or Herdahl families; these were devout, religiously observant Christian families who suffered intense public hostility, even violence, because they objected to the religious observance taking place in their schools. Just as significant, though, like most religious liberty incidents involving public schools, these families did not object necessarily to the *kind of* religious exercise practiced—they did not want to substitute one religious exercise for another—they objected to the school system imposing religion on their children.

Other incidents of persecution against religious dissenters involving public schools have not engendered the same level of hostility as the above examples, but the effects have been equally damaging. One does not have to suffer physical abuse before violation of their civil liberties occurs. In the early 1990s a Jewish high school student and member of the school's choir, Rachel Bauchman, objected to singing two religious songs planned for the school's graduation. Rachel had previously been excused from the December "Christmas concert" at which all of the songs praised Jesus as the Lord and Savior, but she was told by the choir teacher, a devout Mormon, that attendance at the May graduation was mandatory. In the meantime while her case worked its way through the federal courts, Rachel was called a "dirty Jew," "Jew bitch," and told that Hitler should have finished what he started. On the day before graduation the Tenth Circuit Court of Appeals ordered that the religious songs be replaced, and two substitute songs were selected. However, at graduation song lyrics of the prohibited songs were distributed to audience members. When the choir finished singing the replacement songs, audience members were encouraged to join in singing the prohibited songs—in direct violation of a federal court order. As Rachel fled from the graduation ceremony she was spat upon by audience members[9] (Alley, 1996; Ravitch, 1999).

In another incident a few years later, again involving a Jewish family, while no physical torment occurred, the indignities suffered were just as invidious. Here the school regularly performed religious assemblies with the nativity as its theme, and at one assembly the students were told that if they did not accept Jesus as their savior they were doomed to hell. Just as disturbing, during prayer time the children were required to bow their heads—if not, physical force was used—and once a Jewish child was disciplined by having to write an essay entitled, "Why Jesus Loves Me" (Ravitch, 1999).

Clearly the preceding examples of intolerance violated what Justice Black in *Everson* described as "a wall of separation between Church and State" and the civil liberties of the religious minority groups should have been more sensitively protected; still, the question remains: what is the limit to legal protections for religious minority groups, and to what extent can the majority continue to ignore those protections? In the fall of 1993, Stephen Feldman learned that the school where his daughter was about to begin pre-kindergarten had displayed and decorated a Christmas tree the previous year. Stephen, who is Jewish, sent a letter to the school principal requesting that the school refrain from celebrating *any* religious holidays. In his request, Stephen acknowledged that an ornamental pine tree could be a secular symbol, but it clearly denoted the Christian religion to any non-Christian. Attempts to balance Christmas celebrations with seasonal Jewish festivals like Chanukah, Stephen contended, only trivialized both holidays and cast Chanukah in an undeservingly prominent light. The principal responded that the tree was not a "Christmas" tree, but rather a "holiday" tree, the art decorations adorning the tree were not meant to be "ornaments," and Stephen should consider himself lucky to be in a school district where nativity scenes were not on display. Rather than entertain the proposition to have the tree on display year-round, school officials informed Stephen he was being ridiculous (Feldman, 1997). In that same year, fourteen-year-old Sarah Coles was invited to attend a local school board meeting to be recognized for her high scores on a standardized test. Feeling proud of herself, she went to the meeting expecting it to begin with a welcome. Instead, it began with a prayer. "I was shocked," Sarah remarked, "Prayers at a school board meeting? I couldn't believe it....Together with others who felt as I did, I asked the board to drop the prayer from its meetings, but they said they wouldn't" (as cited in Strossen, 1995, p. 609).

This last example demonstrates how school authorities persist in condoning activities outside of constitutional bounds and remain intolerant towards dissenters. It was this type of intolerance that parents in Church Hill, Tennessee, expressed when they objected to the school's use of a reading series that exposed children to different religions *without* instructing them that diverse views were *incorrect*. Although they were from different denominations, all the parents considered themselves born-again Christians. Strenuously objecting to religious toleration, one parent testified in court that her religion would not accept "other religious views on an equal basis with ours" (Fenwick, 1989). The intolerance suffered by religious dissenters is so keenly felt that one family seeking an end to school commencement prayers and prayers by team coaches requested complete anonymity, even threatening to dismiss their lawsuit if their names were revealed. The judge in the case agreed to the secrecy, but local residents still responded with bitter commentary in the newspaper. One writer remarked, "I say if they can't like it here, they have the free agency to move away. There are plenty of places where they can find the godless society they want. They have no right to deny us our right to freedom of religion and of speech" (as cited in Alley, 1996, p. 149).

The Return of Prayer to Public Schools?

This theme of deprivation, or somehow discriminating against the will of the majority—particularly denying Christians the right to pray at school—has become a prevailing argument for defying the federal courts. Ravitch (1999) has described how television channels or programs devoted to Christian messages, such as the 700 Club, exhibit a familiar pattern: the viewer is told that "Christians," meaning certain evangelical Christians, are the victims of discrimination. They are prevented from freely expressing their beliefs through school prayer. In the Christian Coalition's newspaper, *Christian America*, victimization is a common feature. One story from 1993 went so far as to compare the destruction of Jews during the Holocaust to the kind of exclusion leading to extermination that Christians face in America. In that same year leaders of conservative Christian groups—known collectively as the Religious Right—began issuing new challenges to their adherents. The founder of the Christian Coalition and the ACLJ, Pat Robertson, told his followers, "They have kept us in submission because they have talked about separation of church and state. There is no such thing in the Constitution. It's a lie of the left, and we're not going to take it anymore." Jerry Falwell, the founder and president of the Moral Majority, admonished his listeners,

> Modern U.S. Supreme Courts have raped the Constitution and raped the Christian faith and raped the churches by misinterpreting what the founders had in mind in the First Amendment of the Constitution. [W]e must fight against those radical minorities who are trying to remove God from our textbooks, Christ from our nation. We must never allow our children to forget that this is a Christian nation. (as cited in Cantor, 1994, p. 4)

These exaggerations were similarly expressed by Pat Robertson in 1995 when he charged the Supreme Court with completely banning prayer from public schools and removing religion entirely from the schools. Robertson decried "the judicial distortions which have forbidden little children to pray or read the Bible in school" and declared that prayer should be "returned" to the public schools (as cited in Strossen, 1995, p. 625).

This concern over "returning" prayer to the public schools mistakenly presupposes that children are prohibited from praying at school, but such is not the case. The Supreme Court has made clear that within the reasonable need for order and decorum, children *do have the right* to pray during the school day as his or her conscience dictates. Going back to *Engel*, the Court declared that the decision should not be interpreted as showing hostility toward religion or toward prayer. Nothing, the Court stated, could be more wrong. Over the next three decades, however, a majority of Americans continued to press for a change in the Court's decision. Polls since the 1960s consistently show that Americans support public school prayer[10] (Ravitch, 1999).

Similarly, a large number of schools continued practicing what was clearly prohibited by the Court. After *Lee v. Weisman* prohibiting graduation prayer, a Gallup poll found that over 45% of respondents still had student- or adult-led prayers as part of the official commencement exercise. In the South, 76% reported graduation prayer while in the East 34% reported commencement prayer, with anywhere from 65% to 85% following the ACLJ recommended "student-initiated" practice (Ravitch, 1999). By 1994 the *New York Times* was reporting that despite Court rulings, "prayer is increasingly a part of school activities from early-morning moments of silence to lunchtime prayer sessions to pre-football-game prayers for both players and fans. Particularly in the South, religious clubs, prayer groups and pro-prayer students and community groups are making religion and prayer part of the school day" (as cited in Feldman, 1997, p. 269).

Of course, the prevalence of prayer in public schools is not indicative of wrong-doing by students or school administrators. There is no question that students may bring a Bible to school, may pray privately before tests or say grace before meals, and may engage in private religious conversations with their classmates so long as it does not infringe on the rights of others and does not "substantially interfere" with school functioning. Public schools are not nor should they be considered religion-free zones (Ravitch, 1999). What school prayer advocates argue is missing from public schools, though, should not be confused with what they want— namely, they want the return of school-sponsored, teacher-led prayer, but only if it conforms to the beliefs of the *prevailing religious majority*. What school prayer advocates argue is missing is any opportunity for prayer in school, which they believe is detrimental to the development of America's youth. For example, at the trial involving the Bell and McCord families, a clinical and Christian psychologist, Dr. Paul Schmidt, testified that the moral principles taught in church would become irrelevant if religious teaching were not allowed in the public schools. It was necessary to keep religious observance in the schools, Schmidt argued, to instill the "higher moral standard" of regular church goers. Unless religious activity were permitted in schools, "God would be seen as impotent, an irrelevant figure. He doesn't have power to come to school" (as cited in Alley, 1996, p. 113).

Such an argument fails to recognize what the Supreme Court actually said in its school prayer decisions, and, more importantly, it tends to demean the faith that many people have in the omnipotence of God. Senator John Danforth of Missouri, himself a priest of the Episcopal Church, eloquently addressed this issue when he spoke in opposition to the 1984 proposed school prayer amendment. He stated,

> Opponents of a school prayer amendment might further argue that the sacredness of prayer and the holiness of God are debased by the often heard statement that the Supreme Court has removed God from the classroom, and a constitutional amendment will put God back in the classroom. To many religious people, God is not dependent on the Supreme Court or the Congress. Objects may be kept out of the classroom, chewing gum for example. God is not chewing gum. He is the Creator of heaven and earth. (as cited in Swomley, 1996, p. 29)

Add to this what President John Kennedy said when asked what he thought about the *Engel* decision:

> We have in this case a very easy remedy and that is to pray ourselves. And I would think that it would be a welcome reminder to every American family that we can pray a good deal more at home, we can attend our churches with a good deal more fidelity, and we can make the true mean-

ing of prayer much more important in the lives of all our children. (as cited in Swomley, 1996, p. 33)

When one considers the question—"What should the role of religion be in 21st–century public schools?"—we should remember the question asked most often of the ACLU whenever they seek to enforce the Supreme Court's school prayer decisions: "What's wrong with a little prayer in school?" This is the same question Deborah Weisman received during her trial experience. Her response typifies the experience of all victims of religious tyranny in the battle over school prayer. She said,

I don't think a little prayer is a small thing. It excludes. They forced me to pray to someone else's God. That is a big deal...When I am forced to participate in a ritual...it's an attempt to make me different from what I am—to change my identity, to make me conform. (as cited in Strossen, 1995, p. 624)

The First Amendment religion clauses were designed to prevent any attempt by majorities from imposing their religious views on dissenters. Justice Robert Jackson powerfully defended the fundamental rights of dissenters who held unpopular minority views; he wrote, "The very purpose of a Bill of Rights was to withdraw certain subjects from the vicissitudes of political controversy, to place them beyond the reach of majorities and officials and to establish them as legal principles to be applied by the courts. One's right to life, liberty, and property, to free speech, a free press, freedom of worship and assembly, and other fundamental rights may not be submitted to vote; they depend on the outcome of no elections" (*West Virginia State Board of Education v. Barnette*, 1943). Our response to the question of prayer in public schools will depend largely upon how sensitive we are to the rights of all—religious majorities and dissenters—and to the role that religion has played in our schools.

NOTES

1. In a wave of violence from May to July, 1844, in what became known as the Philadelphia Bible riots, more than 50 people were killed and over 140 wounded

when the local school board complied with a request by a Catholic bishop that children not be required to read from the King James Bible. Fearing religious pluralism and fueled by anti-immigrant zeal, Protestants had imposed their prayers, hymns, and Bible readings on the public schools, and, as a result of anti-Catholic fervor, the Catholic school system was founded as the only practical means to avoid persecution.

2. Specifically, Jefferson used it in a letter he wrote to the Danbury Baptist Association, in which he stated: ". . . I contemplate with sovereign reverence that act of the whole American People which declared that their legislature should 'make no law respecting the establishment of religion, or prohibiting the free exercise thereof,' thus building a wall of separation between church and state."

3. The six states were Alabama, Arkansas, Delaware, Florida, Georgia, and Idaho, and the nine states were Indiana, Kansas, Mississippi, North Carolina, Oklahoma, South Carolina, Tennessee, Texas, and Virginia, respectively (*U.S. News & World Report*, May 18, 1964, pp. 63–64).

4. *DeSpain v. DeKalb County Community School District*, 384 F.2d 836 (1967), *certiorari* denied 390 U.S. 906, meaning the Supreme Court did not hear the appeal.

5. The "Becker" amendment, introduced in 1963 by Representative Frank Becker of New York, stood the best chance but failed by 50 votes to move out of committee.

6. 98 Stat. 1302, 20 U.S.C. 4071-4074. The Supreme Court had earlier considered equal access as it applied to college students in *Widmar v. Vincent*, 454 U.S. 263 (1981). The Court later upheld the constitutionality of the Equal Access Act in *Board of Education of Westside Community Schools v. Mergens*, 496 U.S. 226 (1990).

7. *Jones v. Clear Creek Independent School District*, 930 F. 2d 416 (1991) is regarded as *Jones I*. Following the Supreme Court decision in *Lee*, the holding in *Jones I* was vacated and remanded back to the Fifth Circuit for further consideration. On remand, the Fifth Circuit again upheld the school policy in *Jones II*, 977 F. 2d 963 (1992).

8. The decision in *Jones II* was denied review at 508 U.S. 967 (1993), while the decision in *Harris* was denied review at 115 S. Ct. 2604 (1995). The rationale for denial in *Harris* related to standing, which meant that the family could no longer present a justiciable claim since the youngest child had already graduated high school at the time the Court was asked for an appeal.

9. The temporary injunction used to prohibit the use of religious songs did not stop the Tenth Circuit Court of Appeals from later dismissing Rachel Bauchman's case because she, too, had already graduated high school. See *Bauchman v. West High School*, 132 F. 3d 542 (1997).

10. In a 1962 Gallup poll, 79% of respondents approved religious exercises in public schools; in 1975, 77% of respondents favored a constitutional amendment to permit school prayer; in 1983, 81% of respondents aware of a proposed constitutional amendment to permit voluntary prayer in schools favored it; and in 1995, 71% of respondents supported a constitutional amendment allowing prayer in schools.

BIBLIOGRAPHY

ACLU v. Black Horse Pike Board of Education, 84 F. 3d 1471(1996).

Allegheny v. ACLU, 492 U.S. 573 (1989).

Alley, R. S. (1994). *School prayer: The Court, the Congress, and the First Amendment*. Buffalo, NY: Prometheus Books.

Alley, R. S. (1996). *Without a prayer: Religious expression in public schools*. Amherst, NY: Prometheus Books.

Brennan, W. J. (1960). State court decisions and the Supreme Court. *Pennsylvania Bar Association Quarterly*, *31*, 393–403.

Cantor, D. (1994). *The religious right: The assault on tolerance & pluralism in America*. New York: Anti-Defamation League.

Cantwell v. Connecticut, 310 U.S. 296 (1940).

Coyle, P. (1995). The prayer pendulum. *American Bar Association Journal*, *81*, 63–66.

Engel v. Vitale, 370 U.S. 421 (1962).

Everson v. Board of Education, 330 U.S. 1 (1947).

Feldman, S. M. (1997). *Please don't wish me a merry Christmas: A critical history of the separation of church and state*. New York: New York University Press.

Fenwich, L. B. (1989). *Should the children pray? A historical, judicial, and political examination of public school prayer*. Waco, TX: Baylor University Press.

Greenburg, J. C. (2007). *Supreme conflict: The inside story of the struggle for control of the United States Supreme Court*. New York: Penguin Press.

Harris v. Joint School District No. 241, 41 F. 3d 447 (1994).

Jones v. Clear Creek Independent School District, 930 F. 2d 416 (1991).

Lee v. Weisman, 505 U.S. 577 (1992).

Lemon v. Kurtzman, 403 U.S. 602 (1971).

Lynch v. Donnelly, 465 U.S. 668 (1984).

Maryland v. Baltimore Radio Show, 338 U.S. 912 (1950).

McCollum v. Board of Education, 333 U.S. 203 (1948).

Ravitch, F. S. (1999). *School prayer and discrimination: The civil rights of religious minorities and dissenters.* Boston: Northeastern University Press.

Reynolds v. U.S., 98 U.S. 145 (1879).

School District of Abington Township v. Schempp, 374 U.S. 203 (1963).

Strossen, N. (1995). How much God in the schools? A discussion of religion's role in the classroom. *William & Mary Bill of Rights Journal, 4,* 607–37.

Swomley, J. M. (1996). *Myths about public school prayer.* Silver Spring, MD: Americans for Religious Liberty.

West Virginia State Board of Education v. Barnette, 319 U.S. 629 (1943).

Zorach v. Clauson, 343 U.S. 306 (1952).

CHAPTER NINE

To Hell and Back: Teaching Faith-Based Literature to the Devout

Ryan Kennedy, Centralia High School
Centralia, Missouri

It didn't take long for my cover to get blown. It was during the first week of my teaching career. Still wearing a tie to help those around me differentiate students from their teacher, I was delivering some notes on mythology. I was trying to get my students to understand *why* myths exist, what drove ancient man to compose them.

They exist to answer questions, those questions that can only be answered via imagination, and not through actual scientific discovery. They helped explain the birth of the world, the creation of humanity, the origins of death, why there is evil, and why that evil sometimes happens to good people.

Upon hearing that last one, one of my students interrupted me and asked, perhaps demanded, "You don't believe in God, do you?"

I knew better than to use this opportunity to inform them of my actual religious views. I was still a stranger to this community, but I knew one truth very well: Christians don't listen to non-Christians.

I am not devoid of Christian thought; I was once a regular attendee of a Baptist church, until an evil happened to a good person and I went cold turkey on faith. My wife tells me now that that window of piety is what keeps me afloat in a town so religious and conservative. Biblical names and places go completely over her head. On the other hand, while I may have to look them up to jog my memory, I can recognize these things as biblical. I could teach the biblical creation story and know which lines not to cross (never, no matter how true it is, suggest that there are two creation stories in Genesis, and that one of them was influenced by the Babylonian creation story). Overall, I fancied myself fairly intelligent in matters of theology; I had taken classes, I had been to church, and I had watched *SuperBook* and *Flying House* as a kid.

But perhaps my radar had gotten rusty. I must have forgotten a few of the boundaries that I couldn't cross when discussing religious matters. I definitely forgot that everything is a religious matter with some people.

I was once explaining to my students why most experts believe that human existence originated in Africa, millions of years ago. A month later, when students turned in a three-page research paper, one of them was attempting to convince the reader that the Earth was 5,000 years old. This was only the second time I'd heard of this (the first time, a comment on a paper I wrote about dinosaurs for a college class–I thought it was someone trying to be funny). Turns out, people believe this "Young Earth Theory." It is important to point out, however, that not every Christian does. Several students, ones that I knew were religious, had looks of confusion, even condescension, at the suggestion that the Earth was not billions of years old.

This was a major lesson for me. Christians don't believe the same things. I had heard the words Methodist, Episcopalian, Presbyterian, Catholic, and others as I grew up in a Baptist church, but I never understood any difference in philosophy, save for women being forbidden to preach in some faiths, and Catholic priests being celibate. In that stack of research papers, however, one of my most brilliant students educated me, in a paper that spanned seven pages, on what it was like to be a Catholic in a Protestant community.

Tickets to Hell

I had thought that any piece of literature that mentioned God and Jesus was going to be welcomed with open arms by my students and their parents. Dante's *Inferno*, the first part of his *Divine Comedy*, proved me wrong. Some were captivated by Dante's journey; that brilliant Catholic girl even read *Purgatory*, the second part of the comedy, for her independent reading book.

The reaction was not all positive. Many students stared blankly at me as we discussed the poem. I could sense that they wanted to know where I thought I received the authority to teach *Catholic* things in school.

Those things that offended my students were things for which I was not prepared. The mere mention of Purgatory, the place Dante's character ascends to after exiting Hell, immediately was welcomed with a hail of: "What's Purgatory?" Students would answer, sometimes Catholics but most of the time Protestants with Catholic friends, "It's a place where souls go to work off their sins before going to Heaven."

"That's dumb," is the most common response to that.

I hadn't realized that Catholics and Protestants had this sort of relationship with one another. It was truly a new discrimination, for me at least. It is quite old; Martin Luther nailed his protests to the door centuries ago, but I had always thought of their split being more about corruption than any difference in beliefs. Love God? Love Jesus? Mary was a virgin? Check, check, check. We can be friends, right?

Wrong! You idol worshipping, salvation buying, Mother Mary loving too much, I'll just work it off in the afterlife...*CATHOLIC!*

Dante awakened these prejudices and gave them a place to be voiced: my classroom. Dante became a representative of all Catholics, so he even gave Protestant students new reasons to doubt the piety of every Catholic.

A chief reason for that is Dante's use of classical authors and mythological characters in his poem. Dante is guided though Hell by Virgil, the ancient Roman poet who composed *The Aeneid*. Dante refers to Virgil as "my true master and first author" and "the sole maker from whom I drew the breath," (Ciardi, 1993, Canto I, lines 82–3) thus elevating Virgil to almost divine status. John Ciardi translated these lines, and it is this translation that is anthologized in my world literature textbook.

These lines, so early in the poem, rub my students the wrong way, but they shouldn't. Mark Musa translates those lines as "You are my teacher, the first of all my authors,/and you alone the one from whom I took/the noble style that was to bring me honor" (Canto I, lines 82–4). Musa's translation makes it far clearer that Dante is thanking Virgil for influencing him, for making him a poet. I tell my students that it is like Dante is meeting his idol; Jerry Rice for the football players, Michael Jordan for the basketball players, Celine Dion for the choir kids.

The fact that he is Roman should not be ignored, though. Dante's relationship with Virgil is a manifestation of Dante's love for classical authors like Homer and Virgil (though he never actually read Homer) and philosophers. He banishes these people, these "virtuous pagans," to a level of Hell that seems almost like a paradise, showing that, while he knows they can't go to heaven, he wants their afterlife to be painless. Dante was one of the first Christian Humanists (Holt, Rinehart, & Winston, 1993, p.744). He was torn between his strict Catholic beliefs and his interest in classic culture. Many of my students can identify with this situation, although they rarely if ever feel any guilt as a result of their enjoyment of mythology. Dante did feel guilty, and he made amends by limiting Virgil's powers, comparing him allegorically to human reason and showing that reason alone can't get someone into heaven unless it is paired with faith. Though Dante loves Virgil, he *willingly* sends him back to Hell.

The more bothersome characters, the Greek ones, are those who help run Hell, namely Charon, the ferryman, and Minos, judge of the damned. I know that word of this kind of blasphemy gets back to parents, as I was once confronted by a parent who told me that I had no right to teach "some Greek mythology about the Christian Hell." I didn't even know where to begin in her misconception of what *Inferno* was. I appeased her by informing her that it was one man's, a Catholic man, not an ancient Greek (you do know B.C. stands for before Christ, right?), opinion of Hell, and that he never claimed divine inspiration for the poem. It was primarily an excuse to banish his contemporaries to various levels of Hell, thus making the poem one big political cartoon. The characters of Charon and Minos are, on one level, an homage to Dante's interest in the classics, and, on another, a necessary evil in this *fictional* journey. If Dante stuck to the biblical description of Hell and those who occupy it, he wouldn't have enough to write one canto, let alone 33 cantos, as it is only mentioned a handful of times and described as a lake of fire. He takes liberties with his poem because it is not claiming any importance in theological matters: he names it a comedy because comedy, in Dante's age, meant that it was not a lofty, 'important' work.

Other objections to the poem are that it is gruesome and punishes those who may not deserve condemnation. It is gruesome, even in the five cantos excerpted in our textbook. There are naked bodies being stung by hornets, the wounds they inflict dropping blood and pus to feed the worms below (Canto III). In Canto XXXIV there is Ugolino, who hungrily gnaws on the skull of Ruggieri, the man who betrayed him, for eternity. In the years that the National Council of Teachers of English (NCTE) has kept track, there has only been one challenge lobbied against the *Inferno*, for being "grotesque," and the challenge was never followed through. Students cringe, of course, but the main objection to the violence is not the violence itself, but rather the violence being coupled with a religious context: gruesome violence is allowed in school, as long as God is not involved. Nevermind that the Bible is incredibly violent, or that churches sent buses of parishioners to go see *The Passion of the Christ*. If you make this argument, you open yourself for charges of lacking faith and insulting the people you are trying to convince (never a good idea, as tempting as it is). The best defense is this: it's Hell. If Hell were puppies, kittens, and rainbows, nobody would mind going there, but it's symbolic torture for not obeying God. Sometimes violence is done gratuitously. In that case, a challenge might be justified, even if it doesn't deserve to be upheld. Sometimes, however, the violence serves a purpose; sometimes it teaches. The gruesome deaths of the disciples (decapitation, stoning, boiling) are rarely downplayed. Why? Because they show the faith of those who endured those deaths. The punishments levied against those in Hell illustrate their lack of faith and what happens to those who don't believe; what else could a Christian parent want?

Those in Hell who suffer condemnation are a diverse population. Achilles is in Hell, Judas Iscariot is in Hell, and more than one pope is in Hell. On the surface, even my Protestant students see this as an attack on Christianity. It's not; it's an attack on the church. This is where students need context. The pope is not in Hell for being a pope; some popes are in for greed (Canto VII, Lines 46–8) others for lying and crusading against fellow Christians (Canto XXVVII, lines 85–93). At this point, most students in high school know that the church during the Middle Ages was corrupt, one of the catalysts for the Protestant Reformation. However, students have trouble transferring what they learn in history class into a class that reads literature. Simply reminding them that Protestants and Catholics alike recognized the corruption will help solve the problem of viewing Dante as anti-

Christian. It will also provide an opportunity to point out that being a Catholic does not mean supporting corrupt popes.

Catholics are a large minority in the community where I teach, and I preach tolerance of all cultures, Catholics included. I could care less what religion my students follow, as long as they don't discover my lack of one, and in the end get me fired. That's the kind of district I work in. I have to play to the crowd in order to stay employed. It's easy to do that with *Inferno*. All of the less than obvious protests are accounted for now that I've taught it a few times, which is crucial, since there are no published rationales for teaching it. The NCTE has compiled hundreds of rationales for frequently challenged books and other books publishers have made compilations, but nowhere do they mention Dante. It appears that, since it is such a classic, no challenge could hold water, but, while a book may survive a legal battle, often there will be a private agreement between teacher and administrator to cease teaching the book. *Inferno* is a classic, but that explanation doesn't mean much to my sophomores or their parents, many of whom work in a plant forging housing anchors. The poem is an artifact, a culmination of medieval thought, and a precursor to renaissance literature. An education is of lower quality if this poem is banned, as it is referenced in numerous other classics, and even in everyday life. To deny any district of students the opportunity to read the poem is to put them at a disadvantage to the rest of the Dante-reading world and is "an infringement of intellectual freedom" (NCTE and The International Reading Association, qtd. in Burress and Karolides and Kean). Besides its cultural importance, the banning of any book is the first step to what Elmer Gertz (1965) described as "a bovine existence." We need books; "[w]hen the word is killed, life dies. Without speech, spoken and written, life is meaningless; we become only as the animals...I hope we are men, not cattle" (p. 19). We damage our students when we restrict what they read.

Paradise Can be Hell Too

Another faith-based poem that has never had a recorded challenge, and hence, has never had a rationale created to defend its teaching, is John Milton's *Paradise Lost*. I looked into Milton for different reasons than Dante. I have never taught Milton, so I wasn't certain what kind of reaction I would get from a class of devout students. The time may be coming when I will teach it, however, since our current British literature teacher is nearing her retirement and I may be pushed to take over her classes. Milton had always fascinated me as a student, too, since my senior English teacher in high school had told my class that Milton's poem had greatly influenced the conception that many people have of Satan, Hell, and the Fall. She said this right before turning over the discussion of the poem to our principal. I always wondered why she did this, and my only guess was that it had something to do with her being a Methodist reverend.

I felt obliged to contact her about this, as her reluctance to teach the poem due to religious conflicts, while still recognizing it as important enough to have somebody other than her teach it to us, would be perfect for my research. Alas, that's not why she opted out of teaching it personally.

"I don't have the maturity and the grasp of the language to tackle it!" she wrote to me. Apparently, my principal had taken a class on Milton, and she felt that we would get more out of it if we learned from him.

Many expletives ran through my head. "Then who would argue against teaching it?" I asked myself. I reminded myself that it's not about the teacher; it's about the kids. Why would a kid object to it? This came much more easily.

I was having dinner with a friend of mine who happens to be a Catholic. I asked her if she'd ever read the poem, and she admitted that she hadn't. I was a little disappointed, since I had an ulterior motive of discovering her thoughts on parts of *Paradise Lost* that can be seen as anti-Catholic (more on that later). I told her this. She asked what it was about, since she knew nothing about it, and I told her that it was an epic account of Satan's fall from heaven, the creation of man, and the fall of man. I said that Milton's characterizations of Lucifer, God, and Jesus were fascinating.

She stopped me. "So Jesus is a character? Before the fall of man? Well I don't believe in that, if that helps you at all."

It most certainly did. One of the issues that comes up in *Paradise Lost* is that it doesn't just offend large groups of people; it has the potential to offend individuals and small groups in little ways. My friend could be an anomaly. As a Baptist, I read John 1:1 "In the beginning was the Word, and the Word was with God, and the Word was God" (KJV). I was taught that 'Word' was a metaphor for Jesus, meaning that Jesus has always existed. During my church-going days, I believed this, and until recently I thought all Christians believed this. Milton shared this belief and put it in his epic. Four hundred years later, he has annoyed my friend with his belief. Now I had something.

I wrote back to my Methodist Reverend English Teacher (MRET) and asked her what her own theological problems were in regards to Milton. "They are Legion!" she wrote back. She had a problem with Milton's view that Jesus was a blood-for-blood atonement for mankind's sin. "I believe that God was saving the world through Christ" but she was "not big on the idea that Jesus had to be sacrificed for sinners." Jesus came to show a way to salvation; he didn't have to die to do that, but the fact that it happened helped his message to influence far more people.

Satan is another bone of contention, and a widespread one at that. "People think they know [Satan] from scripture, but they describe to me the Satan of Milton." A personified Satan is not a universal belief. Milton turns Satan into the perfect being, fallen from grace and set up to reign in Hell. Even in Sunday school, we were taught that Satan was not a red, horned creature with a pointy tail and a pitchfork, but rather had the appearance of an angel. (I remember a handsome dark-eyed man with an Elvis pompadour in one of our workbooks.) This is Milton's Satan; once perfect, who turned down Paradise out of jealousy of God's power and his arrogance in thinking that he could conquer Heaven. The biblical foundation for this belief can be found in Isaiah 14, in which Isaiah speaks to "Lucifer" and describes his jealousy and fall from grace. Similarly, in Ezekiel 28, an address is made to one who had been in Eden and was once perfect but was then cast out. Literally, however, these addresses are being made to the King of Babylon and the Prince of Tyrus, respectively. Even the name "Lucifer," which means morning star, was referring to Babylon's rise and fall, in the same way that Venus (the morning star) rises and falls quickly. Metaphorically speaking, these passages could be about Satan, but suggesting a metaphoric reading of the Bible is another controversial issue.

Satan does pop up in the Bible in other places, and he is referred to by name. In the Book of Job, Satan argues that Job wouldn't love God if Job weren't so blessed. It is only with God's permission that Satan is able to torture Job. In *Paradise Lost*, Satan seems quite independent of God and, while, theologically speaking, everything Satan does is done with God's permission (since God is omnipotent and omniscient) Satan never asks for permission, and he even is deluded enough to think that he is operating outside of God's knowledge.

This example poses a couple of problems. First, it would seem that, in the Book of Job, Satan is a personified being, but only as much as God is, since they converse with one another. Suggest that God is a being, and you've got problems. Then you open up some more scriptural cans of worms.

One might hear, "Of course Satan is independent of God, he convinced Eve to eat the apple!"

Two things that I would be petrified to respond with: 1) nowhere in the Bible is the forbidden fruit referred to as an apple. You have accepted something Milton wrote as something biblical; shame on you. 2) Nowhere in the Bible is it said that Satan is responsible for the Fall of Man. In Genesis, the serpent tricks Eve. In Revelation 20:22, Satan is referred to as "that old serpent" (KJV) which alludes to Satan having possessed the snake, but literalists would not view that as evidence enough to post blame on Satan. Again, Milton's imagination has wreaked havoc with religious beliefs.

But whether it's Milton's theories on Christ's existence, Satan's personification, or Satan's role in the Fall, one cannot excuse his musings as being merely imagination gone wild. Dante wrote from imagination, and he also wanted his poem to be an allegory that taught Christians how to attain salvation; everything in his *Comedy* is a symbol, and meant to be treated in a nonliteral way. On the other hand, Milton claimed divine influence, he prayed to a muse to tell him the tale of man's fall, and he even stated his purpose as being to "justify the ways of God to man" (Book 1, line 26). Furthermore, Milton would wake up from a night's sleep and dictate the lines that had come to him in his sleep that night. This serves to emphasize the idea that the epic was divinely inspired and meant to be read literally. The former fact is one that students will pick up on fairly quickly, especially since most students have read at least one epic (*The Odyssey*), two if they have been through the district where I teach (*The Iliad*). Invocations and their purposes would be quite familiar. The latter fact would come up in the interest of full disclosure.

Is Milton a man who talked to God and was given this information so that we can read it and feel better about our fall? Or is Milton a heretic, who was either insane to believe what he was writing, or was flat out lying throughout the epic? The better question is: who cares? This question will come up, undoubtedly, but not every question needs to be answered in the academic setting. My MRET told me, "It needs to be viewed in the English classroom as a work of literature. The kid can go talk to a priest about the challenge to his/her theology."

It is most definitely a piece of literature. Its influence on culture for years to come, and its role as an artifact of its time, is undeniable. It is staunchly anti-Catholic, but that speaks to the time from which it came. It needs to be put in the historical context, when England was terrified of going back to Catholic rule. With this kind of approach, "Catholics can learn to regard [Milton's] anti-Catholicism as more historically and politically than theologically significant" (Nardo, 1986, p.50). If done with careful precision, one will not awaken the anti-Catholic sentiment that has been instilled in the students by their parents.

It's there; even my colleagues have that bias. Only a couple of years before I began teaching in my district, it had 100% enrollment in a particular teachers' association. By the time I came along a few teachers had defected to another organization. In an e-mail calling for peace between the groups, one of the teachers in the original association pointed out that she understood that there are always going to be differences, even if she thinks other people are following the wrong paths. "After all," she said, "I think everybody should be Baptist, but I accept that that will never happen." I had never thought that Christians would discriminate against Christians, but it happens, and reading what might come across as hate literature will only stir up controversy.

With all of that controversy, do kids need *Paradise Lost*? Well, it's going to end up being fairly optional whether a student ever reads it. Few teachers would ever think of teaching the poem, with its lofty language and countless allusions, to a class of ninth or tenth graders. It will only be taught in small doses, as well, usually just the first two books. But it does belong in the halls of public education. It is a unique poem. Milton wanted to bring respect to the English language, so he modeled the style used by the great epic poets. (Milton too, it seems, had an appreciation for the 'virtuous Pagans.') No one had tried this, and no one has ever succeeded in such a degree. "It's ours. It's a great contribution to the body of world literature. It's part of being culturally literate," says my MRET. Others agree, "Milton and his epic...summarize the great literary traditions filtering down to the Renaissance in England and...they provide the monument with which much later literature must cope" (Crump, 1986, p.1).

As teachers, 'cope' would be a word that applies to our relationship with our students' religions. I came to the district in which I teach as an outsider. Despite the city in my address, I had only entered the limits of that city a handful of times, and I probably doubled that number during my interviewing process. I had just come off of an internship at a school where the population of the senior class alone was larger than the entire high school population where I was hired. I hadn't expected religious students; I thought that had gone out of style in the 1990s. In my days in the College of Education, we had discussed teaching books with bad language, racially controversial themes, and those with high levels of violence. My peers and I graduated with the NCTE's belief that no book should ever be off limits to someone who wants to read it.

That's not the hard part. The hard part is getting kids to read things they may not feel comfortable reading. Most people are against censorship, I hope, and when someone else decides that something is too harmful to teach and that it should be removed from the curriculum, that is most certainly censorship. Are all books safe to teach to students? Of course not. Don't teach using Madonna's *Sex* or Ian Fleming's James Bond books, but put them in the library and let kids check them out as they please. In the classroom, some trust needs to be put into the hands of teachers to know what will benefit their students. Alternate texts? There are no alternate texts for *Paradise Lost* or *Inferno*; that is what makes them so teachable, their matchlessness, their lack of anything comparable in subject, style, or cultural impact.

In 1964, Elmer Gertz (1965) delivered an address defending all banned books and condemning all forms of censorship. At the time, he said, "I think that one of the great needs of our day is to overcome this fear of books, this fear of words, this dread of the unorthodox, the unpopular" (p. 11). We have not overcome this dread, even after 40 years. Now, though, sex and violence, the scourge of Gertz's day, have become more acceptable than religion. Religion, in all of its forms, has become unorthodox in schooling, even in the most religious communities, and to protest has become the only reaction. If we decide that including these works in the curriculum exposes our children to unorthodox and unpopular thinking towards religion, and react by "protecting" our children from them, we have done those students a disservice. A student who never ponders his/her faith is a robot; faith is a wonderful thing, but no man, woman or child should accept their beliefs based on what another person has told him or her to believe. Reading these books may cause students to pick up their Bibles and actually read what other people have been interpreting for them. That's one of the positive things about the Protestant Reformation: people began to think and philosophize for themselves. Isn't independent thinking the goal of educators, whether they're thinking about politics, science, literature, or faith?

As educators we have a duty. Sometimes we must venture out of what is safe and take a stand for not only what feels right to us, but also what is beneficial to our students. To try and protect them from the controversial is to produce a mass of complacent, unquestioning automatons. There may come a day when there is a showdown, and what might be the only thing saving us from intellectual insulation is people coming to our aide and understanding that what we are trying to do is not evil; on the contrary, it is us showing that we have our students' best interests at heart. If we don't stand up, "[t]hat is how freedom dies—when one does not stand up for the crackpot, the crank, the extremist, the one who is so unused to life that he thinks he can do as he pleases, regardless of the community. He is the man who is going to make the world safe for our children...; and he is the man who is going to give birth to freedom everywhere" (Gertz, 1965, p. 13). Am I so smug that I believe I am "giving birth to freedom" in my classroom everyday? Of course not. It's more like every other day.

BIBLIOGRAPHY

Alighieri, D. (1995). "The Divine Comedy: Inferno." *The Portable Dante*. (M. Musa, Trans.). New York: Penguin. 3–191.

Alighieri, D. (1993). "The Divine Comedy: Inferno." *World Literature*. (J. Ciardi, Trans.). Austin: Holt, Rinehart, & Winston, Inc. 747–69.

Burress, L., & Karolides, N.J., & Kean, J.M. (1993). Introduction. *Censored Books: Critical Viewpoints*. Metuchen, NJ: The Scarecrow Press. xiii–xxii.

Crump, G.M. (1986). Introduction. *Approaches to Teaching Paradise Lost*. New York: The Modern Language Association of America. 1–8.

Gertz, E. (1965). *Censored Books and Their Right to Live*. Lawrence, KS: University of Kansas Libraries.

Holt, Rinehart, & Winston, Inc. (1993). "Introduction: The Divine Comedy." *World Literature*. Austin: Holt, Rinehart, & Winston, Inc. 742–46.

Milton, J. (1674). *Paradise Lost*. (2004). New York: Barnes & Noble Classics.

Nardo, A.K. (1986). Their Faith Is Strong, but Their Prose Is Weak: Teaching *Paradise Lost* at Louisiana State University. In G.M. Crump (Ed.) *Approaches to Teaching Paradise Lost*. (pp. 48–52). New York: The Modern Language Association of America

CHAPTER TEN

The Necessary Role of Religion in Civic Education

Craig S. Engelhardt, Baylor University

Public school students should learn about the ideals that drive many national and international events; they should understand the source of others' values and motivations, and they should be familiar with the plurality of perspectives reflected by their fellow citizens. Thus, it is important to *study* about religion. Forums to acknowledge the multiplicity of our cultural and religious beliefs are also good in that they recognize our diverse heritages. Thus, it is also important to *celebrate* religion. However, academic study and celebration fail to engage religion as a formative core of moral and civic identity. I will argue that greater engagement with religious views[1] will advance the mission of public education to propagate the moral and civic qualities of our democratic society.

After a brief discussion of the civic relevance of religion, I will present the philosophic role of religion within nineteenth-century common schools, public schools of modernity, and contemporary public schools. Through this discussion, I will demonstrate how early public education recognized and attempted to build upon the philosophic connection between religion and the needs of democratic society for morality and civic unity. However, when faced with growing diversity within the ideal of the common school model, secular alternatives of moral and civic formation came to replace those dependent upon religious views. Thus, I will reflect on the historical role of religious/comprehensive views in civic education against the background of religious disestablishment.

Next, I will argue that secular alternatives of civic education curricula have not demonstrated a superior value toward the achievement of public civic interests, while religiously grounded civic education curricula have provided successful models for moral and civic education.

Finally, with this background, I will propose ways in which public education can reengage the formative and motivational qualities of religion for civic purposes within publicly operated schools and within religious schools strategically joined with the state to facilitate the public's civic education vision.

The breadth and conceptual nature of this essay requires a brief address of each component of the discussion, but I have concluded that the expansive argument is of value for future discussion.

Religion's Civic Relevance

Education scholar Warren Nord has reflected the growing concern that religion be taken seriously in public education (Nord, 1995; Nord & Haynes, 1998). In agreement, I have noted that merely to study or celebrate religion overlooks its significant potential. Taken broadly, religion reflects comprehensive beliefs and values that are more than just academic holdings; it provides an intellectual and emotional frame of reference through which individuals interact with information and society. Functionally, religion is "an encompassing world-view that answers the big questions about life, dignifies daily exertions with higher significance, and provides a rationale for meaningful collective action" (Kurtz in Berkowitz, 2003, p. 31). It provides a stable, but not stagnant, ground for analysis and understanding as well as a potential source of hope, compassion and motivation.

In a civic environment concerned with the development of autonomous individuals, I hold that religious beliefs are not presumptuously held, and that religious individuals relate with their beliefs in a bi-directional manner. In other words, religious thought has a rational (though not necessarily strictly scientific) base. From a young age, children are formulating the degree of conviction they hold regarding their family's beliefs even as these beliefs influence their development. When older, the independence of religious "followers" often serves to frustrate the efforts of religious leaders. Nevertheless, beliefs, once deeply held, are life influencing. The biblical sage Solomon wrote, "As he thinketh in his heart, so is he" (Proverbs 23:7, KJV). The religions of history have helped to form the convictions and inspire actions that have freed slaves, educated children, supported human value, and brought aid to the suffering. They have also persecuted heretics, oppressed moral dissenters, and supported authoritarian control.

Thus, prior to the conceptualization of the liberal democratic polity, religious beliefs produced mixed civic effects. Their visions of truth tended to oppose individual liberty, but they also provided transcendent ideals, powerful motivations, and common ideologies that provided for social cohesion. Liberal democratic philosophy saw that the problem was not necessarily with religion, but with the alignment of government power with particular religious conceptions. Alignment not only armed religious conflicts, but denigrated individuals by treating them as incompetent to discern truth for themselves. The liberal political solution for both concerns was to neutralize government respecting issues of faith.

The Constitution famously institutionalized America's conception of religious liberty in the two religion clauses of the First Amendment. Together, they freed private conscience from government coercion and recognized a special place for religious expression; the wars of religion were disempowered while sources of private social formation were un-encumbered.

Sociologists have long worked within a paradigm of increasing secularization that predicted the decline and death of religious belief. "Scholars have agreed that science-driven secularization gnaws steadily at the roots of faith. However, anyone who glances in newspapers sees that religion continues to affect deeply a wide range of human activities, and it is hard to discern extinction in a phenomenon as varied and vigorous as faith" (Bainbridge, 1997 p. 404). Religious beliefs have adapted and flourished, prompting a growing body of sociologists to refute the secularization thesis (Finke & Stark, 1992; Young, 1997). Thus, religious beliefs remain common and contribute to the formation and motivation of future citizens.

Some argue that civic education should be formed around childhood autonomy rights (Brighouse, 2000; Dwyer, 1998; Levinson, 1999). Others argue that public civic education should be actively formed around the needs of democratic society (Gutmann & Thompson, 1996; Macedo & Tamir, 2002). I lean toward the concerns of the latter and believe that civic interests should be preferentially supported by public education. Thus, if public education supports the teaching of common moral and civic ideals, the question remains as to religion's role. This question will be addressed through a historical survey of religion in public civic education.

Role of Religion in the Common School

In the wake of an evolving concern for private conscience, American public education began with the vision to utilize state power to propagate the civic concerns of the day to poor and immigrant populations without access to education. Further, and of greater concern, the choice was driven by a fear that Roman Catholicism encouraged views that were potentially unsupportive of the new nation. The American public saw a need to propagate its civic values and beliefs with the aim to unify a growing diversity of people and form them with the morality of good citizenship. The strategy of the common school model was to make the public's civic education environment religiously noncontroversial so that the greatest number would attend and grow to reflect enlightened American ideals associated with moral behavior, democratic government, and social unity.

Prior to the common school, civic education held a strong concern for the development of religious faith. Most Americans saw a distinctive role for Christianity. Founder Benjamin Rush reflected this in his writings on education. After affirming that any religion was better than no religion, he wrote: "A Christian cannot fail of being a republican." He argued that Christianity undermined the "divine right of kings" and supported

> the original and natural equality of all mankind. A Christian, I say again, cannot fail of being a republican, for every precept of the Gospel inculcates those degrees of humility, self-denial, and brotherly kindness which are directly opposed to the pride of monarchy and the pageantry of a court. A Christian cannot fail of being useful to the republic, for his religion teacheth him that no man "liveth to him self." And lastly, a Christian cannot fail of being wholly inoffensive, for his religion teacheth him in all things to do to others what he would wish, in like circumstances, they should do to him. (in Milson, Bohan, Glanzer, & Null, 2004 pp. 83–84)

With the development of common education, the conscientious problem was that American ideals of the day were largely indebted to Protestant rather than Catholic beliefs. The Catholic faith could not be directly opposed, but civic concerns mandated the exposure of Catholic and all other children to "republican" ideals within their supporting philosophical context. Thus, for the founding generations, effective civic education had to either compliment or modify the comprehensive views of students. A coherent link between private faith and public civic values provided the highest degree of civic buy-in; thus, common school leaders pressed legal and conscientious limits to impart a religiously grounded view of American civic morality and truth.[2]

Horace Mann (1848) labored to strengthen moral propagation as a public interest, and he argued that the common school could accomplish this without it becoming a state religious establishment. He declared in his final annual report, "Religious instruction in our schools, to the extent which the Constitution and the laws of the State allowed and prescribed, was indispensable to the highest welfare, and essential to the vitality of moral education" (p. 125). Continuing, he said, "Our system earnestly inculcates all Christian morals; it founds its morals on the basis of religion; it welcomes the religion of the Bible; and, in receiving the Bible, it allows it to do what it is allowed to do in no other system—*to speak for itself*. But here it stops" (1848, p. 127).

During the 1840's, immigration to America tripled the number of Catholic citizens who were an already marginalized group. The Protestantism of the common schools became a point of contention. In New York, when the Catholics asked for public money to run their own schools, heated debates arose that reflected a general anti-Catholic sentiment (Macedo & Tamir, 2002, p. 111). It was "insisted that public funds should not be used to teach superstition and disloyalty" (McConnell as cited in Macedo & Tamir, 2002, p. 111).

The proposal became a law that excluded all sectarian schools from public funds; for the first time, taxation became available exclusively for the functioning of the Protestant leaning public schools. This act reflected a powerful move to define not only the essential characteristics of American civic identity, but to define their effective propagation. The state was to be trusted to guide the parameters of civic formation in a common religious environment, but sectarian faiths were not.

Initially, Mann's "nonsectarian" solution to the problem of religious differences was unacceptable to most of the Protestant population. "Opponents of state school systems began as a majority in many states, and in 1860 they remained a strong minority, even in the Northeast" (Kaestle, 1983, p. 136). That which many viewed as a Catholic threat served, in part, to draw Protestant opponents to the cause of common public education.

Soon after the Civil War, animosity toward Catholics increased. In a nativist climate inflamed by fear of un-Americanized Catholicism, the nation launched a campaign to insure the preeminence of what they conceived to be a nonsectarian American civic ideal—an ideal that still reflected general Protestant truths. After the failure of a politically embroiled attempt at a federal amendment, many states adopted constitutional amendments largely intended to prohibit state support of Catholic schools. What became known as "Blaine Amendments" standardized the policy of the exclusive use of taxation for public schools across the nation.

Though diversity forced a decline in religious instruction, the common school maintained its reliance upon religion. Education scholar Charles Glenn (1988) finds that "there seems to have been an almost universal conviction that schooling should have some form of religious character. It was not hostility to or avoidance of religion, understood in the most general terms, that fueled the [secularization] debates of these decades" (p. 178). Not only did this religious character make public schools agreeable to the majority of citizens, but also it provided a context of understanding and value that aligned the civic mission of the schools with religious motivations.

The nineteenth century's vision of nonsectarian American civic ideals alienated Catholics to such a degree that they began their own school system (B. McClellan, 1992, p. 47). The significance of the common school's alliance with Protestantism will be lost if one conceives of it simply as religious prejudice expressed through majority control of the schools. The diverse Protestant population had seen the efficacy of their faith towards public moral and political formation (P. Smith, 1976). Enlightened Protestant ideas had produced democratic liberty while the Roman Catholicism of the day seemed to reflect a legacy of control. Charles Glenn (1988) surmised that if not for the specter that linked Roman Catholic immigrants with immorality and authoritarianism, both antithetical to democratic liberty, the common school ideas might never have won acceptance (pp. 205–6). Thus, nonsectarian Protestant beliefs and values were viewed as vital to the public interest as civic supports and came to be protected by the exclusive public funding of common schools.

Catholics recognized that the common school was linked with a Protestant civic identity. Thus, it could not be truly common and was, as to be expected, most acceptable to those who already embodied the traditional American ideals. Common education held a public imposition upon conscience relative to one's distance from the philosophically "common" mean. This mean "centered on republicanism, Protestantism, and capitalism, three sources of social belief that were intertwined and mutually supporting" (Kaestle, 1983, p. 76). Most Americans came to accept this mean as the nation viewed its identity in Protestant conceptions of truth and value, whereas, "Catholics were tolerated, even welcomed, but only on Protestant terms. It was not an arrangement designed to make the new immigrants or their religious leaders happy" (Fraser, 1999, p. 51).

Thus, the common school relied upon nonsectarian Protestant religion to elicit the support of Protestant citizens who believed that education should reflect religious beliefs that were valuable to the formation of public morality and provided a ground for unity around shared beliefs.

The Declining Place of Religion in Modern Civic Education

Under the driving influences of increasing religious diversity and scientific progress, modernity revamped the common school from its philosophically religious foundations to acceptable secular or scientific ones. But even as curriculum and methodology increasingly reflected the secular scholarship of the twentieth century's modern world, much of this was acceptable to large numbers of Christians who believed in "the inherent and inevitable harmony of public education and the Protestant cause" (Lynn, 1964, p. 121). The locally advocated garnishments of prayer, Bible reading and civil religion influenced residents to feel that the schools were generally aligned with their deepest beliefs and values.

These points of attachment served to facilitate public buy-in to public schools, but little was actively done within the curriculum to establish a connection between public civic concerns and private religion. Children often heard a chapter read from the Bible and listened to a prayer, but the moral and civic program increasingly departed from understanding and motivations grounded in religious beliefs and values.

Public moral concern grew with the depersonalization and disorientation of a changing society. While private religious schools maintained their faith-grounded moral instruction, public moral education philosophy had diverged from its comprehensive base by 1910. Traditional character education would predominate in the classroom until the mid-1920s, but its progressive competitor anticipated an entirely new base for moral education (McClellan, 1992, p. 55).

Early modern character educators advocated virtues similar to those of past generations. However, more secularized settings avoided premises of faith as schools strove to form the civic character and beliefs of children. They taught civic values as true and right with little appeal to religious ideology. As part of their civic strategy, they started clubs such as the Boy Scouts, the Campfire Girls, and 4-H designed to instill and encourage good civic behavior and values.

Behavioral codes were key tools of this character education movement. Generally free of the appeal to controversial tenets of faith, these codes listed virtues and defined behavioral expectations. Group activities that utilized the pressures of peer influence became the means of imparting the codes within the organization. Schools published behavioral codes and developed strategies to teach them in the classroom. "The aim was to use the codes as a way of suffusing every facet of school life with moral education" (McClellan, 1992, p. 58).

Character education declined in the face of its competitor from the progressive education camp through the 1930s (Leming, 1997). Progressive moral education gained the support of "liberal Protestant clergy, intellectual leaders, professional elites, and educators associated with major universities and large urban and suburban school systems" (McClellan, 1992, p. 61).

Progressives called for a ground-up redesign of public civic education. They stood against tradition and moral absolutism. "Rejecting the notion that the school should teach specific moral precepts or encourage particular traits, progressive educators hoped to cultivate in students both a quality of open-mindedness and a general ability to make moral judgments" (McClellan, 1992, p. 63). They advocated a dynamic ethical process in which relative values were judged and decided upon in accord with differing situations. Though progressives brought many beneficial qualities to civic education, I argue that their view of the child as an independent decision maker disconnected their programs from the extensive understanding and meaning that could have resourced their civic efforts.

John Dewey argued that democratic citizens should be formed to think like scientists to address the reality of social and moral change; "without initiation into the scientific spirit one is not in possession of the best tools which humanity has so far devised for effectively directed reflection" (Dewey in Westbrook, 1991, p. 169). Whereas proponents of character education avoided religion for the sake of unity, progressive moral educators avoided religion as a hindrance to rational social progress. However, this avoidance was to become a source of conflict; "the new moral philosophy...was conceived of as a potentially closed system, which eventually would make special revelation superfluous, at least for ethics" (Marsden, 1994, p. 51). Many religious believers were not willing to separate this realm from their faith perspectives.

Secular character education and progressive methodologies were widely adopted to replace religion as the ground of moral and civic formation, but the general ethos of many schools remained acceptable to the Protestant majority through the continuance of prayer, Bible reading, and restrictions regarding the teaching of evolution. Thus, religion continued to play a role in public education by linking (in a small way) the public mission of education with the deepest beliefs of the majority of citizens. These secular civic education programs of the character educators and the progressives were soon abandoned for new programs.

The decade of the 1960s was to witness a further disassociation of public concerns from religious/comprehensive views as the faith linking garnishments of prayer and Bible reading were separated from public education by the Court.

Moral and Civic Education in a Pluralistic Setting

Though some midwestern state courts upheld bans on public school Bible reading, as late as 1949, Bible reading was still required in the public schools of twelve states and permitted in twenty-one others. "Only when the Supreme Court declared school prayer illegal in 1962, and Bible-reading illegal in 1963 did such religious activities disappear from the public school classroom" (McClellan, 1992, p. 47).

The removal of even relatively benign and nondenominational official school prayer was met with broad negative reaction by public officials. It was denounced by President Eisenhower (Jeynes, 2007, p. 338), found no vocal support in Congress, was described by former president Hoover as representing the "disintegration of a sacred American heritage" (Jeynes, 2007, p. 338) and moved Congress toward an unsuccessful attempt to impeach Supreme Court Chief Justice Earl Warren (Jeynes, 2007, p. 338).

The private sector was equally condemning. A 1963 Gallup Poll survey found that Americans disapproved of these court decisions by a margin of three to one (Jeynes, 2007, p. 338). One of the results of this disapproval was to be the Christian day school movement. This represented not only a loss of trust in the public education system, but the partial civic alienation of a broad segment of the public that felt the nation had rejected its transcendent source.

The disestablishment of religion from the public schools barred civic education programs from aligning with any religious or comprehensive view. This led to the curricular avoidance of religious beliefs. Though this may have been a necessary transitional step away from Protestant hegemony, the avoidance of private ideological motivations distanced public education from a strong source of civic formation.

The social turmoil and legal reorientation of the 1960s has been marked as America's transition to a pluralistic culture (Ellwood, 1994). Accompanying this transition was the recognition that American public institutions could no longer align with a single source of ultimate truth, whether it be broadly Christian or comprehensively scientific. This removal of trusted (by most) religious symbols from the public's civic education agenda was proper for institutions of the state, but it could be argued that it was destructive of civic and educational ends. The curricular bookends of religious expression that had served through modernity to assure most parents and children that public schooling aligned with their beliefs, understanding, and values were no more.

The ripple effects of the removal of prayer and Bible reading in combination with Rawlsian interpretations of public neutrality

(Rawls, 1971) left public educators uncertain as to how to conduct their civic moral mission. Into this vacuum, educators conscientiously attempted to promote the moral and civic development of children apart from any worldview.

In many schools, Values Clarification and Moral Reasoning filled the void of the 1970s and 1980s. Proponents argued that they were ideologically neutral, but neither was particularly effective and inflamed contentions with segments of the public that believed morality had religious grounds (Hunter, 2000). William Bennett, a current proponent of character education, argued that these systems of moral education promoted shallow values and self-centeredness (Leming, 1997), qualities of questionable civic value.

As other methods of moral and civic development have been introduced, many public schools, supported by scholars such as Nicholas Wolterstorff (1980, 2002), James Arthur (2003), and Kevin Ryan (1998), have returned to systems of virtue and character education. The reaffirmation of common moral and civic goods within many schools provides evidence that some educators have lost confidence in Dewey's belief that children, when provided with adequate experience and reason, could be depended upon to act in a positive civic manner.

Over the past century and a half, public education has moved from civic presentations that aligned with religious conceptions of truth and value to an academic exposure to common civic ideals and values. This truly fulfills the First Amendment's requirement that "Congress shall make no law regarding an establishment of religion," but apart from comprehensive frames of understanding, value, and motivation, public education is challenged to accomplish its mandate to shape the civic identity of children.

Common Education's Dilemma

The formation of civic identity is in large measure the formation of a moral identity; they both reflect the encouragement of proper behaviors, attitudes, duties, and beliefs. Work in this realm of conscience runs the risk of being superficial or objectionable. Education historian Carl Kaestle (1984) succinctly describes this difficulty long associated with public education: "How do you conduct moral education in the schools of a pluralistic country, with no established church and with protected dissent, when almost everyone believes that moral principles must be rooted in some cultural tradition and some transcendent values?"(p. 101).

If moral civic education was peripheral to the mission of public education, then this concern could be overlooked, but many consider it central. Meira Levinson (2002) is not alone when she writes, "Civic education is a primary aim of American schooling. Its general purpose is relatively uncontroversial: to educate children to participate in a democratic *polis*" (p. 262). Though its purpose may stir little controversy, its civic efforts frequently do, and its methodologies seem to lean toward superficiality in the face of what some consider to be our nation's civic decline (Allman & Beaty, 2002; Glendon & Blankenhorn, 1995; Jeynes, 2007).

I propose that two primary causes hamper the mission of public education to build the civic identity of children. 1) Publicly presented civic ideals have become disconnected intellectually from comprehensive beliefs that provide the scaffolding for understanding, value and motivation. 2) Ungrounded civic ideals maintain a distance from the strongly influential formative effects of communities.

Proposal One: Reconnect Civic Ideals with Private Beliefs

Americans look to public education to form civic character; they "seem perpetually predisposed to look to reform of the common school as a means to help create cohesion and unity out of self-absorption and diversity" (Arons, 1997, p. 2). I argue that contemporary public education has the opportunity to explore the value of religion toward a reflective citizenship in a pluralistic society. Schools aim to encourage reflection and promote action. However, reflection that neglects privately recognized grounds of truth and value promotes inconsistent and shallow reasoning and neglects a strong source of motivation. These grounds can be engaged even if they cannot be critiqued by the state.

Education by its nature is comprehensive, and, thus, traditional education was religious at its heart. It is natural for all aspects of life and knowledge to fit together into a comprehensive and meaningful whole. It is as individuals develop their worldviews that they locate themselves and answer the questions of ultimate concern regarding the nature of reality, personal identity and purpose. Under government administration, today's public schools cannot answer ultimate questions, but they can encourage their reflection and facilitate the integration of democratic ideals into the deeply motivating beliefs of their students.

The concern of the public school is how it facilitates this integration. Left ungrounded, it is up to the child and the home to integrate civic ideals with their comprehensive views and motivations. Unfortunately, without school initiatives, these civic ideals may not arise at home for comprehensive discussion. By leaving the initiative with the child, or by presuming the child to be capable of self-integration, current educational procedures overlook the opportunity for a deep integration of civic ideals with private faith.

I propose that teachers routinely send children home with the assignment to discuss particular moral and civic issues in light of their religious beliefs. Since state involvement in these areas can become contentious, I propose that its role be one of asking questions and proposing topics without judging home discussions. These discussions hold the potential to facilitate the grounding, integration, and motivation of civic concerns from comprehensive perspectives.

For example, a public school discussion of the value of honesty may leave a student with a range of possible conclusions. Truthfulness could be pragmatic, valuable when it benefits the self, or just generally right. The civic interest of an honest citizenry would likely benefit from a home discussion that linked truthfulness with the high value of loving God and one's neighbor. Similarly, when learning about our nation and the claims of democracy, students could be encouraged to explore their own faiths with the help of family, religious authorities, and friends as to how their beliefs support, analyze or advance our liberal democracy. They can even discuss how their own religious group has a stake in maintaining religious freedom—especially in pluralism (Eberle, 2002). I maintain that moral and civic supports formed within settings of comprehensive reflection provide a deeper attachment for public concerns than secularized classroom reflection alone.

Civic concerns that schools respectfully attempt to link with student religious views may take on greater meaning, reflective value, and motivational force. Thoughtful assignments can provide opportunities for students to grow in both their religious and civic understanding. Tapping into the dynamics of deep beliefs is also an educational opportunity that links public education with the power of extended communities.

Studies have found that close community, as found in Catholic schools, fosters higher expectations and greater effective character development (Coleman & Hoffer, 1987). Though public schools may have difficulty forming ideological communities, this proposal may provide a means by which public schools can create closer supportive community attachments that may grow with increasing dialogue.

Undoubtedly, the discussions I propose will not always affirm the general stance of the public school, but I argue that the discussions themselves will have been of value. A sector of the public is alienated by public education that it perceives as hostile to communities and conscientious religious beliefs. Reflecting this perspective, scholar Stephen Arons (1997) writes,

> The bureaucratic culture of education has become hostile to the rights of conscience and to the growth of community, behaving as if each were a threat to successful schooling. Conscience—its exercise by teachers, its development in children, and its place in our primary institution for transmitting culture—has been rendered nearly irrelevant. Community—its maintenance within schools as a necessary context for learning, and its support by schooling as an essential part of a free and meaningful life—has been subverted. (p. 123)

As public education acts to value religion and religious views, it will facilitate the disarming of this claim and facilitate the building of public trust and cohesion.

Further, religious discussions that counter the general concern of the public school will have been of value in that students will have a greater understanding of the grounds of their differences. From this base, they will wrestle with the claims of the public and the tenets of their faith. It is my opinion that the rational claims that undergird public moral and civic concerns will tend to encourage the conscientious adaptation of faith holdings toward a greater understanding and support of our democratic life. Further, I believe this reflective process will promote civic involvement as students relate their religious beliefs with public involvements.

A further public benefit stemming from this civic-religious engagement is a greater accessing of the experiences of other successful communities. Learning requires a discernment of truth, and whereas scientific analysis provides a repository of accepted truths in many areas, religious traditions (viewed as evolving with the experience and understanding of each generation) may be the repositories of truth in realms of morality, value and social order. Thus, as students increasingly converse with the authorities of their traditions, they will grow in their understanding of that which has been found to be of value to others.

Before leaving this proposal, I note that these suggestions are to compliment, not necessarily replace, existing moral and civic education programs. In addition, I note that this proposal is dependent upon the initiative of students and parents as to the degree of its effect. Nonreligious, moderately religious, and devoutly religious families are expected to provide differing degrees and depths of religious thought and motivation. Educators, as representatives of the state, are able do little more than facilitate discussions that students voluntarily carry out. Thus, though this proposal facilitates the formation of links between civic concerns and religious beliefs, it faces certain limitations in public school settings.

Proposal Two: Revise the Concept of Public Education

The heart of my thesis has been that the public interest toward the promotion of good citizenship can be strengthened when public ideals are integrated into the comprehensive views of students. I have proposed ways in which common schools can facilitate this, but the practical and legal constraints under which they must operate limit what they can accomplish. Private religious schools are much more able to integrate civic concerns with religious beliefs when the two are viewed as compatible. Religious schools, which far predate secular schools, are not restrained in their advocacy of higher than common ideals. They do not promote the social disunity often associated with common education because they are chosen for their compatibility with family beliefs and values. Additionally, they are generally tied into the broader communities and social networks within which social capital is built (Putnam, 2000).

Since public education is centrally driven to form the moral and civic qualities of good democratic citizens, and my analysis supports active integration of civic concerns with the comprehensive views of students, then it follows that public education should seek ways to facilitate this type of civic-religious engagement both in common and religious school settings. However, accessing religious schools requires a change in the traditional concept of public education. Where public education has been associated only with common or secular schools, I argue that its secular trajectory was a byproduct of its civic mission and not an educational ideal in itself. If the joining of religious schools with public school efforts strengthens the moral and civic mission of public education, then the public should pursue and publicly support this effort.

Religious schools differ widely, but they offer the opportunity to do more than just add prayer, scripture reading, and theology to an otherwise standardized curriculum. Ideally, they reflect a community of committed educators who desire to pass along not only the knowledge and skills of economic and political survival, but also a vision of life that they, the child's family, and their community have found to be of highest value. This meaningful vision integrates the curriculum and provides a greater depth of understanding that is expressed in the school community.

Some assume that religious educations deny the child the opportunity to become autonomous, but good educators are fully aware of the independence of their students and know that they will reject or hold lightly those values and beliefs that the child perceives as wrong, superficial or irrelevant. Thus, recognizing that students are ultimately choosers, effective teachers present beliefs in a context of options, experience, and reason. Rather than denying a student choice, religious schools provide the child with an opportunity for deep insight into the comprehensive nature of life in a manner that is unattainable in a common school setting. Indeed, various scholars argue that a "primary culture" is essential to becoming an individual and as a foundation for growth towards autonomy (McLaughlin, 1984).

The public has long idealized common education as *the* source of a common civic formation supportive of social cohesion. The fear of "Balkanization" and of the "danger of a rupture of the delicate social fabric that binds society together" (Paquette, 2005, p. 580) are often attributed to religious schooling. But, "these claims are most often made without any concern for empirical backing" (Thiessen, 2001, p. 32). "Throughout our history," writes Charles Glenn (1987), "millions of American children have attended private religious schools without a publicly divisive effect" (p. 285).

Contradicting the exclusive civic claim associated with common education, a recent analysis of studies regarding civic values shows that private schools (most of which are religious) tend to equal or exceed public schools in their ability to impart values considered beneficial to the public (See Patrick Wolf, "School Choice and Civic Values" in Betts & Loveless, 2005).

Civic identities commonly reflect religious identities, but common education can hinder the integration of the two. Sociologist Terence McLaughlin finds that children need uniformity within their learning environment and a primary culture in which to grow. Too early an exposure to a diversity of beliefs will inhibit the development of abilities later necessary for functioning within a pluralistic environment (McLaughlin, 1984). Common school founders viewed the religious grounding of American ideals as essential to the stability of the nation; and they believed they were preserving it in the common school. However, they failed on multiple counts. 1) They failed to recognize that those of other faiths could identify and integrate democratic concerns into the fabric of their faiths and even strengthen democracy through contributing from their unique understandings. 2) In their zeal to build national cohesion and unity, they failed to adequately recognize the divisive effects of a public school system grounded in only one view of truth (McClellan, 1992, p. 47). 3) They exclusively linked public funding to a nonsectarian education model that was destined to disconnect from all comprehensive views with growing diversity.

The cumulative effects of these failures have alienated good citizens and, as I claim, obstructed public efforts of civic propagation. Thus, I propose the formation of "joint venture schools." Under the umbrella and light oversight of the public education system, religious schools would be privately operated and publicly funded. The public would not be bound to support all religious schools; it would recognize only those accredited as "joint venture schools." Accreditation standards could insure that religious schools aligned with the public's general education interests, and a public commitment to light regulation would protect religious schools against gradual state encroachments that would undermine their religious missions.[3]

In proposing this, I do not suggest that common public education be abolished, but that it be complimented to better facilitate civic development among those desiring a civic education in a comprehensive religious setting. Philosophical orientation has proven to be one of the most divisive forces in public education. Currently ten percent of the population has chosen to remove itself from today's common school, mostly for religious reasons.[4]

Scholar Charles Glenn (1988) notes this difficulty: "We may have set ourselves an impossible task in seeking to provide a single model of education that is to be at once capable of nurturing character and civic virtue and yet inoffensive to the convictions of any parent" (p. 285). The current idea that public education must be secular sends an alienating message to those who contend that their beliefs are relevant to education. It sends the same message to religious school parents of today's faiths that it sent to nineteenth-century Catholics: "Your faith is insufficient to form good American citizenship." This further implies that the parents who have chosen a religious school are less than good citizens. Civic cohesion demands that public education send the exact opposite message.

At a time when America still viewed itself as having deep philosophical roots to which its identity was indebted, sociologist Will Herberg proclaimed that these roots must no longer be viewed as only Protestant. "The same basic values and ideals," Herberg (1960) wrote, "the same underlying commitment to the American Way of Life, are promoted by parochial school and public school, by Catholic, Protestant, and Jew, despite the diversity of formal religious creed" (p. 242). A broader system of public education can capitalize on the strengths of common and religious schooling while reducing the social tensions associated with secular education. I propose that this is the direction for religion in the twenty-first-century public education.

Pandora's Box or an Opportunity?

With the proper reticence of our liberal democratic polity to step into the realm of private beliefs, it is little wonder that few have explored the trajectory that I advocate. Many view religion as too socially contentious to encourage its reflection, let alone to bring into the classroom as a source of civic motivation. To encourage an examination that would surely bring to light our deep differences would be ill conceived even if the examination were conducted primarily outside of school. Surely, the resultant social divisions would be cause enough to reject any attempt to carry out an overt plan to facilitate the linking of civic and religious concerns.

Can religion be engaged in a pluralistic setting for the public good? Many may be skeptical at the assertion that a broader place for religious engagement could promote social cohesion. The answer, in part, is that engagement does not necessarily increase religion; we are already a very religious people. Thus, deep religious diversity and its resultant philosophical divisions already exist in our culture. Most religions advocate for peace, justice, and concern for others from positions of deep conviction. Providing a greater place for religion in civic formation (as it once had) should promote these qualities in society. Thus, I suggest that civic-religious discussion will strengthen our unity as it draws in fractionally alienated groups, strengthens the public moral fabric, and draws from the social resources of religious wisdom.

Thus, I find little evidence that the "Pandora's box" of sectarian meltdown will be opened by the encouragement of civic-religious discussion. To the contrary, I find that religious belief strengthens the civic character of individuals and the nation.

Conclusion

It seems that human limitations may destine every generation to be acutely perceptive of some concerns and blind to others. The nineteenth century clearly saw that the flourishing of particular social and political ideals required the fertile soil of compatible beliefs and values, but it was blind to the religious coercion the common schools presented to dissenting traditions. Modernity clearly saw that secular academic mythology provided a stable source of technological discovery, but it was blind to the degree to which the vast realms of value and motivation were inaccessible to its methods, yet vital to its civic project. Lastly, from the late twentieth century to the present, the American public has clearly seen that a concern for conscience demands that the state be unaligned with any comprehensive view, but in its zeal over the success of secular government, it has been blind to the fact that healthy democracies rely upon the supportive alignment of meaningful and motivating religious conceptions.

The twenty-first century inherited a public education model intended to promote basic citizenship qualities, democratic attachments and cohesion. Whereas early American educators considered religion vital to their civic mission, the neutralization of state power regarding comprehensive advocacy shaped public education to avoid religion as a civic source. Modern educators posed alternate civic methodologies that claimed to address higher public values, but these have often been contentious and of nominal effect. Research links the successful propagation of values most closely with ideological communities, which lends credence to the common school's concern that civic education address a religious ground.

Public education must view religion as a resource of civic value rather than of fear. Religion is a motivator, a framework for knowledge, value and reason, as well as a source of private meaning. It has not diminished with scientific discovery. To engage it respectfully opens the possibility of winning its strong support, to overlook it is to neglect a historic source of civic formation, and to oppose it as publicly destructive is to encourage its opposition.

Where the common school chose to endorse nonsectarian Protestant faith as the unifying and effective ground of civic motivation and truth, the twenty-first century must actively engage a plurality of faiths toward the support of our liberal democratic society. There are areas in which public schools can engage religion by promoting private discussion and reflection, but a joint venture with the private school sector promises the greatest opportunity for civic-religious engagement.

NOTES

1. The word "religion" will frequently be used throughout this discussion, but it will generally be used expansively to include all comprehensive systems of belief, both theistic and nontheistic. Since our democracy does not prefer religion to nonreligion, I advocate that the comprehensive qualities of nonreligious views be engaged. When I intend to refer to traditional religion, further clarification will make it apparent.
2. Educational dissenters, generally compelled by conscientious concerns, argued that the common school education model overran conscientious limits of state interference regarding the education of their children.
3. The possibility of calling upon private schools to fulfill public educational interests is broad, and its scope is beyond the reach of this paper. However, I

propose that any state program that seeks to accomplish this joint venture must value religious schools for the unique characteristics that they bring to the public system. They have access to the realm of deep beliefs in ways that the state does not, and their privately chosen ideological orientations provide the opportunity for community formation far beyond the evidenced capacity of the state. Apart from a concern that restrains the state, the state will surely destroy the good that it seeks to draw from through its private school partnership.

4. Only 16.9% of private school students are in nonsectarian schools. Source: U.S. Department of Education, National Center for Education Statistics, Private School Universe Survey (PSS), 2001–2002.

BIBLIOGRAPHY

Allman, D. D., & Beaty, M. D. (2002). *Cultivating citizens: Soulcraft and citizenship in contemporary America.* Lanham, Md.: Lexington Books.

Arons, S. (1997). *Short route to chaos: Conscience, community, and the reconstitution of American schooling.* Amherst, Mass.: University of Massachusetts Press.

Arthur, J. (2003). *Education with character: The moral economy of schooling.* London; New York: RoutledgeFalmer.

Bainbridge, W. S. (1997). *The sociology of religious movements.* New York: Routledge.

Berkowitz, P. (2003). *Never a matter of indifference: Sustaining virtue in a free republic.* Stanford, Calif.: Hoover Institution Press.

Betts, J. R., & Loveless, T. (2005). *Getting choice right: Ensuring equity and efficiency in education policy.* Washington, D.C.: Brookings Institution.

Brighouse, H. (2000). *School choice and social justice.* Oxford; New York: Oxford University Press.

Coleman, J. S., & Hoffer, T. (1987). *Public and private high schools: The impact of communities.* New York: Basic Books.

Dwyer, J. G. (1998). *Religious schools v. children's rights.* Ithaca, N.Y.: Cornell University Press.

Eberle, C. J. (2002). *Religious conviction in liberal politics.* Cambridge, U.K.; New York: Cambridge University Press.

Ellwood, R. S. (1994). *The sixties spiritual awakening: American religion moving from modern to postmodern.* New Brunswick, N.J.: Rutgers University Press.

Finke, R., & Stark, R. (1992). *The churching of America, 1776–1990: Winners and losers in our religious economy.* New Brunswick, N.J.: Rutgers University Press.

Fraser, J. W. (1999). *Between church and state: Religion and public education in a multicultural America* (1st ed.). New York: St. Martin's Press.

Glendon, M. A., & Blankenhorn, D. (1995). *Seedbeds of virtue: Sources of competence, character, and citizenship.* Lanham, Md.: Madison Books.

Glenn, C. L. (1987). The new common school. *Phi Delta Kappan,* 69(4), 290–94.

Glenn, C. L. (1988). *The myth of the common school.* Amherst: University of Massachusetts Press.

Gutmann, A., & Thompson, D. F. (1996). *Democracy and disagreement.* Cambridge, Mass.: Belknap Press.

Herberg, W. (1960). *Protestant, Catholic, Jew: an essay in American religious sociology* (New ed., completely rev. ed.). Garden City, N.Y.: Anchor Books.

Hunter, J. D. (2000). *The death of character: Moral education in an age without good or evil* (1st ed.). New York: Basic Books.

Jeynes, W. (2007). *American educational history: School, society, and the common good.* Thousand Oaks: Sage Publications.

Kaestle, C. F. (1983). *Pillars of the republic: Common schools and American society, 1780-1860* (1st ed.). New York: Hill and Wang.

Kaestle, C. F., (1984). Moral education and common schools in America: A historian's view. *Journal of Moral Education, 13,* 101–111.

Leming, J. S. (1997). *Values and character education in public schools: Should the schools teach moral and civic virtue?* Retrieved August, 25, 2007, from http://www.uensd.org/USOE_Pages/Char_ed/fed_proj/utah/hist/values.htm

Levinson, M. (1999). *The demands of liberal education.* Oxford; New York: Oxford University Press.

Levinson, M. (2002). Dilemmas of deliberative civic education. *Phil Education Society Yearbook.*

Lynn, R. W. (1964). *Protestant strategies in education.* New York: Association Press.

Macedo, S. & Tamir, Y. (2002). *Moral and political education.* New York: New York University Press.

Mann, H. (1848). *Twelfth annual report.* Massachusetts State Board of Education.

Marsden, G. M. (1994). *The soul of the American university: From Protestant establishment to established nonbelief.* New York: Oxford University Press.

McClellan, B. Social Studies Development Center. (1992). *Schools and the shaping of character: Moral education in America, 1607–present.* Bloomington: Social Studies Development Center, Indiana University.

McLaughlin, T. (1984). Parental rights and the religious upbringing of children. *Journal of Philosophy of Education, 19*(1), 119–127.

Milson, A. J., Bohan, C. H., Glanzer, P. L., & Null, J. W. (Eds.). (2004). *Readings in American educational thought: From Puritanism to progressivism* (First ed.). Greewich, Conn.: Information Age Publishing, Inc.

Nord, W. A. (1995). *Religion & American education: Rethinking a national dilemma.* Chapel Hill: University of North Carolina Press.

Nord, W. A., & Haynes, C. C. (1998). *Taking religion seriously across the curriculum.* Alexandria, Va.; Nashville, Tenn.: ASCD; First Amendment Center.

Paquette, J. (2005). Public funding for "private" education: The equity challenge of enhanced choice. *American Journal of Education, 111*(4), 568.

Putnam, R. D. (2000). *Bowling alone: The collapse and revival of American community.* New York: Simon & Schuster.

Rawls, J. (1971). *A theory of justice.* Cambridge, Mass.: Belknap Press of Harvard University Press.

Ryan, K., & Bohlin, K. E. (1998). *Building character in schools: Practical ways to bring moral instruction to life* (1st ed.). San Francisco: Jossey-Bass.

Smith, P. (1976). *Religious origins of the American revolution*. Missoula, Mont.: Scholars Press for the American Academy of Religion.

Thiessen, E. J. (2001). *In defence of religious schools and colleges*. Montreal: McGill-Queen's University Press.

Westbrook, R. B. (1991). *John Dewey and American democracy*. Ithaca, N.Y.: Cornell University Press.

Wolterstorff, N. (1980). *Educating for responsible action*. Grand Rapids, Mich.: CSI Publications: Eerdmans.

Wolterstorff, N., Stronks, G. G., & Joldersma, C. W. (2002). *Educating for life: Reflections on Christian teaching and learning*. Grand Rapids, Mich.: Baker Academic.

Young, L. A. (1997). Rational choice theory and religion: Summary and assessment. New York: Routledge.

CHAPTER ELEVEN

Seeking Spaces for Emotionally Connected Rationality Amongst Dogmatic Belief Systems

Andrew N. McKnight, University of Alabama Birmingham

Introduction

This paper philosophically addresses a few of the quandaries and difficulties educators have when trying to teach certain subjects to those who hold what I refer to in this work as dogmatic belief systems. These beliefs are usually rooted in received incontrovertible interpretations of texts attributed with extranatural or divine authority and authorship, and often manifest themselves in absolutistic and often normative determinisms concerning certain truths about human existence and behavior. Although this paper does not seek to analyze these beliefs specifically as they relate to the spheres of science, politics, and culture, it may be instructive here to address an example of each generally, as they set the tone for, and are mentioned throughout what follows.

With regard to science, the predominant controversy seems to revolve around the biblically interpreted idea that the Earth was created some 6,000 years ago, and that therefore scientific theories like the Big Bang and Evolution, which each posit that the Earth is vastly older, are necessarily false. As it turns out this is, in one form or another, a decidedly mainstream belief among Americans as evidenced by recent polls, which reveal that just over fifty percent "reject the theory of evolution, stating that God created humans in their present form" and that over a third "believe that creationism should be taught instead of evolution" (Collins, 2005, p. 1). Additionally, three out of ten participants in the first Republican Party presidential primary debate raised their hands when asked if they did not believe in evolution (Nagourney & Santora, 2007). Consider this also within the context of survey data from the National Science Teachers Association "that a third of teachers were challenged on evolution, mainly by parents and students" (Winerip, 2006, p. 3).

A recent example from the cultural front involved a mother in Georgia who wished to ban Harry Potter books from her child's school library based on two separate and partially contradictory arguments. The first was that the books were being used to indoctrinate children into witchcraft, and the second that the library's holding of the books constituted a violation of the separation of church and state because they endorse an extant religion, witchcraft (Yahoo News, 2007).[1]

Additionally politics, and the thought processes by which we make decisions concerning policy and governance, are also being colored by adherence to dogmatic belief systems and enforced by in-group/out-group dynamics. A salient example of how those beliefs enter the political milieu can be found in the story of a North Carolina pastor who declared to his congregation before the 2004 federal election that "if you vote for John Kerry, you need to repent or resign" (Jonsson, 2005, p. 2). One might glean from these three examples that dogmatic belief systems tend to pose critical problems for those educators who would take the Deweyean stance that "school life should grow gradually out of the home life" (Dewey, 2003, p. 245).

What follows gives some notable exceptions, which seem to indicate that dogmatic beliefs are far from monolithic in their actual manifestations in consciousness and in practice. For instance, there are instances where scientists who participate in dogmatic religious traditions also engage in scientific inquiry within a specific scientific narrative, e.g., evolutionary biology, paleontology, etc., and hold these competing beliefs in abeyance without evident cognitive conflict. As example take paleontologist Marcus Ross, an admitted "young earth creationist," who believes that the Earth is less than 10,000 years old, but who wrote his dissertation according to what he describes as "a particular paradigm of Earth history" (Dean, 2007, p. 3). His justification involved, as he put it, "separating the different paradigms" of paleontology and literal scriptural theology. Another example comes from Dr. Steve Abrams, strict creationist and chairman of the state school board in Kansas who recently stated in the *New York Times* that his personal religious belief "doesn't have anything to do with science." When asked about the apparent conflict between the two he stated that "I can separate them...my personal views of Scripture have no room in the science classroom" (Krauss, 2006, p. 1). Although this may seem to some logically untenable, or even absurd, it does reflect a salient feature of human consciousness: the ability to be self-contradictory.[2] Of course, this is often not an acceptable position for others within similar circumstances, and these contradictions may not only be a site of psychic discord, but also may lead to the pursuit of falsehoods or ethically questionable behavior. However, one might take the position that in the face of alternatives, i.e., the reification of dogmatic positions or the justification of bigotry or ignorance due to the former, a benign contradiction borne out of the compartmentalization of competing narratives might just be tolerable.

I find a similar dissonance echoed by many students when asked about their emerging teaching philosophies. Many of them report having a belief in an absolute truth, but see their day-to-day lives in more materialist and pragmatic terms. I suspect these students are performing a less concerted and intentional version of what I discuss in what follows, namely that they have managed to separate aspects of their world view from an emotionally laden desire to retain their received belief system. Put another way, they see a need to hold on to those things that helped to define them in their upbringing, and yet adopt new and even contradictory views as their consciousness develops via experience. So if we deem cultural tolerance, political pluralism, the development of imagination *and* rationality, and the pursuit of scientific discovery to be important goals for public education, then perhaps we should pay more attention to repositioning dogmatic belief systems. That would allow students to hold these mystical and/or deterministic ideal beliefs in a super structural abeyance while analyzing everyday existence and problem solving through a more concrete and rational base consciousness.

Some Philosophical Premises

Covaleskie (2008) has written an interesting piece in which he posits that much of the "civil strife of the teaching of science in public schools" (p. 7) is due to the conflation of scientific "why's" with what he refers to as the "*Ultimate Why*" and the "*Teleological Why*" (p. 8). These are defined respectively as "ultimate or first causes" and "ultimate ends or purposes" (p. 8). I tend to agree with the author that science is incapable of telling us the pure nature of our creation or for what purpose we are ultimately here. Science, however, can tell us much of the practical mechanics of how our material existence came to be and also how it exists now. So we begin with two premises that depart from different paradigms of thought. The first follows what Covaleskie states with regard to the scope of science aforementioned, and the acknowledgement that the ultimate and teleological are not scientific. The second admits the limitations of science with regard to moral issues and leans on the humanly created concepts of democratic rights and tolerant civil society. Toward pursuing scientific understanding and just society what follows suggests an emotional vehicle for the segregation of dogmatic mystical and spiritual beliefs, specifically those that infringe upon the purview of science or that are at odds with the inclusive and respecting goals of democracy.

This paper posits that the development of an emotionally connected intellect could serve as both an analytic and affective tool of social analysis for students who may be hindered by intellectually limiting fields of cultural context and scopes of imagined inquiry. For the purposes of this paper an emotionally connected intellect denotes the development of powers of rational ordering as a habit that directs and allows us to examine and question an event, interaction, action, or text in terms of its cultural and emotional context, but that also does not forsake or mistake the emotional for the rational. This means that the rational does not become a retreat from the realm of the affective, the sensual, the spiritual, i.e., the aesthetic, but exists in tension as one makes sense of the other and guides its actions toward some perceived communicative understanding, psychic rest, or material benefit. This reflex is developed contrary to potential alternatives such as interpersonal ignorance and strife, psychological discord or dysfunction, and physical privation, as might occur if all sensory data were forced to conform within an interpretative scope that is narrow and doctrinaire.

Even if our experience is limited and this experience is sufficiently foreign as to cause cognitive confusion, the developed mental reflexes that spur us toward inquiry are almost always preferable to those that immediately seek judgment out of ignorance. Put another way, and by way of example, if the individual intellectual being in question inquires about the cause of the behavior of another, and holds the sensory data in tension with her experience and her emotional reactions in a way that is both critical and reflective, she may move toward more accurate counsel concerning judgment and reaction.

With regards to those aforementioned who may be impeded by reductive systems of thought, this method need not generally or specifically be disrespectful of their spiritual aesthetics, the sacred myths that are part of their identities. What is proposed here is the pragmatic rational ordering of dogmatic belief systems, not limited to religion, as a compartmentalized axiological space that acts as a general moral center or aesthetic that comforts, creates meaning, or gives us a feeling of solidarity with others. Through this students can begin to separate physical, ethical, and aesthetical inquiries, respectively, and hopefully turn the lens of analysis upon those dogmatic systems and their relationship to what they want those systems to provide. Via this process the dogmatic beliefs may remain intact, but also become relativized as a category under aesthetics, the emotional and intangible yet purposeful and meaningful aspects of human existence. This category would coexist along with ethics (defined here as the demonstrable and arguable fairness and beneficence of our social arrangements) and physics (defined here as pragmatically determined cosmology and ontology) with each providing feedback upon its rational manifestations in flux with the more emotional and social aspects of identity formation. Some may argue that this marginalizes religious beliefs, relegating them to a purely affective extrarational realm. I, however, feel that this compartmentalization puts these questions concerning the human condition, and what gives us purpose regarding ourselves and the greater whole, in its right perceptional place within the various fields of inquiry. This piece argues that while the distinctive field of human inquiry known as theology exists in conversation with other categories of human investigation, it is limited in its scope, as are the expert cultures of physical and social science. What follows discusses the philosophical context of rational-emotional deliberations and their relation to the repositioning of dogmatic orientations.

Categories of Emotions and Limits of Scope

It is probably instructive to set the boundaries for this reconstruction from the onset. First of all this work will not attempt to contextualize the myriad types of emotions connected to dogmatic belief systems, or their possible permutations or interconnections. However, this piece does distinguish between two *categories* of emotions using Nussbaum's (2001) distinction between those emotions that are background or ongoing on the one hand, and those that are situational or episodic on the other. Respectively, the former could represent our feelings about how we were raised, or the persisting communicative dynamic with a friend, lover, or associate; the latter might involve something that arises in a specific context like a new work environment or something grossly outside of one's emotional ken like an unfamiliar trauma (pp. 70–71). I suspect that possessing an emotionally connected rationality can assist in the ordering of experience and the informing of reaction concerning both of these categories, but it is likely more effective concerning those emotions that have been with us for a time as opposed to abrupt episodic encounters that we may not yet fully understand. However, this is not to say that the training toward a particular kind of response could not likely render such reactions, in the case of a yet unexperienced emotional context, at least *more* informed simply by encouraging a minimal degree of reflection. What is at issue here is the ability to examine an emotionally embedded belief system and allow for narratives that counter the former to be taken into consideration based on their own merits and within the confines of their own spheres of inquiry and understanding.

It should also be stated that I am not suggesting some kind of intellectual detachment from our sentient experience and corporeal constitutiveness, or some sort of retreat into mind in the Cartesian sense, unlike Dewey (1916) who cautioned the intellect is a pure light—the emotions are a disturbing heat (p. 335). Rather I posit that since humans exist in a constant emotional context, and that unlike most other life forms we have the capacity to alter our circumstances via rational processes, that we not forsake one for the other. The point is neither that we must walk the earth being emotional for the sake of it or sublimate everything sentient into hyperrational categorization. I am simply suggesting two things. The first is that emotions at their core often do not fare well when held to rational analysis concerning their context, origin, and intended purpose; and second, that rationality by itself ignores the inevitable emotionally laden nature of everyday life. The latter potentially denies the pleasure much of this affords, including the solace and certainty often granted by having reified beliefs concerning the nature of the universe and our place therein. However, this becomes problematic when the pursuit of beneficial human knowledge, like that of evolutionary biology, which serves as the basis for much of modern medicine, is quelled when the emotionally sustaining belief system closes off all potential of rational inquiry within another area of human inquiry.

This said, it appears that often in the pursuit of rationality we eschew the emotional life as something not useful, savage, annoying, prurient—something to be overcome. Indeed, our murderous urges and those of unproductive shame, resentment, or paranoia may be categories of urge we wish to overcome, or at least subdue. But, attempts at absolute rationalization alone ignore more real and positive emotional categories like the desire for community, love, and the creative spirit, many of which may serve as foundational parts of dogmatic belief systems. We often forget that our labor whether artistic, spiritual, social, or practical begins with a desire to connect, create, or destroy. These desires may be influenced, modified, and even perverted by the dynamic of our culture. Examples of this range from shifts in beliefs about the place of individual human beings in European society brought about by the Enlightenment, or the manipulation seen throughout history of those disempowered by those who control the means of communication and thus have the power to determine and enforce dominant narratives. Regardless of their particular social context, they remain at their base emotional and are not necessarily apprehended rationally. Glibly put, love, hate, apathy, etc. are not rational constructs. Whether we believe in God, respond to the art of Paul Klee, or the literature of Andre Malraux, or whether we like puppies, the base explanations for these connections remain irrational. The real, palpable rationally tempered connection lies in the recognition and acknowledgment of why these things give us pleasure, meaning, hope, resolve, or purpose. Reason can analyze and destroy any one of these things, and not necessarily toward benefit. The point is to be judicious in how we apply our analytical capacities. Put another way, and by way of example, we should probably affirm love and address the various constructs and conditions that create and foster hate. It might be useful to deploy this tool for ordering and counsel we call *reason* toward augmenting beneficial human sentiment and action—toward aesthetics desired. We commence this by addressing that which is not expressly rational, and not wholly interpretable not by mechanical analytics, but in the middle ground between confusion and randomness and the expressly useful and knowable. What follows expands upon this notion of an emotionally connected rationality via an examination of aesthetic expression and the potential place of dogmatic beliefs within the former.

Exploring Emotions as an Aesthetic

Dewey (1934), in commenting on the nature of artistic expression, stated that without emotion there may be craftsmanship, but not art (p. 69). Craftsmanship here might refer to those things of routine or the mechanical application of rational ordering to complete a necessary but not emotionally stimulating task. What follows deploys Dewey's sentiment concerning the purposeful expression of artistic pursuits to denote a deliberate and connected use of our emotional capabilities toward more accurate and beneficial projections and interaction within our human community and natural world. The creation of art may be a suitable metaphor here for describing the purposeful connection between emotion and intellect. However, two questions remain concerning this metaphor: is art a purposeful performance of emotions, and is it sufficiently analogous in terms of emotional import to dogmatic religious expression to be of use to us here? First I will need to speak further about the nature of this expression and then provide context concerning the rational compartmentalization of dogmatic beliefs into aesthetics.

Pursuant to the former, Dewey (1958) states that not to view art as deliberately emotional is to strip it of its connection to subject matter, and thus renders it either a mere medium of expression of emotion or the art itself a mere accident (p. 390). Taking a materialist stance Dewey continues,

> For emotion in its ordinary sense is something called out *by* objects, physical and personal; it is response *to* an objective situation. It is not something existing somewhere by itself which then employs material through which to express itself. Emotion is an indication of intimate participation, in a more or less excited way in some scene of nature or life; it is, so to speak, an attitude or disposition which is a function of objective things. It is intelligible that art should select and assemble objective things in such way as to evoke emotional response of a refined, sensitive and enduring kind; it is intelligible that the artist himself [sic] is one capable of sustaining these emotions, under whose temper and spirit he performs his compositions of objective materials. (pp. 390–391)

The connected aspect of this both rational and emotional method lies in the space between the performer and an objective material world and a simultaneously material and communicatively intersubjective world of other life forms. Art also serves as an example of the connection between a material world, and the movements therein, and the individual organisms ability to perceive and form rational explanations and rationally driven purposeful action. In this sense it can be described as a nexus of expression and circumstance. As art embraces material as intimate stuff of our creation and expression, this emotionally pointed expression becomes intellectually engaged when we listen to emotions, embrace them and their context, and point reaction with connection to others.

As alluded to previously, aesthetics and the emotions that they engender are not always beneficial, indeed some are quite destructive. Reflection upon these emotions and their manifestations is paramount to purposeful projection. Again, we need to through creative production name the origins of these emotions in an attempt to move toward something topically effective and beneficial. The potential analogue to religious beliefs surrounds this notion of purpose. If these beliefs give us meaning so much the better; if they hinder us from comprehending our physical world or ethically negotiating our social world, respectively, then the emotional situation may be disjointed.

In reference to the situational aspects of emotional contexts and their import for our responses to these contexts Dewey (1929) states:

> The emotional aspect of responsive behavior is its *immediate* quality. When we are confronted with the precarious, an ebb and flow of emotions marks a disturbance of the even tenor of existence. Emotions are conditioned by the indeterminativeness of present situations with respect to their issue. Fear and hope, joy and sorrow, aversion and desire, as perturbations, are qualities of a divided response. (p. 225)

Yet it is precisely this confusion that human knowing subjects must address if they are to extend responses that elicit favorable physical and communicative interplay. For, as Dewey continues, emotion is a hindrance or an aid to resolute will according as it is overwhelming in its immediacy or as it marks a gathering together of energy to deal with the situation whose issue is in doubt (p. 226). At question is the potential for repositioning emotional contexts arising from dogmatic beliefs into something affectively tenable yet rationally justifiable.

The quality of what is projected by individuals, within the context the physical and social world, resides in the human potential to reflect accurately upon what experience we already possess with powers of rational ordering toward an extension of the beneficial emotions aforementioned. This in the case of the person who retains dogmatic beliefs means separating aesthetics that nurture our identity and grant us peace, but that also allow us to engage in social and material problem solving, e.g., the aforementioned promotion of cultural tolerance and accurate scientific inquiry.

As with our art metaphor we seek purposeful expression by using what we are given by the situation and through our senses to cultivate an empathy that guides our rational actions. Concerning aesthetics, and for our purposes here a method of conceptualizing these rational-emotional dialectics, Dewey (1934) asserts that,

> In the development of an expressive act, the emotion operates like a magnet drawing to itself appropriate material; appropriate because it has an experienced emotional affinity for the state of mind already moving. Selection and organization of material are at once a function and a test of the quality of the emotion experienced. (p. 60)

So in its function here we deploy this method as a vicissitude, swirls of thought and action fusing emotional response with rationally fostered perspectives toward purposeful action as an effort to create the space for more harmonious, pleasant and just modes of existence, and a more accurate understanding of our material world. We do this with full recognition of its potential limitation whether these emotional catalysts are background or ongoing, or situational or episodic. With Dewey (1934) we can acknowledge the shifting ground of interpretive analysis and rational aptitude as a complex experience that moves and changes...[and that] all emotions are qualifications of a drama and they change as the drama develops (p. 41) and still stake our best attempt at mutual understanding, interpersonal reconciliation, and ethical interaction. I will now discuss examples stemming from my teaching that may help to illustrate this process as they relate to both ongoing and spontaneous emotionally laden situations previous discussed.

The Rational Ordering of Physically Verifiable Inference and Ethically Connected Consciousness

Pursuant to attempting this emotional-rational project I must be honest and confess my own ongoing emotional dissonance concerning the nature of many of my students' beliefs. My frustrations stem from what I perceive as a hindrance to honest rational inquiry regarding all sorts of topics from gay and lesbian issues, the separation of church and state, to questions of evolutionary theory versus other *faith*-based devices for making cosmological judgments. My frustration is not borne out of aggression but rather exasperation. I am not angry with these students, for they are on the whole quite pleasant people. I am, however, indignant concerning many of their perspectives, specifically their willingness to hold as absolute truth what they have been told by members of their family or community whom, I confess, I often view as either motivated by desire to maintain hegemony or who are just theologically naive. I am personally baffled by the platitudes of powerful and wealthy right-wing religious zealots like James Dobson, Pat Robertson, Ralph Reed, and Roy Moore, and the recently late D. James Kennedy and Jerry Falwell. My mind reels with cacophonous damnations of the liberal media, the mortal dangers of secular humanism, the religious absolutism of the founding fathers' as justification for a biblical commonwealth as a matter of heritage, and how gay marriage will corrode the sanctity of that institution and open the gates of hell in the form of natural disaster or terrorist attack. I cannot begin to wrap my mind around the logical possibility of weaving deterministic patriotism, an abstracted notion of freedom as somehow absolute yet inextricably tied to biblical law, literal interpretations of the Bible in its totality, and the notion that capitalism is congruent with the preceding, all into the same pious mantel. I cannot fathom how, for instance, The Sermon on the Mount, can be held in the same analytical space as present day capitalism without explosive contradiction, or how one can participate in the political system to change policy based on often spurious sociological and scientific evidence pursuant to a religiously based agenda and then deny much of the rest of science, because God is somehow in control of melting the polar ice caps, but not of Congress' actions concerning economic equity.

However, this emotional context for many of my students, in my interpretation, not only provides them with what might be considered beneficial emotions, but in some cases the most meaningful expression of their selves. For me, on the other hand, it impedes my ability to actively pursue particular lines of inquiry due to what I perceive to be their belief without sufficient argument or evidence. This ongoing conflict, however, has found some resolution in how I now conduct my classes. For one thing, although it still confounds me, I no longer try to refute biblical truths. I also have tried to better understand the perspective of these students through what they say about their communities and personal histories. I have looked at the objective situation, in so far as it is objective, and have come through experience to the conclusion that it is not likely my arguments and evidence will alter some parts of the aforementioned belief systems in their expression. However, via my teaching art, such as it is, I can assess my parameters and assemble those materials that first reflect my rationally tempered emotions about these beliefs, and second pursue my convictions concerning what I deem to be right, true, and beautiful in the classic philosophical sense. It is also possible that through honest dialogue they can begin to compartmentalize their more dogmatic beliefs with a certain theological umbrella and see other discourses on their own terms, like those of social tolerance and scientific inquiry.

In this, I hope to create an instructional space with an emotionally disruptive component, like the notion that gay and lesbian students have a right to be protected in public schools, or even that the schools have an obligation to create an environment that is tolerant of gay and lesbian students. Other lines of inquiry might include constructing a working definition of scientific method and scientific theory and then apply these definitions to other areas of human study, like theology. I then try to help them rationally order this disruptive content via inquiry and hopefully help them mentally shape the experience so that it becomes a more durable point of reflection and at least a partial reconstruction of consciousness. Although the parameters in which I can work are in many ways finite, I can still create a situation where certain types of biblical truth, for instance, are decentered via emotional indeterminativeness, and criticality is encouraged. Ultimately, we seek to foster an experience where Dewey (1934), using an interesting metaphor states,

> an act of expression is a squeezing out, a pressing forth. Juice is expressed when grapes are crushed in the wine press; to use a more prosaic comparison, lard and oil are rendered when certain fats are subjected to heat or pressure. (p. 64)

This is not to suggest that I wish to destroy the conscious matter of my students, but rather to apply the pressure that might create an emotional and rational context that then might lead to different forms of expression.

On the other hand, episodic instances of outright homophobic or homomisic[3] statements, or outright acritical dismissal of certain scientific theories, for instance, are less tenable, more spontaneous, and significantly harder to address due to their unpredicted nature and immediate rawness in a given dialogue. They are, however, systematic of the former belief system ongoing in its projection and reception, although they disrupt the pedagogical space in a different way given their more spontaneous qualities. Like with those more ongoing expressions of consciousness, direct condemnation on the part of the pedagogue will make it easier for those students who sit on the precipice of credulity to disregard; and ignoring or sidestepping the issue might simply lead to a more trivial shade of disregard. Left unattended they can serve to relativize the disruptive counter-narrative concerning protection and tolerance, or honest investigation of the physical world; overcorrected for, they can alienate the audience and lead them to ignore most related points of inquiry. What addresses the emotionally raw nerve at this moment are questions that seek to connect these reactions to some type of rational explanation that disrupts the emotional reaction. We do this, for instance, by asking about the fairness of a given premise based on democratic principles, or those of care, respect, or love, or by reflecting the spirit of scientific discovery as a means to understand, predict, control, and protect nature, including human health. Another possibility, hopefully, is that other students will provide the counter-narratives themselves, and that the instructor will simply mediate. What has to be maintained, however, is the rational connection to the emotional space with a purposeful and preferably beneficial end in view.

To conclude, I am not suggesting that we should diminish the pursuit of social justice and verifiable scientific knowledge, or an examination of cultural aesthetics, under the presupposition that there are necessary or absolute pedagogical limits to what we may effectively address in the classroom discourse. To do this is defeatist and probably would lead to largely banal classroom dialogue. However, if one wants to pursue greater degrees of emotionally connected rationality we need to guard against emotional exposure that may be beyond the ken of our students, just as the artist is bound by experience, its effect upon imagination, and the materials available. It is paramount to our pedagogical attempts to understand and acknowledge the import of our students' cultural identity and commitments, even if we disagree with their position and want to expand their consciousness past this experience. Certainly first we need to ascertain who they are in terms of identity, where they are with regard to social cognition, and where we feel we can take them responsibly. Pursuant, we need to incrementally address the emotional contexts we create. For if as Dewey (1934) states, a person overwhelmed by an emotion is thereby incapacitated for expressing it (p. 69), then it should follow that we create spaces where students' emotions can near the edge of their ability to rationally interpret sentient things and beliefs toward a more complex and hopefully ethical reconstruction of consciousness, even if contradictions remain due to the retention of certain dogmatic beliefs.

NOTES

1. The plaintiff expresses a pretty salient contradiction by in the same breath pining for a time where, in her own words, "God will be welcomed back in our schools" (Yahoo News, 2007), and proposing the censorship of other religious traditions because of a separation of church and state. I contend that even if the Harry Potter books did depict witchcraft as a religion it would simply join other books, which include the discussion of religious traditions, faiths, and contexts, e.g., works by Shakespeare, Milton, Dante, Dickens, Hawthorne, Dostoevsky, etc. So her argument regarding separation is specious unless we remove all texts that mention, describe, or advocate religious ideas. In reference to the former premise, she is on logically firmer ground, if it is indeed demonstrable that indoctrination is taking place, a point that is dubious.

2. Michael L. Dini, a biologist at the Texas Tech University, for instance, believes that "scientists do not base their acceptance or rejection of theories on religion, and someone who does should not be able to become a scientist" (Dean, 2007, p. 1).

3. I feel the need to draw a distinction between those who may *fear* what might happen to the fabric of society should homosexuality become normalized, e.g., fears of the breakdown of traditional marriage and family life, increased promiscuity or disease, or divinely decreed damnation to an unpleasant afterlife for those who are not saved, and *hatred* visited out of naked xenophobia or perceived challenges to the power engendered in one's identity construction of masculinity or femininity. Thus I have adopted the term homomisic, which derives its construction from the Greek verb *miseo* meaning to hate. However, the possibility that someone is both fearful and hateful should be acknowledged, especially in so far as these traits are exhibited in times of immediate emotional reaction. The only previously published reference to this term that I have been able to locate appeared in a *Psychology Today* editorial by then-editor Robert Epstein (2003). He proffers that "a more appropriate term would be *homomisic*, from the Greek term misos ("hatred"), since many Americans actually hate gays" rather than simply fear them.

BIBLIOGRAPHY

Collins, G. (2005, November 7). An Evolutionist's evolution. *New York Times on the Web*. Retrieved November 7, 2005, from http://www.nytimes.com/2005/11/07/nyregion/07darwin.html

Covaleskie, J. (2008). Three why's: Religion and science in school. *Educational Studies, 43*, 7–16.

Dean, C. (2005, June 21). Opting out in the debate on evolution. *New York Times on the Web*. Retrieved June 21, 2005, from http://www.nytimes.com/2005/06/21/science/21evo.html

Dean, C. (2007, February 12). Believing scripture but playing by science's rules. *New York Times on the Web*. Retrieved February 12, 2007, from http://www.nytimes.com/2007/02/12/science/12geologist.html

Dewey, J. (1916). *Democracy and education*. New York: Free Press.

Dewey, J. (1934). *Art and experience*. New York: Milton, Balch, and Company.

Dewey, J. (1958). *Experience and nature*. New York: Dover.

Dewey, J. (1980). *The Quest for certainty*. New York: G.P. Putnam.

Dewey, J. (2003). My pedagogic creed. In H. S. Shapiro, S. B. Harden, & A. Pennell (Eds.), *The Institution of Education* (pp. 243–249). Boston, MA: Pearson Custom Publishing.

Epstein, R. (2003, January/February). Am I anti-gay? *Psychology Today*. Retrieved November 1, 2007, from http://www.psychologytoday.com/articles/pto-20030123-000001.html

Ga, Judge: Keep Potter books in schools. (2007, May 29). *Yahoo! News*. Retrieved May 29, 2007, from http://news.yahoo.com/s/ap/20070529/ap_on_re_us/potter_protest

CHAPTER TWELVE

Holding Tight With Open Hands—Education at Humlehaveskolen: A Majority Christian Culture and a Minority Muslim Culture Together in a Danish Public School

Karla J. Smart-Morstad, Concordia College
David P. Morstad, Jr., University of North Dakota, Grand Forks

Purposes and Methodology

The crosswalk light turns green, illuminating a figure of Hans Christian Andersen with his walking stick rather than the familiar "WALK" signal. We are in Odense, Denmark, home of the beloved fairytale writer. Waiting for a flood of bicycle riders to pass—women and men in business attire—we cross and board a city bus for the twenty-minute ride from downtown. Our stop is Vollsmose Kirke (Vollsmose Church), where a short walk past open ground, a shopping mall and high-rise apartments, takes us to Humlehaveskolen (Hŭm'·lĕ·hă·və·skō´·lĕn). This multiethnic, multireligious public school serves elementary through secondary students. After an exchange of e-mails over several months prior to our visit, Olav R. Nielsen, school principal, meets us at the front door.

On our first visit, May 2007, we simply want to learn about Danish educational philosophy and practice. Ethnographic research, including interview, observation, and photojournalism, provides inquiry tools. What we witness at Humlehaveskolen is a school actively accepting minority religious and cultural values while simultaneously practicing and teaching strongly held traditional Danish values. How can these two different, and sometimes contradictory, belief systems both be valued so highly in a coherent way? How can a school be successful when the teachers and students, seemingly, have so little common ground in their common path?

We return in June 2007 to focus on the role of religion in public education as experienced at Humlehaveskolen. The majority of students are Muslim immigrants from numerous countries, and the majority of teachers are ethnic Danish Christians. Again, interview, observation, participant observation, and photojournalism support our qualitative study.

At our invitation Olav Nielsen comes to the Midwest to visit K-12 schools in March 2008. His particular interest is settings for at-risk students. Making school observations and interviewing American educators together with him deepens our understandings of his purposes, values, and work. In the closing days of Olav's visit, Mads Christensen, a Danish undergraduate at Concordia College, Moorhead, MN, joins us in discussions of cultural perspectives and educational purposes.

What can American educators and public schools learn from Humlehaveskolen, where minority culture students face majority culture teachers, and the seemingly disparate value systems may appear not only contradictory but also antagonistic? To respect; to carry on in pursuit of values in our own culture, yet to find openings for dialogue and recognition of interconnected values, including religious ones. We can learn to explore what it means to be a good person, and we can clarify the cultural and religious beliefs that shape what we understand to be the purposes of education. Students, teachers, and administrators at Humlehaveskolen can teach us to hold tightly to our beliefs while welcoming differing beliefs with open hands. Then, to find a new path from there.

Geographical, Historical, and Ethnic Context

Denmark is comprised of three main landmasses: Jutland, which juts up from northern Germany arching towards its Scandinavian siblings of Norway and Sweden, and two large islands, Funen and Zealand. Funen is centered between Jutland and Zealand, with both islands in the North Sea east of Jutland's southern shore. Odense (population 150,000) is the capital of Funen. The city of Odense is over one thousand years old, but its Scandinavian heritage is thousands of years older. In 965 A.D., Harald Bluetooth, son of Viking King Gorm the Old, Christianized Denmark, and following the Protestant Reformation Denmark converted to Lutheranism in 1536 (WorldAtlas.Com Denmark, n.d.).

Streets lined with 16th century shops, inns, and carriage houses; streets with quaint houses that could be found in fairytale illustrations; bustling streets full of bicycles and small cars; green parks and public sculptures; an occasional McDonalds; and, walking streets closed to cars so shoppers and tourists can amble unimpeded from store to store—Odense seems the idealized version of an old European city blending past and present. How does a city like this, especially with its millennia-long Scandinavian and centuries-long Lutheran lineages, find itself with public schools that are 95% non-Danish, non-Christian?

Humlehaveskolen serves Vollsmose, an economically depressed borough of Odense. In the 1960s Vollsmose was nearly 100% traditional Danish families, as were the students at Humlehaveskolen. The students were known to be difficult, many from troubled and poor homes. Teachers and administrators dedicated and skilled in working with these students gravitated to Humlehaveskolen. Principal Olav Nielsen was one such teacher.

Immigrants came to Denmark in the 1960s and 70s because there was a worker shortage. They continue to come because Danes understand there is a humanitarian need for families to relocate from wars and political instability. Turkish immigrants were the first refugees to come to Vollsmose. Danish social policy, at the time, encouraged them to live together in the same area. Most of the immigrants moved into Vollsmose with its lower cost of living and subsidized apartments. When some of the Turkish residents moved on, they emptied apartments for Vietnamese boat people rescued by Danish sailors. When the Vietnamese, now third generation Danes, emptied the refugee apartments in Vollsmose, Iranians fleeing the Ayatollah Khomeini arrived. Then Palestinian immigrant refugees came from the Lebanese civil war; next, immigrants from Iraq after the Kurds were attacked; then from the Balkans, Somalia, Afghanistan, and Sri Lanka. "I like to say that these are the children of the American presidents' wars, but I know it is more complicated than that," Olav tells us (interview, May 7, 2007). The students at Humlehaveskolen and their families, are "damaged by the atrocities they have witnessed," Olav explains (interview, June 20, 2007). "Some of them have seen their parents killed," (O.R. Nielsen, interview, June 20, 2007).

Over the past thirty years, Humlehaveskolen has evolved from 100% white ethnic Danish Christian students to 95% multiethnic Muslim. This has not been a linear evolution. First Turkish, then Vietnamese, and so on, and now the majority of students are Lebanese-Palestinian and Somali. Humlehaveskolen serves students from mixed cultures while the teachers remain 85% white ethnic Danish Christians. (The Lutheran Church is the state church in Denmark, and, while certainly not all Danish nationals are churchgoing and secularism is well accepted, even those teachers who said they do not attend church spoke of the Christian faith and values that were part of their childhood upbringing.)

Religion and Culture of Humlehaveskolen's Students

A significant aspect of the current students at Humlehaveskolen is this: religion *is* their culture and identity. A Gallup Poll survey of Muslims worldwide finds that "for overwhelming majorities of Muslims (who are also the moderates), Islam is a fundamental source of identity, guidance, and spiritual and psychological security" (Esposito & Mogahed, 2007, p. 162). At Humlehaveskolen, it does not make sense to talk about multicultural education apart from religion. Although students come from different cultures, their Muslim religion is present in their cultural practices and traditions (O. R. Nielsen, interview, May 7, 2007).

Parents as well as the students at Humlehaveskolen are conflicted and feel the pull of two cultures and belief systems. A desire to maintain traditional values while also hoping for their children to succeed in Western culture is certainly not unique to Islamic parents in Odense. Indeed, Haddad, Smith, and Moore (2006), writing in *Muslim Women in America: The Challenge of Islamic*

Identity Today, report that American Islamic mothers struggle with "keeping their children isolated from what the parents perceive to be dangerous Western secular values at the same time that they acknowledge their children's citizenship in the west and want to prepare them to be able to live their lives in a Western culture" (p. 14).

Olav, a realist, tells us that some Palestinian students at the school would not like us because we are American, and that the school likely would not be a welcoming place for a Jewish child given the political and religious beliefs of these students. Yet, Muslim families in Vollsmose respect people of faith over those who are atheistic (O.R. Nielsen, interview, June 21, 2007). Because faith is a commonality, it is possible for Christian teachers to educate Muslim students in this setting. The majority of families in Vollsmose are willing to trust people of faith, a concept that holds true for the majority of Muslims everywhere (Esposito & Mogahed, 2007). But, Islamic fundamentalism, in Olav's experience, makes communication "impossible," and he tell us, "I cannot talk with fundamentalists" (interview, June 21, 2007). Al Qaeda terror cells have been uncovered in Odense (Bilefsky, 2006). Many Muslims share Olav's rejection of fundamentalists. As Esposito and Mogahed (2007) point out, "the 'terrorist fringe,' far from being glorified, is rejected by citizens of predominately Muslim nations just as it is by citizens in the United States" (p. 96).

Culture and the Purpose of Education

Olav explains that, because Islam is a religion of law, many Muslim parents in Vollsmose do not rear their children to think independently or to find and exercise freedom (interview, June 21, 2007). An aim of these families is to have children and adolescents remain committed to extended family, with patriarchal authority and religious law shaping behavior and expectations. Olav and Liselotte Sunesen, a veteran teacher of over 30 years with 15 years of service at Humlehaveskolen, understand that these families value and practice their religious and cultural traditions in family life and community life. Both educators recognize that the immigrant Muslim students at Humlehaveskolen, and their families, are living in two worlds (O.R. Nielsen and L. Sunesen, interviews, June 20, 2007).

One example of Humlehaveskolen's students' need to negotiate the pluralism of their current West/East circumstance can be understood by considering the differing cultural traditions surrounding conversation between adults and children. Mads Christensen, a Dane attending college in the United States, describes to us a Scandinavian cultural expectation. In Danish homes and schools, Mads tells us, children and adults converse, question, debate, express and examine opinions, engage together in some decisionmaking and planning, and share humor (interview, March 13, 2008). In the varied cultures of Humlehaveskolen's students, however, there is no expectation that children and adults will converse in these ways in their homes (L. Sunesen, interview, June 20, 2007). Instead, talk in students' families is expected to focus on adult directions and reprimands. "It is not good upbringing to discuss with your parents, if you are Muslim," Liselotte adds (interview, June 20, 2007). Questioning—perhaps challenging—parental opinion or religious authority is not culturally acceptable for Humlehaveskolen's students when talking with their families.

Liselotte shares another example of how the children she teaches are excluded from conversation with adults in their families. When her students return from summer holidays, they will often have been on a car trip but not know where they have been. "My students tell me they rode in a car, perhaps to visit an uncle, but they have had no conversation to anticipate the trip, or to look at a map, or to understand where they went in relation to where they live in Vollsmose" (interview, June 20, 2007). For Liselotte, narrating, describing, questioning, forming and defending opinions is fundamental to Danish education and engagement in Danish society.

Ethnic Danes, historically since the Protestant Reformation, have understood the goals of education to be toward advancement of the individual and improvement of the social good. Danish parents want their children to gain responsibility and freedom through education, ultimately exercising independence from parents and freedom to make their own decisions about behavior (O. R. Nielsen, interview, June 21, 2007).

"Danish parents want to train their children to think and to make self-decisions, including about their sexual partners and behavior. It is the Danish way to make them independent. The Middle Eastern cultures still want children and young adults under the control of parents, and they consider the *Koran* the law," Olav tells us (interview, June 21, 2007). That is, in Danish culture the goal of education is independence; in the cultures of many immigrant families in Vollsmose the goal is obedience.

Cultural values also influence beliefs about who should be educated, why, and how. The Imams and families in Vollsmose, Olav explains, are most focused on the behavior of girls and how that impacts the family's honor. Muslim boys have freedom in their movement outside of home and school. Being in school affords Muslim girls a respected, trusted place to be where they experience more freedom than in their homes. The Muslim girls excel beyond the boys in their education at Humlehaveskolen. They go to Danish universities in higher numbers, as well. "The Imams and parents are more controlling of the girls, so some of the boys have too little direct guidance. They make some kinds of criminality—robbery and violence. Drugs are not so much a problem for school children. That's a problem for the fathers and older ones," Olav tells us (interview, June 21, 2007).

Principal Olav Nielsen and Compassion and Respect as Educational Tools

How do Humlehaveskolen's teachers and administrators educate a multiethnic, multireligious population? They create an atmosphere of compassion and respect that encourages trust.

The term *respect*, as we use it here, and as we observed its practice by teachers and administrators at Humlehaveskolen, is well described by Sara Lawrence-Lightfoot (1999) in her book *Respect: An Exploration*. She writes, "usually respect is seen as involving some sort of debt due people because of their attained or inherent position, their age, gender, class, race, professional status, accomplishments, etc. By contrast, I focus on the way respect creates symmetry, empathy, and connections in all kinds of relationships, even those, such as teacher and student, doctor and patient, commonly seen as unequal" (Lawrence-Lightfoot, 1999, p. 9). The essence of respect, for Lawrence-Lightfoot (1999), is succinctly paraphrased in the book's cover-notes: "in her vision, respect is not the passive deference offered a superior but an active force that creates symmetry even in unequal relationships" (cover-notes).

One way such respect is apparent is in how Olav makes himself visible, living in Vollsmose where very few ethnic Danes still reside. His community relationships connect him with students' families, providing a foundation to make believable the respect and support shown students. He is a friend, counselor, parent-educator, and trusted leader in the community of Vollsmose. For the summer solstice observance in Vollsmose, a traditional Danish celebration with pagan roots, Olav is the invited speaker at the bonfire.

Olav values relationship so highly that he carries out his promise to himself—what he calls "my punishment"—every student whom he must expel from school he follows for five years (interview, June 22, 2007). Visits to prisons and psychiatric facilities, keeping in contact with former students and their families, are part of what Olav considers his role as principal. Walking through the Fyn Bazaar where former students are grocers and shopkeepers, the enthusiastic greeting "Hi, Olav!" rings constantly. If ever there was a *benevolent godfather*, it is Olav.

Humlehaveskolen's Guiding Philosophy

The underlying school philosophy at Humlehaveskolen is to accept immigrant cultures and religions, as well as Danish culture and religion. Religion and religious differences are faced openly and honestly at Humlehaveskolen. The school does not cultivate an either/or mindset. Rather, the interconnections of major world religions are used as foundational tools for understanding perspectives.

A framed poster near the school's entrance uses the symbol of a tree with roots and branches to show connections between Christianity, Islam, and Judaism. Another poster, titled *My Neighbor's Religion*, traces tenants and shared values between the three branches of Judeo-Christian-Muslim religions, plus Hinduism, Buddhism, and Taoism. For students and teachers at Humlehaveskolen, these are not simply educational posters. The content carries life-skills information as certainly as "wash your hands" notices in the restrooms.

Humlehaveskolen's teachers and administrators recognize that every religion has as its goal helping individuals to be good people. "We talk about what it means to be a good Muslim, a good Christian, a good person," Liselotte explains (interview, June 20, 2007).

She teaches students to better understand humanity and the values of Islam and Christianity, and to use that understanding as a basis for making decisions when thinking about their behavior. "I have become a better Christian by teaching my Muslim students," she says (interview, June 20, 2007).

Compassion and Respect as Cultural Bridges and Educational Tools

The atmosphere of compassion and respect at Humlehaveskolen is seen in two extra-hours programs. Teachers and administrators creatively respond to the social needs of Muslim girls and teenagers within the expectation of their religion and traditions.

Teachers noticed adolescent girls lingering in school at the end of the day. Liselotte explains that in their cultures it is unacceptable for women to be in the casual company of men outside their immediate family (interview, June 20, 2007). So, unlike the Muslim boys at Humlehaveskolen, Muslim girls, once home from school, are not allowed outside of their apartments. The girls stayed after school to talk with each other, teachers, and administrators because, once home, they would be isolated from much of their world. To help facilitate this quest for a greater social life after school, and to honor the parents' concern that girls not be with boys, the school created The Pink Room. The Pink Room is an after school environment for girls and female teachers only: no boys or men allowed. It is evidence of the parents' trust that the school will honor their concerns that these Muslim girls now enjoy a safe and trusted environment in which to talk, form friendships, and pursue activities (O. R. Nielsen, interview, May 7, 2007).

Another example of the administrators and teachers responding to Muslim girls is found in the Girls Soccer Team. Families make the final decision as to whether or not their daughters are able to play on the team. Liselotte tells us, "If the families say no, then that is that" (interview, June 20, 2007). But, for the girls on the team, there is physical activity and teamwork through competitive sports. Olav, wisely, builds interest in the school through the team, lobbying for financial and moral support for the young women athletes. The Girls Soccer Team from Humlehaveskolen, coached by a male kindergarten teacher, successfully competes both regionally, with Danish school teams, and internationally.

The Girls Soccer Team has traveled to play in China. Without exceptional trust in the school, these Muslim parents—just as any parents—would not allow their daughters to participate.

Soccer can serve as a cultural bridge and an educational tool. "Everywhere in the world they play soccer with the same rules—when someone knows soccer anywhere, they know it everywhere," Olav explains (interview, March 15, 2008). The players, individually and, ultimately, collaboratively, create a team. For Olav, soccer allows players and fans to transcend labels such as Christian, Muslim, immigrant refuge, and Danish national. However, as Franklin Foer (2004) argues in *How Soccer Explains the World*, although the rise of soccer coincides with globalization, paradoxically, it also heightens nationalism through pride in national or local teams. Olav understands the soccer field as providing common ground for students at Humlehaveskolen. Without abandoning their cultural identities, soccer players can find a structure in the game where they all know the code of interaction, respect each other as athletes, and communicate without, necessarily, even a shared spoken language (O.R. Nielsen, interview, March 11, 2008).

Compassion and Respect in the Adult-Student Interactions

Compassion and respect are visible in the classroom environments and teaching styles at Humlehaveskolen. In Danish schools, an elementary teacher remains with the same class of students for up to nine years, allowing relationships to deepen and the needs of individual children to be understood over time. Liselotte tells us that including students in conversations with adults is a crucial aspect of teaching and relationship building. She says, "we *have* to talk with them" (interview, June 20, 2007). The urgency of the need, from her perspective, is academic as well as social.

Liselotte engages students in conversation—with her and with their own parents—by asking them to ask their parents for information or an opinion for her. "'Ask your father,' I say to students. 'Tell your father *I* want to know'" (interview, June 20, 2007). And, she does want to know. This structure she imposes allows the student to enter a dialogue with a parent—but on Liselotte's behalf—not as a child questioning parental authority. Some students tell her they are not allowed to speak Danish at home. "I tell them that is okay, but that they should ask in Turkish or

Arabic and then explain the answer to me in Danish," she tells us (interview, June 20, 2007).

By encouraging students to have conversation with adults, Liselotte creates a context for students to use language to question and discuss. While maintaining respect for students and their families, she redirects a cultural tradition that otherwise limits conversation between adults and children.

Olav focuses on conversation and language in his approach to discipline. A parrot—named Mr. Larson after a Danish pop-singer—lives in Olav's office where sports memorabilia cover the walls. Mr. Larson sings, dances, and squawks to make his presence known, and his presence is purposeful. Mr. Larson helps make the space relaxed for students coming to visit Olav before, during, or after school. The discipline Olav practices relies on open conversation and recognition of students' complicated lives.

While waiting to talk with Olav one day, we watch teachers half-carry, half-drag a distraught boy, about 11-years old, into the office. Olav greets the child, Osama, quietly and calmly. "These students do not need shouting. Their parents shout," he explains (interview, June 22, 2007). Students need a space to gather their composure and to talk with an adult. "I will not allow teachers to describe a child as *ugly* or bad," Olav says (interview, June 22, 2007).

Olav describes the boy we meet in his office as "unlucky" (interview, June 21, 2007). It is how he describes Osama to teachers as well. Olav confides in us that the boy's father is out of the country looking for work and the family faces an uncertain future, compounding the stress of a young boy whose family has already fled war-ravaged Somalia. Olav's compassion sees the boy's uncooperative behavior as a natural manifestation of overwhelming stress and uncertainty. And that compassion is communicated by using the term *unlucky* to describe why the boy was misbehaving, rather than to describe the fact that he was misbehaving.

Later, Olav tells us that walking with the boy after school, they encountered the child's mother who began shouting at her son, telling him what he had done wrong. In response, because Olav is known in Vollsmose; because students and their families gave him an Arabic name meaning "the old man" and symbolizing that he is esteemed as a wise elder; because his moral compass guides him to be both student-advocate and parent-educator; because he can do no less, Olav talks to Osama's mother about the content and the manner of her communication with her son. "I had to tell her that she cannot shout at the boy and tell him that he was violent at school. I had to tell her that he already knows what he did and now he needs to calm himself," Olav explains (interview, June 22, 2007).

The Role of Minority Teachers

Minority staff, including teachers and custodians, plays a role in creating an atmosphere of compassion and respect at the school. Muslim teachers, educated in Danish teacher education programs, are ethnic role models. We hear from teachers and administrators how important it is that students see adults like themselves in professional roles.

Lessons are taught in Danish, with English introduced in the third year of elementary school. Arabic speaking adults are often able to communicate in students' first languages. However, Liselotte explains, Arabic speakers need to be more than language translators. Minority teachers and staff need to model and explain majority cultural values in appropriate settings as well. Liselotte tells us that, to her chagrin, "Danish language and culture courses are not required in teacher education" (interview, June 20, 2007). In her perspective, some non-Danish teachers have limitations in fluency and cultural understanding that, perhaps, Danish higher education could address through the reconsideration of teacher education curricula (L. Sunesen, interview, June 20, 2007).

Distinguishing the Religious from the Traditional

Respecting that the aim of religion is to help people be good human beings, Christian teachers of Muslim students at Humlehaveskolen must determine whether students' beliefs and actions come from their religion or their tradition. "Tradition can change. Religion cannot," Liselotte explains (interview, June 20, 2007). "You cannot question the *Koran*—not at all—but you can question the traditions" (L. Sunesen, interview, June 20, 2007).

If students or families tell Liselotte "well, that is our tradition," she asks how they fit that tradition into their lives in Denmark (interview, June 20, 2007). The tradition of elementary school girls wearing the scarf can be questioned, for example. The scarves are hot when little girls play in the schoolyard during recess. Religion does not require girls under age 18 to wear headscarves, but tradition encourages the practice. Liselotte tells us that even little girls worry that gossip about them could start, if they do not wear headscarves (interview, June 20, 2007).

The fear of gossip, especially for girls in Muslim culture, is traditionally a mechanism of control, Liselotte explains (interview, June 20, 2007). Girls are careful to avoid even the appearance of misbehavior lest gossip reaches their family (L. Sunesen, interview, June 20, 2007). Islamic law does not require that tattletale or fanciful stories be spread if a girl is seen talking with a male. "I teach them that they do not have to gossip, and that they can stand up to stories being told about them," Liselotte tells us. "I teach them that a good Muslim, a good Christian, a good person does not deliberately hurt people" (interview, June 20, 2007).

Danish Nationalism

When Olav met us at the front door that first day, it did not take long for us to recognize the respect he and his faculty held for other cultures, nor did it take long to witness the compassion they had for their students. What took us longer to recognize was their equally strong belief in, and respect for, Christian Danish values and culture.

It is from a deep sense of understanding what it means to be Danish that Humlehaveskolen extends respect and acceptance to others. Immigration and emigration—*invandring* and *udvandring* in Danish—have differing histories in Denmark with 19th century emigration to the United States overwhelmingly more prevalent than immigration during the 19th century and much of the 20th:

> Denmark's long history has contributed to a homogeneity not found in American society. Social conventions have evolved over time that have profoundly influenced the ways that Danes view themselves and those who live in the world around them. It is a view that admits and is open to global diversity but can be rigid when considering what makes one Danish. There are behaviors and assumptions, [religious and] secular, political and social, that one holds if one is Danish. (J. Nielsen, 2007, p. 23)

If you look for it, this strong sense of Danish-ness and Danish nationalism is seen everywhere. The flag, known as the Dannebrog or Danish Cloth, and officially adopted in 1625 (WorldAtlas.Com Denmark, n.d.), is visible in public and private spaces all over Denmark. Public squares and parks, institutions and private homes all display their red flags with the white cross. Danish flags are part of art projects and décor in classrooms.

Danish pride in who they are as a people is easy to understand from a historical perspective. Denmark is the oldest kingdom in Europe. During the World War II occupation of Denmark, King Christian X, in daily defiance of the Nazis, embodied Danish pride in country and culture. To demonstrate his claim of national sovereignty, each day he rode his horse in the streets of Copenhagen, unarmed and without a guard, saying that the citizens of Denmark were his guard ("King Christian X," n. d., ¶ 1). The Danish sense of responsibility to the other, and the Lutheran concept of service to neighbor, came to fruition as Danes smuggled over 7,000 Jews into Sweden during the war. Only 455 Danish Jews were sent to concentration camps (Kjeldback & Thorsen, 1995).

In the United States, pride in American culture at times is tempered by the concern that it may overwhelm other cultures, or the fear that those who display national pride may appear as *ugly Americans*. Danish pride seems different. Danes believe in their values and prefer them to others. The BBC News reports University of Leicester professor Adrian White's study creating a "world map of happiness" and showing Denmark, out of 97 countries surveyed, the happiest nation ("Denmark 'happiest place on earth'" n.d.). The Danes' desire to maintain Danish cultural values appears to contain no fear of overwhelming others—nor any desire to do so. "Only a few million people in the world speak Danish and the country is small," Olav reminds us (interview, May 7, 2007). Indeed, Danes realize they must be proactive to prevent their culture from being subsumed by European or American cultures (M. Christiansen, interview, March 13, 2008).

Interpreting the Compassion and Respect of Olav Nielsen's Third Way

How does Humlehaveskolen find solutions to problems resulting from conflicting cultural values and traditions? It might be assumed that this is accomplished by accommodating both sides through the compromise of give-and-take. But, more than this happens. Everyone at Humlehaveskolen is negotiating a new world. Students are living in two cultural worlds, learning Danish and English as second and third languages. Their lives require them to make decisions that permit them to integrate multiple perspectives. The path many of them are following is what Olav calls his *third way* (interview, June 22, 2007).

Olav's third way is analogous to Pruitt and Rubin's (1986) dual concern model from the field of conflict resolution. It can be visualized as follows. Each culture has its own spectrum of values and traditions. When two cultures have values that conflict, it is easy to assume the only solution is to compromise by meeting in the middle. However, this assumption leads to the false belief that finding a solution is essentially a zero-sum game: that is, for one side to be accommodated, the other must give up something (see Figure 1).

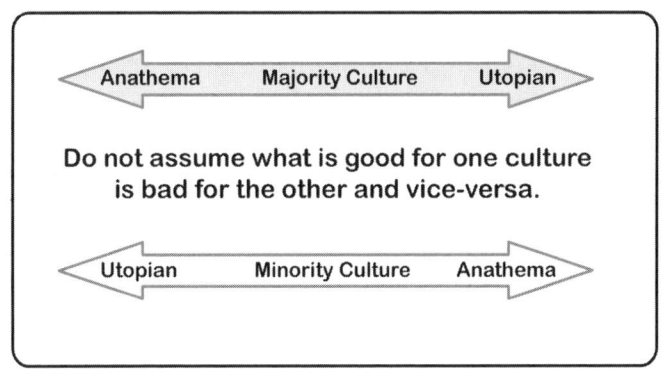

Figure 1. When cultures conflict, it is counterproductive to view differences as zero-sum.

In the dual concern model, the spectra of values are placed perpendicular to one another rather than parallel to one another. Repositioning the spectra helps visualize the theoretical possibility that solutions to conflicts can encompass important values of both cultures (see Figure 2). Such solutions constitute Olav's third way.

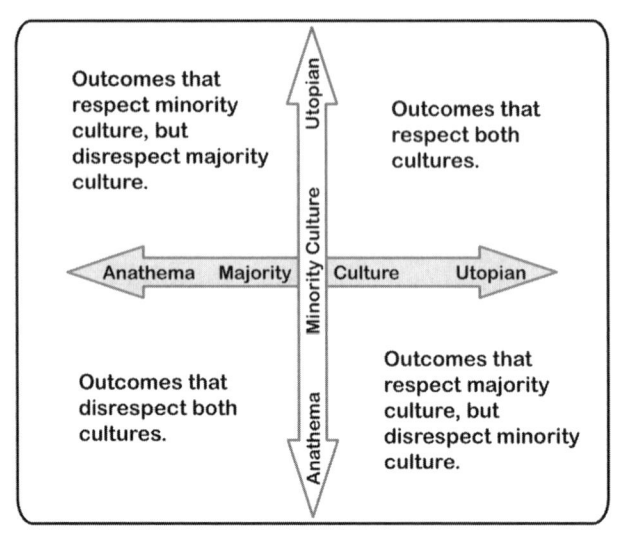

```
                    Utopian
    ┌─────────────────┬─────────────────┐
    │ Outcomes that   │                 │
    │ respect minority│ Outcomes that   │
    │ culture, but    │ respect both    │
    │ disrespect      │ cultures.       │
    │ majority culture│                 │
    │                 │ Minority        │
    │                 │ Culture         │
    ├─Anathema Majority┼Culture Utopian─┤
    │                 │                 │
    │                 │ Outcomes that   │
    │ Outcomes that   │ respect majority│
    │ disrespect both │ culture, but    │
    │ cultures.       │ disrespect      │
    │                 │ minority culture│
    └─────────────────┴─────────────────┘
                   Anathema
```

Figure 2. The dual concern model encourages seeking outcomes that respect both cultures.

Negotiating Olav's third way means to search for paths that honor both cultures and violate neither religion. It requires distinguishing between practices that are religious and those that are traditional. Cultures are changing, but Christianity and Islam need not—indeed cannot be changed—to co-exist at Humlehaveskolen.

It further requires earning the trust and respect of minority cultures so they become partners with the majority culture in finding this new common path. This parallels Lightfoot-Lawrence's (1999) view of the development of respect: "I see [respect] not only as an expression of circumstances, history, temperament and culture rooted in rituals and habits, but also arising from efforts to break with routine and imagine other ways of giving and receiving trust, and in so doing, creating relationships among equals" (p.10).

The Pink Room provides one formalized example of Olav's third way. It honors both Muslim parents' concern that daughters not be in the company of males during after-school activities and Danish educators' concern that extracurricular enrichment and social relationships be an integral part of students' interpersonal development and school-age experiences. Liselotte's practice of asking her students to ask their parents questions on her behalf, another example of Olav's third way, respects the parents' expectation that children not question parental opinion or authority while satisfying Liselotte's desire for students to learn to engage in thoughtful conversation with adults. When Liselotte opens the door for religious discussions in her classroom, she puts into practice Olav's third way. Liselotte helps young students think about religious matters through recognition that the goal of religion is to provide guidance about how to be a good person. It is in this context that neither religion is slighted, both are valued, and common goals are respected.

Successes

When we ask Olav to talk about success at Humlehaveskolen, he redirects the conversation by putting the focus on *faithfulness* instead. Olav tells us, "I do not want to be successful. I do not care about success. I want to be faithful. I care about being faithful" (interview, June 22, 2007). Faithfulness, for Olav and his staff, whether they are ethnic Danes or not, whether they are Christian or Muslim, means establishing trust and continuing the conversation to create spaces for learning and for healthy behavior in the community.

In Olav's view being faithful to students necessitates being faithful to their families as well (interview, June 20, 2007). While learning Danish language and cultural traditions is important for students' current and future lives in Denmark, Olav points out that, for their fathers, the need for employment has a greater immediacy. "What is an unemployed Iraqi father going to do in a Danish village," he asks rhetorically (interview, June 21, 2007). Building trust requires awareness and understanding of a family's struggles and empathy for their plight. Humlehaveskolen—Olav in particular—is not just flexible, but more importantly steadfast in commitment to helping immigrants in their new lives. Olav focuses on being faithful, dwelling on neither successes nor failures. Liselotte tells us, however, that Olav has endured "deep disappointments" when, inevitably for some students and families, his efforts and faithfulness have not been enough (interview, June 20, 2007).

Liselotte is more pragmatic than Olav about what she considers success, saying, "some successes come slowly" (interview, June 20, 2007). For example, she explains that, although girls' marriages are still arranged exclusively to men from their own country, now many marriages are to men already in Denmark, rather than to those in the homeland seeking emigration. The success is that fewer young girls become brides in marriages arranged for the purpose of providing immigration status for much older uncles or cousins. Another example of success, as Liselotte sees it, is evident in the reduction in number of adolescent Somali girls who are sent back to Somalia for circumcision (interview, June 20, 2007). The practice is traditional, not dictated by religious law. Some of the Somali-Danish mothers in Vollsmose now question and prevent this traditional practice (L. Sunesen, interview, June 20, 2007).

At some point, a shared use and understanding of humor also builds community. Mette Nielsen, Olav's wife who also teaches at Humlehaveskolen, tells us that it takes more than a generation for the power and subtlety of humor to be shared and trusted. "Some Turkish Danes now use and understand Danish humor in their personal relationships," Mette explains (interview, June 21, 2007). The Danish newspaper, *Morgenavisen Jyllands-Posten,* is well known for its 2005 editorial cartoons featuring Muhammad (Encyclopedia Wikipedia, n.d.). Danish Muslim immigrants did not share such use of satire as humor. (Ironically, *Morgenavisen Jyllands-Posten* provided the posters representing connections between world religions displayed at Humlehaveskolen. The posters arrived years before the cartoon was published.)

Lessons from Humlehaveskolen

Theologian Dietrich Bonhoeffer said, "The test of morality of a society is what it does for its children" (as cited in McGovern, Dole & Messer, 2005, p. 6). Today this test must include all of a society's children: immigrant and native born, minority and majority culture, religious and secular. It is a test well met at Humlehaveskolen.

As diversity increases in the United States, public schools will enroll more and more students for whom religion *is* their culture and identity. The United States will no longer be able to relegate the role of religion in public schools as so much academic subject matter: religion will be coming in on the backs—in the hearts and minds—of minority students. "We need better education—and not because it is nice to be multicultural but because the world's religions, no longer quarantined in the nations of their birth, now live and move among us; yoga in our church halls, *nirvana* in our dictionary, and Sikhs at our gas stations," Stephen Prothero (2007) writes in *Religious Literacy: What Every American Needs to Know—And Doesn't* (p. 3). The parameters of passing Bonhoeffer's test are changing in this country as they have in Denmark.

Viewing Humlehaveskolen as a model and emulating their successes will require well-informed, culturally respectful teachers. It will also require wisdom and steadfastness. Humlehaveskolen's successes do not come through sacrificing what is valued in Danish culture or in Christianity. Nor do the school's successes come from mandating that immigrants abandon their cultural and religious beliefs.

Success or, as Olav prefers, faithfulness, does not stem from a single idea or practice. It comes from a facing of facts: that immigrant refugee children at Humlehaveskolen are Muslims from varied cultural backgrounds who now need to understand themselves and function in a new country that is both secular and Christian. It comes from focusing on differentiating, through questioning, what is religious and what is traditional. It comes from questioning how minority cultural traditions fit into lives in the majority culture. It comes from recognition that all parties have a stake—all have values, all strive for meaning, and all must negotiate the way forward.

A valuable lesson learned from Olav is that communication is critical. Olav facilitates communication by being present in the lives of students and families. He engenders trust through his visible commitment and by being believable. The importance, indeed necessity, of trusted communication and understanding between Muslims and Western cultures is highlighted by Gallup's research (Esposito & Mogahed, 2007). Surveys of Muslims worldwide "produced a number of insights, but the most important was this: The conflict between the Muslim and Western communities is far from inevitable. It is more about policy than principles. However, until and unless decision makers listen directly to the people and gain an accurate understanding of this conflict, extremists on all sides will continue to gain ground" (Esposito & Mogahed, 2007, p. xi).

Students at Humlehaveskolen, along with their principal and teachers, and together with their families, face the task of learning when, why, and how to hold tightly to what they know, and when, why, and how to grab on to what they are coming to know. Increasingly, this needs to be the goal of schools in the United States.

The goal of finding a path along Olav's third way, which respects *both* cultures, means that each culture should accommodate the other while neither capitulates to the other. United States majority culture teachers will need to respect and understand the values of minority cultures. They will also need a deep and thoughtful understanding of, and respect for, their own cultural values in order to hold them tightly with open hands.

BIBLIOGRAPHY

Bilefsky, D. (2006, September 7). A dark turn for a Danish city. *International Herald Tribune*. Retrieved January 16, 2008, from http://www.iht.com/articles/2006/09/06/news/DENMARK.php

Denmark 'happiest place on earth' (2006, July 28). BBC News. Retrieved July 14, 2008, from http://news.bbc.co.uk/2/health/5224306.stm

Encyclopedia Wikipedia. (n.d.) http://en.wikipedia.org/wiki/Jyllands-Posten_Muhammad_cartoons_controversy

Foer, F. (2004). *How soccer explains the world: An unlikely theory of globalization*. New York: HarperCollins Publishers.

Haddad, Y. Y., Smith, J. I. & Moore, K. M. (2006). *Muslim women in America: The challenge of Islamic identity today*. New York: Oxford University Press.

King Christian X: The king on his horse. (n.d.). Retrieved January 16, 2008, from http://www.auschwitz.dk/docu/King.htm

Kjeldback, E., & Thorsen, K. (Eds.). (1995). The museum of Danish resistance: 1940–1945. Copenhagen: Frihedsmuseets Venners Forlags Fond.

Lawrence-Lightfoot, S. (1999). *Respect: An exploration*. Reading, MA: Perseus Books.

McGovern, G., Dole, B., & Messer, D.E. (2005). *End hunger now: A challenge to persons of faith*. Minneapolis, MN: Augsburg Fortress.

Nielsen, J. M. (2007) The others among us: Immigrants crossing borders, facing boundaries. *Immigrants: Graphic images from Funen graphic workshop*. Odense, DK: Fyns Grafiske Vaerksted.

Prothero, Stephen. (2007). *Religious literacy: What every American needs to know—and doesn't.* New York: HarperCollins Publishers.

Pruitt, Dean G., & Rubin, Jeffrey Z. (1986). *Social conflict: Escalation, stalemate, and settlement.* New York: Random House.

WorldAtlas.Com Denmark description. (n.d.). Retrieved January 16, 2008, from http://www.worldatlas.com/webimage/countrys/europe/dk.htm

Contributors

Steve Broidy teaches foundations, human development, and teaching methods courses in the Education Department at Wittenberg University. His research interests focus on professional ethics, speech act theory, thinking skills, and educational policy issues. He is currently at work on a book on kindness as a teaching ethic.

Daniel Cohen is currently Visiting Assistant Professor in Religious Studies at the University of Missouri–Columbia. Dr. Cohen's research and courses cover South Asian religious traditions, religion and law, religion and film, and most recently religion, spirituality and the brain where he is involved in ongoing multidisciplinary research at the University of Missouri.

Craig S. Engelhardt is a graduate of Baylor University and the foundering director of the Society for the Advancement of Christian Education (SACE). His research and writing focus on religion in public education, the religious nature of citizenship, and the philosophic basis of Christian schooling.

T. Jeremy Gunn is Director of the American Civil Liberties Union's Program on Freedom of Religion and Belief and the Senior Fellow for Religion and Human Rights at the CSLR at Emory University. He is also a member of the Advisory Council on Freedom of Religion and Belief of the Office of Democratic Institutions and Human Rights of the Organization for Security and Cooperation in Europe (OSCE). He has written and spoken extensively on questions of religious freedom within and without democratic societies.

Steven P. Jones teaches educational foundations and methods classes in the department of Reading, Foundations, and Technology at Missouri State University. His research and writing focus on the examination of the purposes of education with special attention to the contributions of the ancient Greeks. He is Director of the Academy for Educational Studies.

Ryan Kennedy teaches language arts with a world literature focus at Centralia High School in Centralia, Missouri. He earned his bachelor's and master's degrees, both in secondary English education, from the University of Missouri–Columbia.

Jordan Lorence is senior counsel for the Alliance Defense Fund. He has litigated First Amendment cases since 1984 in courts across the United States. Mr. Lorence argued the *University of Wisconsin v. Southworth* student fees case before the U.S. Supreme Court on behalf of the students in 1999. He has participated as co-counsel in other cases before the U.S. Supreme Court.

Andrew N. McKnight is an Assistant Professor in the School of Education at the University of Alabama at Birmingham, teaching undergraduate and graduate courses in the social, historical, and philosophical foundations of education. His research concerns the application of philosophical, historical, and qualitative research methods to contemporary educational and cultural issues, specifically with regard to emotional contexts and underserved groups.

David P. Morstad, Jr. is the director of the University of North Dakota, Grand Forks Mathematics Computer Lab and is a Senior Lecturer in Mathematics. He has completed graduate work in special education and is currently involved in developing a new family-centered group home paradigm for adults with special needs.

Nel Noddings is the Lee Jacks Professor Emeriti of Child Education at Stanford University; she also holds the John W. Porter Chair in Urban Education at Eastern Michigan University. She is past president of the Philosophy of Education Society and of the John Dewey Society. In addition to numerous books—among them, *Caring: A Feminine Approach to Ethics and Moral* Education, *Women and Evil, The Challenge to Care in* Schools, *Educating for Intelligent Belief or Unbelief*, and *Philosophy of Education*—she is the author of some 200 articles and chapters on various topics ranging from the ethics of care to mathematical problem solving.

Karla J. Smart-Morstad teaches undergraduate methods courses in literacy education and graduate courses in qualitative research methods at Concordia College, Moorhead, MN. She and her husband, David Morstad, collaborate in working with international education issues, including leading undergraduates on education seminars to Northern Europe to visit schools and examine cultural beliefs, values, and practices in K-12 education, as well as leading Scandinavian educators on education seminars to visit American K-12 settings for at-risk students.

Craig A. Smith teaches historical methods, constitutional law, and social studies education at California University of Pennsylvania. His research and writing interests include the lives of Supreme Court justices and how Court decisions impact citizens. He is currently writing essays about Supreme Court law clerks and researching a biography about Justice Tom Clark of Texas.

Susan E. Waters teaches undergraduate and graduate courses in public relations, ethics, communication and aging/gender, and applied research methods in the Department of Communication and Journalism at Auburn University. Waters has written and obtained several research grants focusing on service-learning and also has research interests and publications in the areas of public relations, aging, and ethics.

COUNTERPOINTS

Studies in the Postmodern Theory of Education

General Editors
Joe L. Kincheloe & Shirley R. Steinberg

Counterpoints publishes the most compelling and imaginative books being written in education today. Grounded on the theoretical advances in criticism, feminism, and postmodernism in the last two decades of the twentieth century, Counterpoints engages the meaning of these innovations in various forms of educational expression. Committed to the proposition that theoretical literature should be accessible to a variety of audiences, the series insists that its authors avoid esoteric and jargonistic languages that transform educational scholarship into an elite discourse for the initiated. Scholarly work matters only to the degree it affects consciousness and practice at multiple sites. Counterpoints' editorial policy is based on these principles and the ability of scholars to break new ground, to open new conversations, to go where educators have never gone before.

For additional information about this series or for the submission of manuscripts, please contact:

> Joe L. Kincheloe & Shirley R. Steinberg
> c/o Peter Lang Publishing, Inc.
> 29 Broadway, 18th floor
> New York, New York 10006

To order other books in this series, please contact our Customer Service Department:
> (800) 770-LANG (within the U.S.)
> (212) 647-7706 (outside the U.S.)
> (212) 647-7707 FAX

Or browse online by series:
> www.peterlang.com